2/93

St. Louis Community College

Forest Park
Florissant Valley
Meramec

Instructional Resources
St. Louis, Missouri

BIOLOGY & FEMINISM

A Dynamic Interaction

The Impact of Feminism on the Arts & Sciences

Claire Sprague, *General Editor*
New York University

BIOLOGY & FEMINISM

A Dynamic Interaction

Sue V. Rosser

Twayne Publishers • New York
Maxwell Macmillan Canada • Toronto
Maxwell Macmillan International • New York • Oxford • Singapore • Sydney

Twayne Publishers
Macmillan Publishing Company
866 Third Avenue
New York, New York 10022

Maxwell Macmillan Canada, Inc.
1200 Eglinton Avenue East
Suite 200
Don Mills, Ontario M3C 3N1

Library of Congress Cataloging-in-Publication Data

Rosser, Sue Vilhauer.
    Biology & feminism : a dynamic interaction / Sue V. Rosser.
      p. cm.—(Impact of feminism on the arts and sciences)
    Includes bibliographical references and index.
    ISBN 0-8057-9770-X.—ISBN 0-8057-9755-6 (pbk.)
      1. Feminism.   2. Human biology—Social aspects.   3. Sexism in sociobiology. I. Title. II. Title: Biology and feminism.
III. Series.
HQ1154.R744   1992
305.42—dc20
                                                         92-36338
                                                            CIP

10 9 8 7 6 5 4 3 2 1
10 9 8 7 6 5 4 3 2 1

Printed in the United States of America

CONTENTS

FOREWORD

After more than two decades of feminist thought and action, it is time to stand back and assess what has been happening to traditional modes of research and evaluation in the universities. The Twayne series on the Impact of Feminism on the Arts and Sciences represents one contribution toward such an assessment. It addresses the complex questions as well as the uncertainties and possibilities that are raised by the meaning of feminist impact. Which disciplines can claim to have been altered as a result of feminism? Which cannot? How can we measure feminist impact? What biases or gaps in scholarly thought are still there? Are we creating new ones? Has a gendered approach developed in the field? What are the major areas of resistance to change?

The scope of the series is ambitious. Over the next several years, we envision the publication of volumes on anthropology, art history, bioethics, biology, classics, education, economics, film, history, law, literature, music, philosophy, political science, psychology, religion, sociology, and theater. These volumes will not follow a uniform format or approach. We anticipate that each one will combine the virtues of accessibility with original interpretations of central issues of gender, genre, methodology, and historical perspective. These are the questions that feminism has explicitly and implicitly unsettled in every field of knowledge, forcing us all to reconsider how we learn, how we choose what we learn, and how we change what and how we learn. We hope that the series will be both charting change and making it happen.

With the launching of the first two volumes, *History and Feminism*, by Judith P. Zinsser, and *Biology and Feminism*, by Sue V. Rosser, the series has become a reality. These two volumes make exciting inaugural companions, for history and biology, apparently so far apart, in fact raise similar crucial methodological questions about an ideal of ''objectivity'' based on value-laden data. They provide a much needed synthesis of feminist thought and efforts at change in the academy. They do not segregate the theoretical from the practical. The place of women in the profession, the politics of the profession, the lives of practitioners, the design and staffing of courses—these matters are not peripheral to an evaluation of the impact of feminism on a particular profession. The awareness that there are feminism*s* but no single, monolithic feminism is axiomatic to both volumes as it is to the series as a whole.

Zinsser's study demonstrates with force and clarity the continuing androcentric character of the practice and teaching of history. It suggests, furthermore, that despite visible changes in outlook, curriculum, and the representation of women in the profession, women's history still occupies a marginal place. If this is true for history, it is even more true for biology.

Women are still not very visible in the biological or physical sciences as students or professionals. Yet women's health and reproductive issues, now at the center of national debate, did, in Rosser's words, unite "biology and feminism at the rebirth of the women's movement in the twentieth century." Rosser's critique of so-called "scientific method" and its androcentric bias demonstrates that the interaction between biology and feminism continues to be unequal and ironic, for while biology as a field has significantly affected feminism, feminism has had very little effect on biology.

Both authors see positive change as a continuing possibility, Zinsser with her assessment of a new approach to history represented by grassroots initiatives, Rosser with her discussion of ecofeminism and the possibilities inherent in a strengthened interaction between biology and feminism.

Claire Sprague
Series Editor

PREFACE

Biology and feminism have been linked since the beginning of the nineteenth-century women's movement. Much of the nineteenth-century feminist scholarship and activism sought to overthrow the constraints of Freud's "anatomy is destiny" (1924, p. 178) and the theories presented by the other eminent male scholars. These theories purported to explain women's passivity, unequal access to education, and inferior position in society by appealing to the biological "evidence" for sexual differences (Darwin, 1896), women's smaller brains (Broca, 1868), and failure to evolve as completely as men because women must use energy to reproduce (Spencer, 1873). Feminists in the first wave of the women's movement refuted the biological evidence used to justify women's inferior social position. They pointed out the flaws in logic and measurements and rebutted Darwin's notion that women were mentally inferior to men (Blackwell, 1875), Broca's misinformation that brain size was dependent on the exercise of intelligence (Gardener, 1887), and Freud's contention that female psychological development is predicated on phallocentrism (Horney, 1926; Klein, 1924).

A small stream of feminist criticism (Hollingsworth, 1914; Tanner, 1896; Thompson, 1903) continued to reveal the biases and flaws in research carried out during the first two-thirds of the twentieth century, which proposed hormonal and anatomical bases for differences in intelligence, performance, and status between men and women. When the second wave of the women's movement began in the 1960s, biology again served as a catalyst around which much of the organization originated. Women's health and reproductive rights united biology and feminism at the rebirth of the women's movement in the twentieth century.

Biology and related issues pertaining to women's health and reproductive rights not only served as an initiating force, but also continues to be a central focus for this wave of the women's movement. Feminist criticisms emerging from disciplines as diverse as literature, history, philosophy, religion, sociology, and psychology have dealt extensively with issues of essentialism—the experience of the female body as it influences women's writing, role in history, conception of self and others, interactions in groups, and psychological development.

Biology has become such an issue in feminist literary criticism that some (Moi, 1985; Marks and Courtirron, 1980; Bannet, in press) have distinguished French feminism from American feminism on the basis that "American feminisms have generally preferred to retrieve women's lost historical experiences by empirical sociological and historical research, while French feminisms have tended, more poetically and philosophically to try to reconstruct the specificity of feminine experience by speaking the mystery of the (m)other body in her absolute biological difference" (Eve Bannet, in press).

Biology and feminism currently shape the parameters for debates and cutting-edge scholarship in literary criticism and in many other disciplines. In that sense biology continues to have a large impact on feminism. Ironically, feminism is having much less impact on the discipline of biology than it is on some other fields.

In 1988 I published a study (Rosser, 1988) in which I explored the impact of feminism and women's studies on the humanities (modern languages) as compared to the sciences during the last two decades. I examined the programs of the last 20 years from the meetings of the American Association for the Advancement of Science (AAAS), the major national multidisciplinary scientific organization, to determine whether or not there had been an increase in papers relating to women's studies or feminism over time. I also examined the titles of papers as listed in the Preconvention Program Issue of the *Proceedings of the Modern Language Association* (PMLA) for 1965–85. The Modern Language Association is the largest multidisciplinary national organization for humanities disciplines and in that sense is comparable to the AAAS for science disciplines. The individual papers on feminist or women's issues were counted.

The results revealed that there has been an increase over the years in the papers on feminism or women's issues presented at the annual meetings of both the AAAS and MLA. Papers centering on women's studies or feminist issues at AAAS meetings have increased from 0.7% in 1966 to 1.8% in 1986. In 1966, 1.17% of the papers at MLA focused on these issues; in 1985 the percentage was 24.22%. The percentage of papers presented at the AAAS meetings on feminism issues and women's studies has increased over the past two decades. However, it has increased significantly less ($t = -5.13$; significant at the 0.0001 level) during the same time period than the percentage of papers on such issues at the MLA.

The survey of the data from the MLA and AAAS suggests that the impact of feminism appears to be increasing in the humanities, whereas it remains constantly negligible in the sciences. This conclusion is based on the premise that the topic of papers presented at the major national meeting serves as an index that can be used to assess the impact of that topic or issue on the discipline.

Although this is undoubtedly a crude index, such a constant trend over a two-decade period makes one question why feminism is failing to have the impact on the sciences that it is on some of the other fields of study.

One reason that feminism has not had much impact on the sciences is that there has been and continues to be a dearth of women in science. Although Vetter's statistics (1988) indicate that more women have received advanced degrees in science and engineering in the 1970s and 1980s than in the 1950s and 1960s, the 1990 Report of the National Science Foundation documents that many fewer women (30.3%) than men (69.7%) receive bachelor's degrees in sciences and engineering (exclusive of the social sciences in which women receive 53% of the bachelor's degrees). The salaries, promotion, and advancement rates of women scientists are lower than those of men scientists at all ranks (except in engineering) and unemployment rates for women are higher (NSF, 1990). In the 10-year interval 1975–84 women went from 16.9% of National Institutes of Health (NIH) study section members to only 17.9%; during this time the total number of members doubled from 733 to 1,264 (Filner, 1986). The National Academy of Sciences, which has a membership of 2,610, has had only 57 women members elected since the Academy was chartered in1863 (Rubin, 1986). Almost all of them were elected within the last decade. Thus, the women who are in science, particularly those at the higher ranking positions, still find themselves in the vast minority.

Because of their minority position most women fear, and rightly so, that any commitments such as those to women's studies will make them appear more peripheral to traditional science and therefore lessen their chances for promotion and tenure. The documented discrimination against women in science (Vetter, 1980) and the perception of many scientists that good science requires that all of one's energy and thought processes be directed toward pursuing the problem in the laboratory substantiate their fears that involvement with anything outside of science (including feminism) might be detrimental to their careers. Furthermore, it does not appear that the shortage of women will improve any time soon. In fact the dearth of women in science is becoming more critical because of the overall shortage of scientists predicted in the 1990s. Sheila Widnall uses an Office of Technology Assessment Report to explain the pipeline issue quite clearly:

> The report described an initial cohort of 2000 male and 2000 female students at the ninth grade level. Of that original cohort, only 1000 of each group will have sufficient mathematics at the ninth grade level to remain in the pipeline. When the two groups are followed to the end of high school, 280 men and 220 women will have completed sufficient mathematics to pursue a technical career. A major drop in women students occurs with career choice upon entering college, with 140 men and 44 women choosing scientific careers. After a career

choice is made, a larger percentage of women than men actually complete their intended degree in science and engineering: at the B.S. level, 46 men and 20 women receive degrees. Data show that women enter graduate school in the same proportion relative to their percentage of B.S. degrees as do men in the various technical specialties. (The number actually entering graduate school from each cohort is estimated from their current presence in graduate schools since entry data are not available). However, some combination of attrition and stopping at the M.S. level rather than going on for the Ph.D. creates another major drop for the women students in the pipeline. Of the original 2000 students in each group, five men and one woman will receive the Ph.D. degree in some field of the natural sciences or engineering. (Widnall, 1988, pp. 1740–41)

The result of the shortage or absence of women from science is that science becomes a male province. Science is a male province not only in that it is populated mostly by men and excludes large numbers of women but it also reflects a male approach to the world. Fee (1981; 1982), Haraway (1978), Hein (1981), and Keller (1982; 1985) have described the specific ways in which the very objectivity said to be characteristic of scientific knowledge and the whole dichotomy between subject and object are, in fact, male ways of relating to the world, which specifically exclude women. This subject will be explored further in chapters three and five.

Keller (1982) documents the different levels from which women are excluded from science:

1. Unfair employment practices prevent women from reaching the theoretical and decision-making levels of science.

2. Androcentric bias in the choice and definition of problems studied so that subjects concerning women, such as menstrual cramps, childbirth, and menopause, receive less funding and study.

3. Androcentric bias in the design and interpretation of experiments so that only male rats or monkeys are used as experimental subjects.

4. Androcentric bias in the formulation of scientific theories and methods so that unicausal, hierarchical theories that coincide with the male experience of the world become the "objective" theories that define the interpretation of the scientific data.

The implication is that because of these practices, attitudes, and perspective science becomes a totally masculine province that excludes females. Rossiter (1982) also claims that this masculinity has made it doubly difficult for women in science: "As scientists they were atypical women; as women they were unusual scientists" (p. xv).

Biology, in contrast to the other physical and natural sciences, has seen a significant increase in the number of women receiving degrees during the last two decades. For example, in 1986, 48% of the undergraduate degrees (the latest data available) and in 1988, 36.6% of the doctoral degrees in biology (NSF, 1990) were received by women in comparison to 34.4% of the undergraduate and 25.4% of the doctorals in 1978 (NSF, 1990). The percentage of women receiving degrees in biology does not yet approach the percentage earning degrees in the humanities. However, women in biology significantly outnumber women in the other physical and natural sciences (but not social sciences) receiving degrees.

These data may explain why feminism has begun to demonstrate some impact on the discipline of biology. It was not until a large number of women were working in other academic disciplines for a lengthy period of time that the influence of feminism began to be felt. Biology represents the area within the natural and physical sciences on which feminism has had the most impact. This is not surprising as, unlike the other physical and natural sciences, the numbers of women in biology have reached a critical mass large enough to begin to raise feminist questions from a number of perspectives. Feminists in biology have worked extensively on a feminist critique of the androcentrism that permeates biology in general and its subdisciplines—animal behavior, endocrinology, and evolutionary biology—in particular. More recently they have begun to explore changes that might occur in experimental designs, methods of data gathering, theories and conclusions drawn from the data when the lens of gender helps to focus the biologist's examination of the world.

Supporting the new theoretical and methodological critiques, other feminists in biology have concentrated their analysis on the position of women in science and the effects of feminism on curriculum transformation and the practice of science. Recovering the history of women in biology and gathering data on the current status of women in the profession have provided crucial information that explains the current dearth of women in science. Incorporating feminism into curricular content and approaches and into the practice of science may attract more women to fill the shortage of scientists predicted for the 1990s. As more feminists become biologists, the transformative effects of feminism will have further impact on the theories, methods, and practice of the biological sciences. The purpose of this book is to explore the dynamic interaction between feminism and biology—the effects that feminism has already had on biological theory, research, and teaching—and to consider its potential impacts and implications. It also raises the question of the effects that biology might have on feminism.

The first section of the book is Feminist Analyses of the Position of Women in Biology. Chapter one provides a brief recapitulation of feminist work on the history of women in biology. Historians of science have recently begun to recover the lost history of women biologists. This recovery work is difficult because frequently the significance of the work of women biologists is not appreciated, is misunderstood, or was attributed to the man with whom they worked. Until recently historians have tended to adopt the model of emphasizing famous women scientists and their contributions. Some of the newer work, however, examines the lives of ordinary women scientists.

In chapter two, I delve into the considerable current work that centers on the status of women in science. In addition to the statistical reports gathered by the federal government (National Science Foundation) and numerous professional societies about the numbers of women receiving degrees in biology and their attained rank and salary in government, industry, and academia, data are also available from which future trends for women in the profession may be predicted. After presenting this data, I will explore reasons for the dearth of women scientists and measures that are being taken to attract more women to biology.

The second section, Effects of Feminism on Theories and Methods, represents the core of the work by feminists in biology and serves as the centerpiece of the book. The major volume and impact of work on feminism and biology have focused on critiques that demonstrate androcentric bias of current research and theories.

In chapter three, I explore feminist critiques of biology on the organismal level. Critiques of current biological research begin with an exploration of the problems of objectivity and the notion that even scientific theories are human constructs that may reflect the culture and values of the scientists who develop them. Discussing bias in scientific paradigms opens the door to exploring the possibility of androcentric bias. In this chapter I examine the substantial work by feminists demonstrating androcentrism in the theories of the subdisciplines of evolutionary biology, primatology, animal behavior including sociobiology, and ecology.

Chapter four extends the critique begun for research on the organismal level in the previous chapter to the cellular and molecular level. In terms of volume, the feminist critique on this level is less extensive and well developed. However, the work of Bleier on the neurosciences and endocrinology sketches possible parameters for this critique. An evolving critique of developmental biology is being applied as a model to explore bias in cell biology and molecular biology.

Feminist critiques of biological theories raise questions about the possibility of feminist approaches to experimental research. In chapter five I examine the relationship between feminist theories and their links to possible avenues for feminist methods in biology: objectivity versus subjectivity; quantitative versus qualitative approaches; shortening the distance between the observer and the subject of study; valuing women's experience; and use of application to assess the value of basic research.

In the final section of the book, Applications of Feminism to Biology, I explore the actual and potential impact of feminism on biology. Transforming the biology curriculum through feminism is the subject of chapter six. The first challenge to the traditional biology curriculum appeared as separate Women's Studies courses. Some of these, in the form of "Know Your Body" courses, sought to rectify the absence and exclusion of women and women's issues from traditional biology courses. Other courses present feminist critiques of biology. Eventually Women's Studies faculty began to mainstream this information into introductory and advanced biology courses in an effort at transformation. More recently, other feminists who focus on teaching have attempted to apply feminist pedagogical techniques to the teaching of biology to attract more women to science.

Feminism has begun to show limited pragmatic impact on the practice of science, which I explore in chapter seven. Because of feminist critique of the absence of female animals and humans from experimental designs, the National Institutes of Health, encouraged by the National Women's Health Network and American Women in Science (AWIS), recently declared that research protocols must include both females and males if the disease under study occurs in both sexes. The birth of ecofeminism and Feminist International Network of Resistance to Reproductive and Genetic Engineering (FINRAGE) activist groups demonstrate the praxis resulting when feminism is used to critique applications of biology to the environment and women's bodies.

In the conclusion, I initiate explorations of how biology may begin to influence feminism. An examination of the effects of feminism on biology leads to a consideration of the evolution of a biology that is more humane and socially responsive to the needs of all people. Similarly some subdisciplines and principles of biology may provide important information for feminism. I use the subdiscipline of ecology to begin to examine lessons that feminism might learn from biology. As more biologists accept feminist critiques and more feminists become biologists, further transformative effects on theories, methods, and practice will emerge from the dynamic interaction between feminism and biology.

Acknowledgments: I am grateful to Claire Sprague, Series Editor and Carol Chin, Twayne Editor, for the Impact of Feminism on the Arts and Sciences. Mariamne Whatley, Associate Professor at the University of Wisconsin provided excellent suggestions for the manuscript. Their guidance was invaluable in my completing this volume. Without the support of my very able administrative assistant Linda Lien, who typed many versions of this manuscript, it would have been impossible to complete this project. I am also indebted to my family, Charlotte, Meagan, and Caitlin for their continuing inspiration. Thank you to all of these important people in my life for helping me to produce *Biology and Feminism: A Dynamic Interaction.*

REFERENCES

Bannet, E. T. (in press). The logic of both/and in French and American feminism. *Postcultural theory: Critical theory after the Marxist paradigm*. London: Macmillan.

Blackwell, A. B. (1976). *The sexes throughout nature*. Westport, CT: Hyperion Press. (Original work published 1875)

Broca, P. (1868). On anthropology. *Anthropological Review*, *6*, 35–52.

Darwin. C. (1896). *The descent of man and selection in relation to sex*. New York: Appleton. (Original edition published 1871)

Fee, E. (1981). Is feminism a threat to scientific objectivity? *International Journal of Women's Studies*, *4*(4), 213–33.

Fee, E. (1982). A feminist critique of scientific objectivity. *Science for the People*, *14*(4), 8.

Filner, B. (1986, July/August). President's remarks. *American Women in Science*, *15*, 4.

Freud, S. (1924). The dissolution of the Oedipus complex. *Standard edition of the complete psychological works of Sigmund Freud* (Vol. 19). London: Hogarth Press and the Institute of Psychoanalysis.

Gardener, H. H. (1887). Sex and brain weight. *Popular Science Monthly*, *31*, 266–69.

Haraway, D. (1978). Animal sociology and a natural economy of the body politic, Part I: A political physiology of dominance; Animal sociology and a natural economy of the body politic, Part II: The past is the contested zone: Human nature and theories of production and reproduction in primate behavior studies. *Signs: Journal of Women in Culture and Society*, *4*(1), 21–60.

Hein, H. (1981). Women and science: Fitting men to think about nature. *International Journal of Women's Studies*, *4*, 369–377.

Hollingsworth, L. (1914). Variability as related to sex differences in achievement. *American Journal of Sociology*, *19*(4), 510–30.

Horney, K. (1926). The flight from womanhood. Reprinted in J. B. Miller (Ed.), *Psychoanalysis and women* (1973). Harmondsworth: Penguin.

Keller, E. F. (1982). Feminism and science. *Signs: Journal of Women in Culture and Society*, *7*(3), 589–602.

Keller, E. F. (1985). *Reflections on Gender and Science*. New Haven: Yale University Press.

Klein, M. (1924). An obsessional neurosis in a six-year old girl. In *The psycho-analysis of children* (1975). London: Hogarth Press.

Marks, E. and Courtivron, I. (1980). *New French Feminisms*. Brighton: Harvester.

Moi, T. (1985). *Sexual/Textual Politics: Feminist Literary Theory*. New York: Methuen.

National Science Foundation. (1990). *Women and minorities in science and engineering* (NSF 90–301). Washington, DC: Author.

Rosser, S. V. (1988). Impact of feminism on the AAAS meetings. In S. V. Rosser (Ed.), *Feminism in the science and health care professions: Overcoming resistance*. New York: Pergamon Press.

Rossiter, M. (1982). *Women scientists in America*. Baltimore: Johns Hopkins University Press.

Rubin, V. (1986, July/August). Women's work: For women in science, a fair shake is still elusive. *Science, 86*, 58–65.

Spencer, H. (1873). Psychology of the sexes. *Popular Science Monthly, 4*, 30–38.

Tanner, A. (1896). The community of ideas of men and women. *Psychological Review, 3*(5), 548–550.

Thompson (Woolley), H. B. (1903). *The mental traits of sex*. Chicago: The University of Chicago Press.

Vetter, B. (1980, March). Sex discrimination in the halls of science. *Chemical and Engineering News, 58*: 37–38.

Vetter, B. (1988). Where are the women in the physical sciences? In S. V. Rosser (Ed.), *Feminism within the science and health care system: Overcoming resistance*. New York: Pergamon Press.

Widnall, S. (1988). American association for the advancement of science presidential lecture: Voices from the pipeline. *Science, 241*, 1740–45.

FEMINIST ANALYSES OF THE POSITION OF WOMEN IN BIOLOGY

1.

HISTORY OF WOMEN IN BIOLOGY

From most accounts of the history of science, including the discipline of biology, it appears that few, if any, women have ever been biologists or were responsible for significant, fundamental contributions to the field. Because the exposure for most people to the history of science comes from the scant information given in science courses and textbooks, students develop the impression that no women have been biologists. Because of the tradition of referring to famous discoveries by the last name only of the scientists who performed the experiment, stereotypes that scientists are male reinforces the obscurity of women biologists who have made such discoveries. For example, on hearing about the Hershey-Chase experiments determining that DNA was the genetic component in bacteriophage, most students will assume that Hershey and Chase were both men unless the instructor underlines the fact that Chase was a woman or includes the first name of the experimenters.

Although we sometimes labor under the false impression that women have only become scientists in the latter half of the twentieth century, early works by Christine de Pizan ([1405] 1982), Giovanni Boccaccio ([1355–59] 1963), and H. J. Mozans ([1913] 1974) recorded past achievements of women in science. Their works underscore the fact that women have always been in science. However, all too frequently the work of women scientists has been credited to others,

3

brushed aside and misunderstood, or classified as nonscience. There are several classic examples of the loss of the names of women scientists and the values of their work. Eli Whitney was the employee of Catherine Green, the person who really invented the cotton gin. Because Whitney applied for the patent, he is credited with the invention of this important piece of technology (Haber, 1979). Rosalind Franklin's fundamental work on the X-ray crystallography of DNA, which led to the theoretical speculation of the double helical nature of the molecule by Watson and Crick, continues to be brushed aside and undervalued (Watson, 1969; Sayre, 1975). The ground-breaking work of Ellen Swallow in water, air and food purity, sanitation, and industrial waste disposal, which began the science of ecology, was reclassified as home economics primarily because the work was done by a woman (Hynes, 1984). Ellen Swallow is thus honored as the founder of home economics rather than as the founder of ecology.

The recovery of the names and contributions of the lost women of science determined by historians of science who were spurred on by the work of feminists in history, has provided invaluable research. Much of the work has followed the male model, focusing on the great or successful women in science. Olga Opfell's (1978) *The Lady Laureates: Women Who Have Won the Nobel Prize* and Lynn Osen's (1974) *Women in Mathematics* are based on this model. *Hypatia's Heritage* (Alic, 1986) recovers the history of outstanding women in science, medicine, and mathematics from prehistory through the nineteenth century. Alic uses biographic and scientific evidence to document the achievements of women scientists whose work has been overlooked, suppressed, or stolen. Ogilvie's work (1986) *Women in Science: Antiquity through the Nineteenth Century* profiles 186 women who represent the participation of women in the science of their time and culture. Many individual biographies on famous figures such as Marie Curie (Reid, 1974), Rosalind Franklin (Sayre, 1975), Sophie Germain (Bucciarelli & Dworsky, 1980), Mary Somerville (Patterson, 1983), and Sofia Kovalenskia (Koblitz, 1983) have also emerged. Demonstrating that women have been successful in traditional science is important in that it documents the fact that despite the extreme barriers and obstacles, women can do science. This work is what Lerner (1975) calls compensatory history. In the schemes proposed for transformation of the standard liberal arts curriculum by the new scholarship on women (McIntosh, 1983), the works on these famous women scientists would be categorized as heroines, exceptional women, or an elite few who are seen to have been of benefit to culture as defined by the traditional standards of the discipline.

In these accounts of the lives and work of these women scientists who have achieved recognition for their contributions, common themes emerge: their tremendous commitment and love for their work; their pursuit of scientific problems because of their fascination with the organism they were studying or their desire to help people; choices about family versus career; the significant role that male colleagues or mentors played in recognition of the women's work by the scientific community; and the tremendous obstacles and barriers they faced in pursuing a scientific career because of their gender. A brief profile of two famous women scientists suggests how these themes were played out in their individual lives and careers.

NOBEL LAUREATES

Barbara McClintock and Gertrude Elion are two of the nine women scientists who have been awarded the Nobel Prize, the highest honor in recognition of scientific discoveries. Although both are still alive at the time that this book goes to press, their productivity over lengthy scientific careers can be studied as exemplary of the great women biologists who have achieved the highest recognition awarded in a male dominated profession.

Barbara McClintock

Barbara McClintock, the third of four children of Thomas Henry McClintock, a physician, and Sara Handy McClintock, was born on 15 June 1902 in Hartford, Connecticut (Current Biography Yearbook, 1984). After her only brother was born in 1904, she frequently lived for long periods with her paternal aunt and uncle in rural Massachusetts, where she began to enjoy nature and the solitary life.

In 1908, the McClintocks moved to the semirural Flatbush section of Brooklyn, New York, where Barbara received her elementary and secondary education. Although she loved information and solving problems, she also enjoyed sports and solitary experiences, "thinking about things" (Current Biography Yearbook, 1984).

Understanding nature through an intimate knowledge of how a particular organism responds to changes in its internal and external environment provides the central focus for McClintock's life and work. As a child, she "immensely" enjoyed the time she spent in the country and her solitary times spent reading and "thinking about things." McClintock told her biographer (Keller, 1983) that in her science classes she delighted in finding the unexpected answer: "I loved to know things. I would solve some of the problems in ways that weren't the answer the instructor expected. . . . It was a tremendous joy, the whole process of finding that answer, just pure joy" (Current Biography Yearbook, 1984). Unfortunately her mother opposed her attending college. After she had worked in an employment agency for a year while trying to educate herself, her parents relented and sent her to Cornell University in 1919. Because the head of the department of plant breeding in the College of Agriculture did not consider women suitable for the field, McClintock majored in botany.

Soon she became fascinated with genetics and took graduate courses while still a junior. She continued her graduate work at Cornell, receiving her masters in 1925 and her doctorate in 1927 in botany (Current Biography Yearbook, 1984). McClintock became involved in the field of genetics only 21 years after the rediscovery in 1900 of Mendel's principles of heredity (McClintock, 1983). The field of genetics itself and her unique approaches to studying the maize organism in its surrounding environment led her to find many unexpected answers.

When McClintock registered as a graduate student in the Botany Department at Cornell University in 1923 with an intent to major in cytology and minor in genetics and zoology, it was a stimulating time for graduate students at Cornell in the College of Agriculture. Faculty were pioneering work in plant genetics, particularly investigating maize or Indian corn. As an undergraduate studying genetics with C. B. Hutchinson and cytology with Lester W. Sharp, McClintock had already become interested in the structure of chromosomes and their behaviors during meiosis and mitosis. She entered graduate school with the aim of studying cytogenetics or the genetic content and expressions of chromosomes.

During her graduate work and immediately following receipt of her Ph.D. in 1927, McClintock explored the morphology of the 10 maize chromosomes and the correlations between cytological markers and visible genetic traits along with graduate students George Beadle and Marcus Rhoades. This research was fruitful, resulting in nine published papers between 1929 and 1931 (Current Biography Yearbook, 1984).

She remained at Cornell after completing her doctorate to study the relationship between chromosomes, genes, and other aspects of cytogenetics. At that time she worked closely with George W. Beadle and Marcus Rhoades under the guidance of Professor Rollins Emerson, a group of colleagues with whom she retained a warm personal relationship throughout her life. In 1931 she and Harriet Creighton published a famous paper providing the evidence for genetic exchange between chromosomes, or crossing over: that chromosomes exchange genetic information and physical material when they cross over in early meiosis. Encouraged by the famous geneticist Thomas Hunt Morgan, McClintock and Creighton in August 1931, published a cornerstone paper in experimental genetics entitled "A Correlation of Cytological and Genetical Crossing-Over in *Zea Mays*" in the *Proceedings of the National Academy of Sciences* (McClintock & Creighton, 1931).

Receiving a National Research Council Fellowship from 1931 to 1933,

McClintock traveled frequently from Cornell to the California Institute of Technology, stopping at the University of Missouri in Columbia to work with Lewis Stadler on the effects of X-rays in inducing ring chromosomes in maize. Although she traveled to Germany in 1933 as a Guggenheim Fellow to study with Richard Goldschmidt, she returned abruptly, shocked by the rise of Nazism (Keller, 1983).

Despite the acclaim received for her work, because she was a woman Cornell would not give her a faculty position. McClintock remained at Cornell, working in Rollins Emerson's laboratory on Rockefeller Foundation funded research. Although much less qualified male colleagues were receiving faculty appointments, McClintock's gender stood in her way, despite her outstanding reputation. Finally in 1936 she became an assistant professor at the University of Missouri at Columbia.

She remained at the University of Missouri until 1941 while she conducted experiments that led to the publication of a series of papers explaining the process by which broken chromosomes fuse (McClintock, 1938, 1941a, 1941b). She demonstrated that cells are able to sense the presence in their nuclei of ruptured ends of chromosomes and then activate a mechanism that will bring them together and unite the ends. This breakage–fusion–bridge cycle initiated during meiosis continues during the development of the pollen grain and embryo sac. It also may continue during mitoses of the developing endosperm, leading to the variegated colors of the corn kernels.

Although she became vice president of the Genetics Society of America in 1939 (Lewin, 1983), she was not promoted at the University of Missouri. As a female who often demonstrated independent and nontraditional behavior, she remained on the margins of academia and left the University in 1941. She spent the summer of 1941 working with Marcus Rhoades at Cold Spring Harbor Laboratory on Long Island. After a one-year temporary position, Milislav Demerec, director of the Department of Genetics of the Carnegie Institution of Washington at Cold Spring Harbor offered her a permanent position. It was at Cold Spring Harbor in the 1940s that she conducted her initial pioneering experiments on genetic transposition (McClintock, 1944, 1945, 1947, 1948, 1950).

With the stability of a permanent position, McClintock undertook the series of experiments beginning in 1944 that led her to discover the transposable elements for which she received the Nobel Prize almost four decades later. Observation of seedling mutants of approximately 450 plants whose parents each had a newly ruptured chromosome arm convinced her that regulation of pattern of gene expression was associated with an event occurring at mitosis in which one daughter cell had gained something the other had lost. She concluded that transposable elements were the controlling factors for gene expression that were gained and lost (McClintock, 1983).

By 1947 McClintock was investigating the factors responsible for activating the movement of the transposable elements. She determined that the genome responds to the entrance of a newly ruptured end of a chromosome into a telophase nucleus by activating silent, but potentially transposable elements. In any one strain of maize the number of silent but potentially transposable elements, as well as other repetitive DNA, may be observed to change, and most probably in response to challenges not yet recognized.

In 1944 McClintock was elected president of the Genetics Society of America, became the third woman named to the National Academy of Sciences, and was listed among the 1,000 top scientists in the United States by the new edition of *American Men* [sic] *of Science*. These honors were based on her earlier work. However, when her theory of transposition was presented at a Cold Spring Harbor symposium in the summer of 1951, it was neither understood nor accepted. "They called me crazy, absolutely mad at times" (McClintock quoted in *Time*, 1981, p. 84).

Because the view of genes as immovable beads on a string and the central dogma of the Watson-Crick model of DNA predominated for years to come, McClintock became increasingly isolated. Rebuffed by her scientific colleagues, she stopped publishing in major scientific journals, although she continued her research. "In an interview two years ago, Dr. McClintock said that because she received only three requests for reprints of an article on jumping genes that she wrote in a scientific journal in 1953, she decided to confine most of her writing to the annual reports of the Carnegie Institution, which helps finance her laboratory" (Altman, 1983, p. A-1). From 1958 to 1960, she even took time from her research at the invitation of the National Academy of Sciences, to train Latin American cytologists to collect and identify indigenous strains of maize.

Ironically it was from the field of molecular biology—the same field whose prominence and theories had initially led to the lack of understanding and appreciation for the significance of her work—that the sophisticated techniques to vindicate her theory of transposability also emerged. A series of genetic engineering experiments done by molecular biologists demonstrated that pieces of bacterial DNA do "jump around" on the chromosomes (Cherfas & Connor, 1983).

Other research documented that genetic transposition occurs not only in maize and bacteria, but also in viruses, insects, and higher organisms. Transposition may explain diverse phenomena from antibody formation to chromosome changes in cancer cells to species formation during evolution (McClintock, 1983).

When the practical implications for research in medicine, agriculture, and evolution of McClintock's research began to be understood, she was showered with numerous awards. Appointed Andrew White Professor-At-Large at Cornell in 1965, she received the Kimber Genetics Award from the National Academy of Sciences in 1967. In 1970 she received the National Medal of Science, followed by the Albert Lasker Basic Medical Research Award in 1981. The Lasker Award is the highest honor of its kind in the United States and is often seen as a stepping stone to the Nobel Prize. In 1981 she also received Israel Wolf's Foundation Prize and the MacArthur Foundation $60,000 lifetime, tax-free annual fellowship (Wallis, 1983). In 1982 she shared with Susumu Tonegawa Columbia University's Horwitz Prize.

McClintock's receipt in 1983 of the Nobel Prize in Physiology or Medicine was viewed both as very appropriate and quite overdue by both her colleagues and the general public. Several aspects of McClintock and the circumstances of her discoveries particularly appealed to the scientific and popular media: McClintock's work represented significant discoveries in basic research that had enormous practical applications not anticipated initially; the importance of her work was ignored and misunderstood by her colleagues for almost 40 years; she worked alone without the benefit of sophisticated equipment or substantial funding; and McClintock was a woman scientist who embodied other unusual personal characteristics (Wallis, 1983).

When the award was announced, the scientific community expressed its appreciation for the significance of her work. The Nobel Prize Committee itself set the tone by describing her work as quoted in the 24 October 1983 issue of *Time* as "one of the two great discoveries of our times in genetics, the other being the 1953 discovery, by James Watson and Francis Crick of the double-helix structure of DNA" (Wallis, 1983). Watson himself gave further support to the significance of her work: "It is not a controversial award. No one thinks of genetics now without the implications of her work." As director at Cold Spring Harbor, Watson had been her boss for the last 15 years.

Bioscience quoted the Karolinska Institute in Stockholm as stating that "the initial discovery of mobile genetic elements by Barbara McClintock is of great medical and biological significance. It has also resulted in new perspectives on how genes are formed and how they change during evolution" ("Barbara McClintock," 1984). McClintock noted that her work in corn genetics was initially seen as obscure and insignificant: "If I had been at some other place, I'm sure I would've been fired for what I was doing," she noted "because nobody was accepting it" (*Time*, 24 October 1983).

Consistently described as a loner, McClintock captured the attention of the media as the parallel of Mendel as a scientist who worked alone, with plants, and without sophisticated equipment. *Time* (24 October 1983) stated: "Genetics is a science founded by a monk—19th century Augustinian Gregor Mendel—and McClintock is in every sense his disciple. For half a century she has labored in almost monastic solitude over her patch of Indian corn, or maize, much as Mendel did in his famous pea patch. In an era when most scientific work is done by large research teams, McClintock did not even have a laboratory assistant."

In addition to her status as a loner, both scientists and the media appeared to be fascinated by her other "unusual" characteristics. Virtually all accounts emphasized that she was only the seventh woman to ever receive the Nobel Prize in scientific categories. Only she, France's Marie Curie in 1911, and Britain's Dorothy Crowfoot Hodgkin in 1964 won without fellow honorees. McClintock is the first sole female recipient in medicine or physiology (Beck, 1983; Wallis, 1983).

Several accounts also underlined the simplicity of McClintock's life and her lack of interest in material possessions. The 11 October 1983 *Chicago Tribune* quoted McClintock's nephew's wife when asked how McClintock might use the $190 thousand prize money as saying: "Last year she said all she wanted were her glasses and her car. So last year she bought a new car after 30 years" (Sec. 1, p. 4).

McClintock's nature was reflected in her own reaction to receipt of the prize. After learning that she had received the prize from a radio broadcast, as she does not have a telephone in her residence, McClintock went out to take her daily nature walk and pick walnuts along a wooded path near her house at Cold Spring Harbor Laboratories. Later at a news conference she said, "You don't need the public recognition; you just need the respect of your colleagues" (Altman, 1983, p. C-6). McClintock's lack of bitterness after years of being misunderstood and her continued love for unveiling the secrets of nature captured the attention of the scientific and public communities. Nor did fame distract her from her work. Barbara McClintock continued to pursue her research at the Cold Spring Harbor Laboratories until June of 1992. She died, aged 90, on 2 September, 1992.

Gertrude Elion

Gertrude Belle Elion, born in New York City on 23 January 1918, was the only daughter of a dentist and his wife. When she was 15 her grandfather died of cancer. His death influenced her decision to become a scientist to find ways to help other cancer patients avoid the suffering her grandfather endured.

Her parents were supportive and "very anxious" for her to have a career (Kolata, 1988). With Elion's strong determination to become a scientist, she would probably have successfully pursued her major at any college, including a coeducational institution. However statistics documenting that women's colleges produce proportionately more women scientists than coeducational institutions and that a much higher percentage of successful women scientists attend women's colleges would suggest that Elion's matriculation at Hunter provided a supportive environment for her career aspirations. She received her A.B. in 1937 from Hunter College in chemistry.

As a woman, Elion faced obstacles in beginning her career rarely experienced by male scientists. Laboratory jobs with major pharmaceutical companies were then reserved for men. After working as a lab assistant for the School of Nursing at New York Hospital for one year and the Denver Chemical Company for two years, she worked to receive her M.S. from New York University. Still finding laboratory positions closed to her, she taught chemistry and physics in high school (Kolata, 1988). During World War II, the shortage of male scientists available to pharmaceutical companies forced them to give women opportunities (Marx, 1988). She worked for Quaker Maid Company as an analyst in food chemistry from 1942 to 1943 and a research chemist in organic chemistry from 1943 to 1944.

In 1944 she was hired by Burroughs Wellcome Company. Lacking a doctorate she was initially hired to be a laboratory assistant to Dr. George H. Hitchings. He had theorized that it might be possible to stop the growth of rapidly dividing cells such as bacteria, tumors, and protozoa by using antagonists (antimetabolites) of the nucleic acid bases. Elion was assigned to work on the purines, pteridines, and some other condensed pyrimidine systems. Because few chemists were interested in the synthesis of purines in those days, she relied mainly on the methods from the old German literature, specifically Fisher's transformation reactions and Traube's syntheses from pyrimidine intermediates.

"At the beginning it was a question of whether I'd get married or stay at the company" she said. "In those days, women couldn't do both." She never married (Kolata, 1988, p. A-1).

Recognizing that the lack of a doctoral degree might work to her disadvantage at Burroughs Wellcome, she enrolled in a Ph.D. program at Brooklyn Polytechnic Institute. Elion took courses at night, commuting over $1\frac{1}{2}$ hours each way after working all day. Eventually she quit the program because of the institution's requirement that she must attend full time to receive the degree. She could not afford to give up her job to meet the requirement (Kolata, 1988).

Fortunately, Hitchings recognized Elion's talents and worked with her as a colleague rather than an assistant. By 1951 they had made and tested over 100 purines using *Lactobacillus casei* as the test microorganism and had discovered that the substitution of oxygen by sulfur at the 6-position would produce inhibitors of purine utilization. Testing on rodents and children with acute leukemia at the

Sloan-Kettering Institute revealed that 6-mercaptopurine (6-MP) was effective in producing remissions (Elion, 1988).

In 1953, only two years after synthesis and testing, the Food and Drug Administration approved 6-MP. Immediately, the average survival time of children with leukemia was increased from three months to one year; today 6-MP used in combination with other drugs has led to the cure of 80% of children with acute leukemia.

In the early 1950s Elion and her colleagues explored the biochemical pathways and metabolic fate of 6-MP. She used ion-exchange columns and paper chromatography to investigate the fate of 6-MP in vivo and to explore possibilities for modifying its metabolism. While attempting to modify the metabolism and thus increase clinical efficacy, they synthesized azathioprine (AZT). Although AZT was recognized initially to be effective in treating patients with leukemia, today it is more widely recognized as the drug used to treat AIDS.

Robert Schwartz, working with William Dameshek in Boston, had discovered by 1958 that 6-MP was effective in suppressing the immune system. This information coupled with the work by Roy Calne in England on the effect of 6-MP in reducing kidney transplant rejection in dogs led Elion and her colleagues to identify new active agents and synergistic combinations of drugs effective in immunosuppression. 6-MP, thioguanine, and AZT are now used in the treatment of autoimmune hemolytic anemia, systemic lupus, and chronic active hepatitis. AZT is an approved drug for the treatment of severe rheumatoid arthritis (Elion, 1988).

By the early 1960s Elion and her colleagues began to explore methods to increase the activity of 6-MP by producing an inhibitor to the oxidation of 6-MP catabolism. The inhibitor, allopurinol and its derivative, oxypurinol, revealed that they are effective, safe drugs for long-term treatment of gout. They also reduce the joint pain from uric acid and kidney stones that often form in gout sufferers.

About 10 years later, the finding of Joseph Marr that allopurinol inhibits the replication of some protozoans led Elion and co-workers to discover antiparasitic uses for allopurinol. They exploited differences between mammals and protozoans in the incorporation of allopurinol to treat successfully Leishmaniasis and Chagas' disease (Elion, 1988).

Work begun 20 years earlier stimulated Elion and her colleagues to explore in 1968 the antiviral activity of diaminopurine arabinoside. In 1970 Burroughs Wellcome moved their laboratories from Tuckahoe, New York to Research Triangle Park, North Carolina. Howard Schaeffer had synthesized acyclic nucleoside analogs with antiviral activity. Elion and her group defined the mechanisms of action, enzymology, and in vivo metabolism of the analogs. One of these, acyclovir, was effective against the herpes simplex viruses 1 and 2 and varicella-zoster virus both in vivo and in vitro.

Investigations in animals and human beings revealed that acyclovir is a very selective drug. Highly effective against herpes simplex 1 and 2 and varicella zoster, acyclovir is moderately effective against Epstein-Barr and pseudorabies. However, it shows only slight activity against human cytomegalovirus (HCMV) (Elion, 1988).

Intensive research by Elion and co-workers revealed some of the mechanisms that induced this specificity. They turned this information into an effective means for reducing human suffering. For example, acyclovir alleviates symptoms significantly and decreases the time of viral shedding and healing in victims of genital herpes. It also decreases new lesion formation from 23% to 6.5% in individuals with recurrent episodes. In immunosuppressed individuals, acyclovir may mean the difference between life and death. Similarly, in treatment of shingles, acyclovir significantly reduces the pain for most individuals. Acyclovir may save the lives of immunocompromised people by preventing progressive skin dissemination and visceral disease.

The most remarkable aspect of the 1988 Nobel Prize in medicine shared by Elion, Hitchings, and Black was that it was awarded for the development of new drugs. Virtually every piece surrounding the award published in both the popular and scientific press noted that it was extremely unusual for the Nobel committee to give the award to individuals working for drug companies ("Nobel Prizes," 1988). In its 18 October 1988 article the *New York Times* stated, "Only a few times in the 87-year history of the Nobel Prize has the medical award been granted to researchers who discovered drugs and who worked for drug companies" (A-1). In a similar vein *Science* in its 28 October 1988 issue noted: "The Nobel Assembly rarely favors the researchers who develop new drugs with the prize" (Marx, 1988, p. 517).

In awarding the prize, the Nobel Assembly at the Karolinska Institute specifically mentioned that the researchers' drug discoveries grew out of the better understanding of cell biochemistry and physiology generated by their investigations. They emphasized that the research "has had a more fundamental significance" than the discovery of individual drugs (Sjoqvist, 1988). Perhaps the Nobel Assembly emphasized the fundamental understanding of the cell and the basic research involved in their discoveries in an attempt to explain their nontraditional award to individuals in private industry working on applied research.

Colleagues in the scientific community reacted favorably to the choice of the individuals for the award. Experts such as Paul Calabresi at Brown University's School of Medicine noted the significance of their discoveries for cancer chemotherapy, immunosuppression, malaria, viruses, and AIDS. The Nobel Committee, scientific colleagues, and the popular press all underlined the fact that these drugs have withstood the test of time. A Nobel official noted: ''We are still harvesting the fruits of what they determined almost 40 years ago'' (*Time*, 1988, p. 71). Other scientists commented on their amazing understanding and discoveries that occurred at a time when very little was known about cell structure and function: ''Although this is easy to see now, in the 1940's when Hitchings and Elion began their investigations very little was known about the nucleic acids'' (Marx, 1988, p. 516).

The portion of the publicity particularly focused on Elion emphasized the small number of women in science and the different choices that women scientists, including Elion, are forced to make (Kolata, 1988). To appreciate this focus it is important to recognize that Elion was only the ninth woman to receive the Prize in either science or medicine and physiology during the 87 years that the Nobel Prize has been given.

Most scientific journals restricted their comments regarding the scarcity of women scientists and their career difficulties to Elion's initial problems in getting hired. *Science*, for example, stated that Elion had noted that most companies were reluctant to employ women scientists ''but the shortage of men during World War II gave women new opportunities to work in the laboratory'' (Marx, 1988, p. 516).

The popular press, however, gave the issue more attention and emphasized the problem that most women scientists are forced to choose between career and marriage and family. Gina Kolata interviewed and profiled Gertrude Elion for the 18 October 1988 issue of the *New York Times*. Kolata (1988, A-1) noted that as a scientist for over 40 years Elion ''has had to struggle against preconceived notions of what careers were suitable for women.'' Elion was forced to teach high school rather than work in a laboratory after graduation from Hunter, because laboratory jobs were reserved for men until World War II. In 1944, Elion was hired by Burroughs Wellcome Company as an assistant for Hitchings. Hitchings' acceptance of her as a colleague led to their ultimate sharing of the prize. Although she viewed her lack of a doctoral degree as a disadvantage, she stated that she was accepted and respected at Burroughs Wellcome. However, Elion felt that her acceptance as a serious scientist was contingent on her decision not to marry and have children. ''She felt that she would not have advanced in her career if she had chosen to marry and have children because women were not encouraged then to work while their children were young'' (Kolata, 1988, A-1).

Because of their dedication and belief in their work, both McClintock and Elion overcame many of the severe barriers placed in their paths simply because of their gender. As was the case with many of the few successful women scientists, they never married nor did they rear children. Although McClintock shuns questions about gender, family, and relationships, Elion states directly that because she was a woman she felt that she must not marry and have children if she wanted a successful career as a scientist. For both McClintock and Elion, the supportive role played by at least one male colleague who helped to advance her work was significant.

WOMEN BIOLOGISTS RECOGNIZED POSTHUMOUSLY

Rosalind Franklin

The Nobel Prize is never awarded posthumously. Both Elion and McClintock were fortunate to live long enough to receive recognition for work that they had done 40 years earlier. Because of the lengthier period of time it appears to take for the scientific community to recognize the significance of work done by women scientists in particular, some women have died before receiving such recognition. Just as Evelyn Fox Keller's 1983 biography of McClintock was instrumental in bringing attention to her work, which culminated in the award of the Nobel Prize, other feminists have revealed and emphasized to the scientific community the misunderstood and undervalued work of other women scientists.

Ann Sayre's (1975) biography of Rosalind Franklin underscored the fact that the ''discovery'' of the double helix by Watson and Crick could not have occurred had they not used, without her authorization or knowledge, Franklin's X-ray diffraction picture of DNA. Sayre also revealed, by cleverly emphasizing Watson's own words from his account of the discovery in *The Double Helix* (1969), the sexist behavior of Watson towards Franklin. Not only did he use her work without her knowledge, he also falsely assumed that she had been brought into the lab to assist Wilkins. In fact she had been invited to join the group as an equal to Wilkins and held superior experience to his in X-ray diffraction. Hubbard (1990) reinforces Sayre's account (1975) of the disparaging comments made by Watson about Franklin's personality and physical and sexual attractiveness. The lack of recognition of Franklin's significant contribution to the double helical model was aided by her discrediting at the hands of a male colleague. He emphasized her unmarried state as an indicator of her difficult personality and sexual unattractiveness rather than as a signal that she wished to pursue a serious career in science.

Rachel Carson

H. Patricia Hynes (1989) finds that Rachel Carson's unmarried status and emphasis on her personal characteristics were also used by her male colleagues to undermine the significance of her work. Hynes chronicles the events that drove Carson (1962) to write *Silent Spring*, the reaction of the world to her work, including the establishment of the Environmental Protection Agency, and the extent to which the continued failure to heed her advice signals impending ecological disaster for nature and people, particularly women. Hynes's account of Carson reveals a woman whose life was inspired and fulfilled by both her work and her strong friendships with women. Carson's previous male biographers have accepted the negative image of Carson as a lonely spinster, although they rejected the propaganda painted by government and pesticide-industry officials that her work was flawed and exaggerated.

Carson recognized that the pesticides developed for chemical warfare during World War II and marketed as necessary for crop production after the war were biocides harmful to people and animals, although profitable for the chemical industry. Despite the extensive efforts of agribusiness and the chemical industry to discredit Carson's work, the world heard her message. Hynes (1989) documents with detailed examples the evidence accumulated since *Silent Spring* that further proves Carson's case.

The establishment of the Environmental Protection Agency was the result of Carson's call for an agency free from conflict of interest from government or industrial control. However, it has recently come under criticism for failure to protect the environment. Hynes measures the extent to which the Agency has succeeded in developing the ethic of the environment demanded by Carson.

She argues that Carson's work provided tools to "critique and protest a world increasingly dominated by technologies which endanger ecosystems" (Hynes, 1989, p. 24). Hynes recognizes that the agricultural biotechnologies and reproductive technologies are newly endangering the world in the quarter century since the publication of *Silent Spring*. Commercial interests and the scientific enterprise sell the biotechnologies as cures for world hunger and infertility while masking the environmental ravages that result in crop failures in third-world countries and reduced fertility in developed countries. In *The Recurring Silent Spring*, Hynes reveals the biotechnologies as the latest technical turnkeys that exploit nature and women for the benefit of men.

AFRICAN-AMERICAN WOMEN BIOLOGISTS

Women of color who choose careers in science must overcome the double barriers of race and gender when they attempt to enter a profession that is traditionally white and male. James Jay (1971) estimates that approximately 650 black Americans received doctoral degrees in the natural sciences between 1876 and 1969.

He suggests that although the 84,000 doctorates awarded in the fields in the U.S. from 1920 to 1962 may make the number of African-American Ph.D.s appear to be low, in fact the numbers are exceptional given the adversities faced by the recipients.

In addition to the problems of racism and economic hardship faced by black men seeking a doctorate, black women also endured sexism (Patterson, 1989). Although more black women than men graduated from college between 1876 and 1969, only 58 of the 650 natural science doctorates were awarded to women (Jay, 1971). "More than 50% (31) of these 58 natural science doctorates awarded to Black females between 1876 and 1969 were in the biological sciences: zoology— 14; bacteriology—7; botany—7; and general biology—3" (Patterson, 1989, p. 8).

Ruth Moore was the first American-born black woman to earn a doctorate in the life sciences. She received her degree in bacteriology from Ohio State in 1933. Other black women who were the first to receive their doctorates in the life sciences were as follows: Jessie Jarue Mark in botany in 1935 from Iowa State University; Roger Arliner Young in zoology in 1935 from the University of Pennsylvania; Ruth Lloyd in anatomy in 1941 from Western Reserve University; Mary Logan Reddick in neuroembryology in 1944 from Radcliffe and Harvard; and Geraldine Pittman Woods also in neuroembryology in 1945 from Harvard.

Unfortunately during the last decade the number of research doctorates earned by blacks has declined by 27% (*Black Issues in Higher Education*, 1988). Only 64% of 820 doctorates earned by blacks in 1986 were in the life sciences. "In 1986 white females received approximately 37 percent of all life science doctorates as compared to 0.9 percent for Black females" (Patterson, 1989, p. 8).

A knowledge of these statistics combined with an awareness of the obstacles they faced in achieving careers in biology motivated some of the outstanding African-American women biologists. In addition to building exemplary research careers in their own discipline, many have developed special programs to attract women and minorities to science.

Jewel Plummer Cobb

Born 17 January 1924 in Chicago, Illinois, Jewel Plummer Cobb attended Englewood High School where she credits her teachers, particularly Ms. Hyman, her biology teacher during her sophomore year, and Ms. Mordoff, her zoology and botany teacher, with inspiring her interest in biology (Cobb, 1989). Her father, a physician, and her mother, a physical education and dance instructor, encouraged her interest in science at home. Although she began her college career at the University of Michigan in Ann Arbor in 1941, aspects of the social life that prevented black students from living in the dormitory and participating in mainstream fraternities and sororities, caused her to leave Michigan and earn her undergraduate degree from Talladega College in Alabama.

Her bacteriology professor at Talladega encouraged her to attend graduate school at New York University (Cobb, 1989). From NYU she received her M.S. in 1947 and her Ph.D. in 1950 in cell physiology. The thesis for her master's degree involved original laboratory research using a Warburg respirator on a series of organic molecules, aromatic amidines, to determine their effect on the respiration of yeast cells. "My doctoral dissertation dealt with the way melanin pigment granules could be formed *in vitro* (outside the body) using the enzyme tyrosinase" (Cobb, 1989, p. 40).

During a two-year appointment as a postdoctoral fellow at the National Cancer Institute she worked with advanced cancer patients at Harlem Hospital to examine the effects of newly synthesized folic acid antagonists on cells (Cobb, 1989). In 1952 she became an Instructor in the Anatomy Department at the University of Illinois College of Medicine where she directed the Tissue Culture Laboratory. Returning to New York City in 1955, she married and joined the New York University faculty in Research Surgery. In 1960 she went to Sarah Lawrence College where she ultimately became Professor of Biology and head of the Cell Biology Laboratory. From 1969 to 1976, she was Professor of Zoology and Dean of Connecticut College (Patterson, 1989).

During the 24 years from 1952 to 1976, her research was supported by external grants from the National Cancer Institute of the National Institutes of Health, the Damon Runyon Cancer Fund, and/or the American Cancer Society (Cobb, 1989). This research examined factors that influence growth, morphology, and genetic expression of normal and neoplastic pigment cells. She published 36 journal articles on this research. During this period, Dr. Cobb managed to combine a successful career in scientific research with childrearing.

> Perhaps my most interesting work, an in-depth analysis of Thio-Tepa, a promising anti-cancer drug, was a cinematographic analysis of cell division movement behavior photographed through a special phase contrast microscope. I presented my paper on this work at the eighth International Cancer Congress in 1962 in Moscow. As I read my paper there, it was simultaneously translated into five other languages. At that time my son was just five years old and I was most reluctant to leave him at home because I was traveling so far away. However, my husband and son clearly thrived in my absence. (Cobb, 1989, p. 42)

She also successfully combined increasing administrative duties with her research schedule.

> This research was indeed invigorating and for seven years, while dean of the college at Connecticut College, I arranged my schedule to spend early morning hours in my research lab before going to my dean's office or teaching a course. There were several undergraduates interested in my research who, together with two excellent research assistants, formed our group. While this schedule was full, it was rewarding. (Cobb, 1989, p. 42)

In 1976, she stopped active laboratory research to become Dean of Douglass College of Rutgers University and Professor of Biology. From this position, she worked to increase underrepresented groups—women and minorities—in science. She had begun this work while dean at Connecticut College by establishing a new program called Postgraduate Premedical and Predental Program for Minority Students, which prepared highly motivated advanced undergraduates who were minorities and put them on a fast track in science to enter professional schools. "In six years of the program, 90% of the approximately 40 students entered professional schools of their choice" (Cobb, 1989, p. 42).

Perceiving that her position as an administrator enabled her to improve the status of women and minorities, she left Douglass in 1981 to become president of California State College in Fullerton (Patterson, 1989).

> As an educator and administrator Dr. Cobb has focused on analysis of causes of under-representation of women in science, the future of international science in developing countries, and the development of science programs for minority youth. She has published nine articles concerning the advancement of minorities and women in the sciences. In a 1988 interview, Dr. Cobb summarized her views on moving from education into administration: "What happens in this business is that you begin to look outside your discipline at campus-wide policy . . . I found that I was concerned about what happened in biology, but also about what was happening on other levels such as student planning, the handling of faculty. You realize that if you care about those things . . . administration is the way for you to do something about it. (Patterson, 1989, p. 10)

Dr. Cobb is an outstanding role model for all biologists—female or male, black or white. She has achieved success as a scientist, educator, and administrator. She has used her position on policy committees such as the National Science Board of the National Science Foundation (NSF) to establish and chair committees such as Women and Minorities in Science, to expand and diversify the pool of scientists.

LIVES OF ORDINARY WOMEN BIOLOGISTS

In addition to recovering from obscurity and providing new positive interpretations of some individual women scientists, feminism has shaped the history of women in biology in another way. Some historians have rejected the male model emphasizing famous pioneers and sought to examine the lives and situations of women in science who were not famous. Margaret Rossiter's (1982) *Women Scientists in America: Struggles and Strategies to 1940* is a groundbreaking book that examines how the work of the usual woman scientist suffers from underrecognition due to application of double standards and other social barriers inherent in the structure of the scientific community. Vivian Gornick (1983) adopts some of this approach in her popularized work *Women in Science* in which she explores the daily lives, hopes, and frustrations of contemporary women scientists.

A newer work by the historian of science Londa Schiebinger (1989) documents the significant role that women played in the development of early modern science in Western Europe. Margaret Cavendish in England and Emilie du Châtelet in France serve as examples of prominent, upper-class natural philosophers in seventeenth- and eighteenth-century Europe.

Although Schiebinger (1989) discusses these great women in the history of science, the originality of her work rests on her illustration of the involvement of many women in science. Schiebinger depicts the role of aristocratic women who dominated the informal salons of seventeenth-century Paris. Madame Geoffrin, Madame Helvetius, Madame Rochefoucauld, and Madame Lavoisier used their salons for discussions of science and competed with the academies of the day for the attention of the learned (Schiebinger, 1989).

In Germany women of the artisan class who worked alongside their husbands, fathers, and brothers in the family business pursued research in scientific fields such as astronomy and entomology. The craft tradition in seventeenth- and eighteenth-century Germany permitted women such as Maria Sibylla Merian to serve as an apprentice in the workshops of her father and stepfather to learn illustration. She converted this art into a scientific career through her exact observations and depictions of the life cycles of various insects, including the silkworm. Between 1650 and 1710, Germany also produced several women astronomers: Maria Cunitz, Elisabeth Hevelius, Maria Eimmart, Maria Winkelmann, and her daughters, Christine Kerch and Margaretha. Typically these women learned the trade at the side of their fathers and worked alongside their husbands in the guild. Schiebinger (1989) points out that the role of a guild wife was more comprehensive than that of assistant to the husband. Because the observatory was in the home, not in a university, German women astronomers collaborated with their husbands and did more than calculations and computations.

In *Uneasy Careers and Intimate Lives: Women in Science, 1789–1979*, Abir-Am and Outram (1987) also abandon the "great women" approach to the history of science by their exploration of the mutual impact of family life and scientific career. By examining the interaction of domestic life and working life in American and European women scientists over the span of two centuries, they begin to elucidate the changing impact of gender and gender roles on women's lives as scientists at different historical times, different geographic locations, and in different scientific disciplines.

FEMINIST BIOLOGISTS

Feminists have thus revealed the obstacles and forces that mold the lives of ordinary women biologists. They have also been instrumental in bringing the significant contributions of overlooked women scientists to the attention of the scientific community and ultimately to the general public.

Ironically, many women scientists reject feminism. Elion admits that gender affected her career in terms of obstacles and foreclosing the option of marriage and family; she stops short of calling herself a feminist. Keller's feminist biography about McClintock, emphasizing the influence that her gender may have had on her different approach to science, was a factor that contributed to the recognition of McClintock's work and her receiving the Nobel Prize. However, McClintock is adamant that she herself is not a feminist and denies the possibility that her gender might have influenced her work in any way.

Many scientists are feminists in their politics or in their relationships outside of the laboratory. Although they fight for feminist causes in other arenas, they leave feminism at the laboratory door, divorced from their scientific hypothesizing, data gathering, and theorizing. Some scientists who are feminists (Keller, 1984) even question whether or not gender enters into good science.

Most feminists are not scientists. A quick perusal of the women's studies journals and disciplinary affiliations of most feminists in academia yields an overwhelming majority of scholars in the humanities and social sciences. Few feminists outside of academia are scientists. In fact, many feminists openly reject science, which they view as a male-dominant patriarchal approach to the world and women (Holliday, 1978).

Ruth Bleier

Ruth Bleier was one of a small group of individuals interested in both science and feminism, and the interaction between the two. Born in 1923 near Pittsburgh, Pennsylvania, Ruth Bleier was an only child. She saw this as a great help and suggested in a 1984 interview (Martin, 1988) that "I got to do everything the son would do as well as the daughter." After receiving a bachelor's degree in political science from Goucher College, she pursued a medical degree at the

Women's Medical College of Pennsylvania. During this same period she became involved with AIMS (the Association of Interns and Medical Students) whose political purposes included improving the future of civilization by seeking world peace while also improving medical education and practice.

After interning at Sinai Hospital in Baltimore from 1949 to 1951, she practiced medicine for seven years in a working-class racially mixed neighborhood. Here she continued to fight discrimination within medicine and the larger political realm. As one of the leading organizers in the Maryland Committee for Peace, Ruth helped petition to end the Korean War and ban atomic weapons. Because of her political activities during this period of McCarthyism, at age 28 Bleier's name appeared on J. Edgar Hoover's personal, unpublished "wanted list" and she was called to testify before the House Un-American Activities Committee (HUAC) in July of 1951. Her testimony before the Committee included the following statement:

> As a physician, as a woman, as an heir to a great democratic tradition, I will continue to fight for the America I love: one where all peoples have full equality, where our constitutional rights become the unquestionable birthright of all regardless of color, creed, or belief; where all have an equal opportunity to pursue the full development and realization of their potentialities and aspirations; where our science and technology, that produced the boundless resources of atomic energy, will be turned to peaceful construction for the benefit of all. And this is the America that my generation of Americans will achieve. (Martin, 1988, p. 7)

The traditional medical profession in the traditional city of Baltimore would not tolerate left-wing political views during the McCarthy era. Bleier was denied privileges at Sinai Hospital and was not accepted into the Baltimore City Medical Society.

In 1959 she left the practice of medicine to explore the structure and function of the brain with the aid of a postdoctoral fellowship in neuroanatomy at Johns Hopkins. Drawn to Madison, Wisconsin in 1967, Ruth Bleier's initial appointment was with the Department of Neurophysiology in the Medical School. As she stated in the text of one of her last speeches (actually delivered by someone else because of her illness):

> As many of you know, my own history, before the era of women's studies and from my medical school days, was as a political activist, on the left end of the spectrum, and my preferred activity was to agitate and organize. Thus it came to pass that with the advent of the current Women's movement, I decided to leave the President of the United States and his congress to their own devices and became, instead, an agitator of the University administration and an organizer of women on this campus and throughout the State System beginning in 1970. [And that may be a much more gripping history than the one I was asked to

present here.] While my activities were confined to the political, another part of our activist group, the Association of Faculty Women (a misnomer since it included academic and classified staff and students) worked consistently toward the establishment of women's studies on campus and in the U.W. System, a goal that was accomplished in 1975. (Bleier, 1987, p. 4)

At the University of Wisconsin, organized feminist activities were born in the early 1970s when HEW (Housing, Education, and Welfare Department) investigated sex discrimination charges but spoke only to men. This led to the creation of an active, militant organization, the Association of Faculty Women (AFW), co-chaired by Ruth Bleier. Involved in many issues concerning women such as faculty grievances, Affirmative Action, the Committee of Women in the Sciences, and women's athletics, AFW pushed the administration and was largely responsible for the establishment of the Women's Studies Program.

As a founder of the Women's Studies Program at the University of Wisconsin, Bleier was a pioneer who helped develop and co-teach Biology and Psychology of Women, one of the first four core courses in the program. Imbued with "a passionate vision of the struggle for peace, for feminism, and for truth, and justice" (Martin, 1988, p. 7) Bleier continued to be a guiding light for Women's Studies at Wisconsin, where she served as Chair of Women's Studies from 1982 to 1986, and for feminists throughout the world, where her scholarship on feminism and science became well-known.

Ruth Bleier was unique among scientists who are feminists in that she did not divorce her feminism from her science. She spent hours explaining the connections between feminism and science to her colleagues and friends who were not scientists. She used her feminist analysis to critique existing theories of science, to point out racist, sexist flaws in experimental design and interpretation, and to begin to sketch the parameters for a feminist science. Perhaps more importantly she brought the feminist critique to bear on her own research and that of her colleagues in neuroanatomy. By presentations on feminist issues at the American Association for the Advancement of Science (AAAS) and tangling with the editors of the most prestigious professional journal, *Science*, over experimental methods used in papers showing differences in the size of the corpus callosum between male and female brains (Bleier, 1988), Bleier brought feminism to the cutting edge of research science.

Ruth Bleier was unusual among feminists in that she continued to be a practicing scientist while working on and writing about feminism and science during the four years that she chaired the Women's Studies Program at the University of Wisconsin. The small group of feminists interested in questions of science and feminism consists primarily of historians and philosophers of science. Fewer members of the group have Ph.Ds and teach in traditional scientific disciplines. Of those who do, most have changed their research focus toward feminism and science, gradually dropping "hard science," grant-supported research along the way. Ruth Bleier never stopped her "hard science" research. She continued active neuroanatomy research, well-supported by federal grants, while also writing on feminism and science. In fact, her best known single authored Pergamon book, *Science and Gender* , and a monograph on the cat brain were published simultaneously in 1984.

Ruth Bleier was the feminist scientist who could most skillfully use the methods and theories of feminism to critique science; similarly she employed the tools of science to analyze flaws in the methodology and theoretical constructs of feminism. In this respect she was unique. With her death on 4 January 1988, the world lost a scientist, a feminist, and most importantly, a feminist scientist.

Feminist historians and philosophers of science (Fee 1982; Haraway, 1978; Hein, 1981) have suggested that a theory for a feminist science might also develop. Fee has stated that a sexist society should be expected to develop a sexist science. Conceptualizing a feminist science from within our society is "like asking a medieval peasant to imagine the theory of genetics or the production of a space capsule" (Fee, 1982, 31).

Some feminists who are scientists have even sketched some of the parameters that might distinguish a feminist science from the traditional science as it is now practiced in our culture. Bleier (1984) suggests that ideas central to a feminist science might be the rejection of dualisms such as subjectivity/objectivity, qualitative/quantitative, and nature/culture, which focus our thinking about the world. Kahle (1985) believes that changes in elementary and secondary school teaching that will attract more women to science might lead to feminist science. Fee (1986) has hinted that feminist visions of science are similar to visions proposed by other groups who differ in race, class, or tradition (rather than gender) from the white middle- or upper-class Western men who are the major developers of scientific theories. Fee's comment again raises the question of whether or not gender has a particular influence on science. Posed in broader terms, the question is whether or not "good" science really can be objective, or whether, as it is a human pursuit, it will always be laden with human values and biases such as those of race, class, and gender. Birke's vision is perhaps more far-reaching in that she considers the interactive relationship between feminism and science. She recognizes that science will not be changed by feminism as long as feminists remain solely in the passive, critical role. We must be active and engaged in science to cause the change to occur. "If science is to be changed, then it has to be done in ways that take account of gender and other differences, and that does mean that feminists have to engage actively in making that change" (Birke, 1986, 171).

The demand of Birke (1986) is for feminists to work with science and attempt to change it. She recognizes the ultimate failure of feminist theories and feminists who reject science and technology because they have been used to dominate and control women. Rejecting science and technology will not stop its influence in our daily lives and its capabilities for death and destruction. The only way that feminists can really hope to change it is to understand science and its relationships to women and feminism.

REFERENCES

Abir-Am, P. G. & Outram, D. (Eds.). (1987). *Uneasy careers and intimate lives: Women in science, 1789–1979*. New Brunswick, NJ: Rutgers University Press.

Alic, M. (1986). *Hypatia's heritage*. Boston: Beacon Press.

Altman, L. (1983, October 11). Long Island biologist wins Nobel in medicine. *New York Times*, pp. A-1, C-6.

Barbara McClintock, discoverer of 'jumping genes, wins Nobel. (1984). *Bioscience, 34*(2), 131.

Beck, J. (1983, October 12). Genes, corn, prizes and women. *Chicago Tribune*, Sec. 1, p. 14.

Birke, L. (1986). *Women, feminism and biology. The feminist challenge*. New York: Methuen.

Bleier, R. (1984). *Gender and science*. Elmsford, NY: Pergamon Press.

Bleier, R. (1987), December 4). ''*A decade of feminist critiques in the natural sciences.*'' Women's Studies Research Center Colloquium. Unpublished.

Bleier, R. (1988). *Science* and the construction of meanings in the neurosciences. In S. V. Rosser (Ed.), *Feminism within the science and health care professions: Overcoming resistance* (pp. 91–104). Elmsford, NY: Pergamon Press.

Boccaccio, G. (1963). De Claris Mulieribus. *Concerning famous women* (G. A. Guarino, Trans.). New Brunswick, NJ: Rutgers University Press. (Original work published 1355–59)

Bucciarelli, L., & Dworsky, N. (1980). *Sophie Germain: An essay in the history of the theory of elasticity*. Dordrecht, Holland: D. Reidel.

Carson, R. (1962). *Silent spring*. New York: Fawcett Press.

Cherfas, J., & Connor, S. (1983). How restless DNA was tamed. *New Scientist, 100*, 78–79.

Chicago Tribune Wires. (1983, October 11). U.S. botanist wins Nobel. *Chicago Tribune*, Sec. 1, p. 4.

Cobb, J. P. (1989). A life in science: Research and service. *Sage, 4*(2), 39–43.

Current lack of minority doctoral candidates will lead to future minority faculty shortage. (1988). *Black Issues in Higher Education, 4*(23), 2.

de Pisan, C. (1982). *The book of the city of ladies* (Earl Jeffrey Richards, Trans.). New York: Persea Books. (Reprint, slightly modified from the translation by Earl Jeffrey Richards. Original work published 1405)

Elion, G. (1988). The purine path to chemotherapy. Nobel lecture delivered December 10, 1988 in Stockholm, Sweden.

Fee, E. (1982). A feminist critique of scientific objectivity. *Science for the People, 14*(4), 8.

Fee, E. (1986). Critiques of modern science: The relationship of feminism to other radical epistemologies. In R. Bleier (Ed.), *Feminist approaches to science*. Elmsford, NY: Pergamon Press.

Gornick, V. (1983). *Women in science: Portraits from a world in transition*. New York: Simon and Schuster.

Haber, L. (1979). *Women pioneers of science*. New York: Harcourt Brace Jovanovich.

Haraway, D. (1978). Animal sociology and a natural economy of the body politic, Part I: A political physiology of dominance; Animal sociology and a natural economy of the body politic, Part II: The past is the contested zone: Human nature and theories of production and reproduction in primate behavior studies. *Signs: Journal of Women in Culture and Society, 4*(1), 21–60.

Hein, H. (1981). Woman and science: Fitting men to think about nature. *International Journal of Women's Studies, 4*: 369–377.

Holliday, L. (1978). *The violent sex: Male psychobiology and the evolution of consciousness*. Guerneville, CA: Bluestocking Books.

Hubbard, R. (1990). *Politics of women's biology*. New Brunswick, NJ: Rutgers University Press.

Hynes, H. P. (1984, November/December). Working women: A field report. *Technology Review*, 38ff.

Hynes, H. P. (1989). *The recurring silent spring*. Elmsford, New York: Pergamon Press.

Jay, J. M. (1971). *Negroes in science: Natural science doctorates, 1876–1969* (p. vii). Detroit: Balamp Publishing.

Kahle, J. B. (1985). *Women in science*. Philadelphia: Falmer Press.

Keller, E. Fox. (1983). *A feeling for the organism: The life and work of Barbara McClintock*. New York: W. H. Freeman & Co.

Keller, E. Fox. (1984, November). Women and basic research: Respecting the unexpected. *Technology Review*, 44–47.

Koblitz, A. H. (1983). *A convergence of lives, Sofia Kovlevskia: Scientist, writer, revolutionary*. Cambridge, MA: Birkhauser Boston.

Kolata, G. (1988, October 18). Winners of the Nobel Prize in physiology or medicine. *New York Times*, p. A-1.

Lerner, G. (1975). Placing women in history: A 1975 perspective. *Feminist Studies, 3*(1–2), 5–15.

Lewin, R. (1983). A naturalist of the Genome. *Science, 222*, 402–405.

Martin, M. (1988, February). A lifetime of action, of passion. *Feminist Voices*, 7.

"McClintock, Barbara" (1984) ed. Charles Moritz *Current Biography Yearbook*. New York: H. W. Wilson, pp. 262–265.

McClintock, B. (1938). The production of homozygous deficient tissues with mutant characteristics by means of the aberrant mitotic behavior of ring-shaped chromosomes. *Genetics, 23*, 315–376.

McClintock, B. (1941a). The stability of broken ends of chromosomes in *Zea Mays. Genetics, 26*, 234–282.

McClintock, B. (1941b). The association of mutants with homozygous deficiencies in *Zea Mays. Genetics, 26*. pp. 542–571.

McClintock, B. (1944). The relation of homozygous deficiencies to mutations and allelic series in maize. *Genetics, 29*, 478–502.

McClintock, B. (1945). Cytogenetic studies of maize and *Neurospora. Carnegie Institute of Washington Year Book, 44*, 108.

McClintock, B. (1947). Cytogenetic studies of maize and *Neurospora. Carnegie Institute of Washington Year Book, 46*, 146.

McClintock, B. (1948). Mutable loci in maize. *Carnegie Institute of Washington Year Book, 47*, 155.

McClintock, B. (1950). The origin and behavior of mutable loci in maize. *Proceedings of the National Academy of Sciences*, *36*, 344–355.

McClintock, B. (1981, November 30). As quoted in Jumping genes. *Time*. *118*, 84.

McClintock, B. (1983). The significance of responses of the genome to challenge. Nobel lecture, December 8, Stockholm, Sweden.

McClintock, B. & Creighton, H. (1931). A correlation of cytological and genetical crossingover in *Zea Mays*. *Proceedings of the National Academy of Sciences*, *17*, 492–497.

McIntosh, P. (1983). *Interactive phases of curricular revision: A feminist perspective* (Working paper No. 124). Wellesley, MA: Wellesley College, Center for Research on Women.

Marx, J. L. (1988, October 28). The 1988 Nobel prize for physiology or medicine. *Science*, *242*516–517.

Mozans, H. J. (1974). *Women in science—1913*. Cambridge, MA: MIT Press.

Ogilvie, M. B. (1986). *Women in science*. Cambridge, MA: MIT Press.

Opfell, O. (1978). *The lady laureates: Women who have won the Nobel prize*. Metuchen, Scarecrow Press.

Osen, L. M. (1974). *Women in mathematics*. Cambridge, MA: MIT Press.

Patterson, E. (1983). *Mary Somerville and the cultivation of science 1815–1840*. The Hague: Nijhoff.

Patterson, R. M. (1989). Black women in the biological sciences. *Sage*, *4*(2), 8–14.

Reid, R. (1974). *Marie Curie*. New York: Mentor Books.

Rossiter, M. W. (1982). *Women scientists in America: Struggles and strategies to 1940*. Baltimore: Johns Hopkins University Press.

Sayre, A. (1975). *Rosalind Franklin and DNA: A vivid view of what it is like to be a gifted woman in an especially male profession*. New York: W. W. Norton.

Schiebinger, L. (1989). *The mind has no sex? Women in the origins of modern science*. Cambridge, MA: Harvard University Press.

Sjoquist, F. (1988, December 10). The Nobel prize in physiology or medicine 1988. Speech by Professor Folke Sjoquist of the Nobel Assembly at the Karolinska Institute.

Staff. (1988, October 31). Nobel prizes: Tales of patience and triumph. *Time*, 71.

Wallis, C. (1983, October 24). Honoring a modern Mendel. *Time*, *122*, 53–54.

Watson, J. D. (1969). *The double helix*. New York: Atheneum.

2.

THE CURRENT STATUS OF WOMEN IN BIOLOGY

Even a casual examination of the history of science reveals that science has been dominated by men: Only nine women have ever won the coveted Nobel Prize in science or medicine. Despite recent recovery work done by historians that reveal lost contributions and achievements of women scientists, much work done by women in science has been brushed aside, misunderstood, or attributed to male colleagues. The male domination of the profession led to an inhospitable environment for the few women who braved the obstacles to become scientists; it also prevented most women from entering scientific professions.

One of the initial goals of feminists in this phase of the women's movement that began in the late 1960s and early 1970s was access for women to careers, particularly in the male-dominated professions. Correctly perceived as supreme male bastions, science and medicine served as primary targets. Legal actions initiated by qualified women applicants to medical schools were successful in ending the quota system that had held the number of women physicians to less than 7% of the profession until the 1970s (Altekruse & McDermott, 1988). Concurrent efforts by women scientists led to the formation of women's caucuses within the professional organizations and national organizations such as American Women in Science (AWIS). A major focus of these groups included attracting more women and improving the lot of women in the profession. In order to achieve these ends, the groups began to collect data on the status of women in the profession and to insist that federal agencies such as the National Science Foundation (NSF) and the Office for Technology Assessment (OTA) gather data on the status of women that might be compared across the fields within science. Proceedings of several national conferences and workshops such as the 1964 MIT Symposium on Women in the Scientific Professions (Mattfield & Van Aken, 1964), the 1978 New York Academy of Sciences national conference: Expanding the Role of Women in the Sciences (Briscoe & Pfafflin, 1979), the 1981 Purdue Conference on Women in the Professions: Science, Social Science, and Engineering (Haas & Perrucci, 1984), and the 1986 Workshop on the Underrepresentation and Career Differentials of Women in Science and Engineering (Dix, 1987) also contributed to the data base.

Because of the efforts of these groups, considerable data are available on the current status of women in science. Analyses of these data indicate that the scientific professions continue to be male dominated. Although more women have entered scientific professions since the 1970s, the overall number still tends to be small. Data expressed as percentage increases tend to look deceptively positive because of the small numbers of women involved. For example, the number of women receiving doctorates in engineering increased from 53 to 286 from 1978 to 1988 (NSF, 1990)—a 540% increase; the fact that 286 women compared to 3,904 men received a Ph.D. in the same year does not mean that the number (or percentage) of women in the profession has improved very much. The numbers and status of women in science also vary substantially among the subdisciplines and fields. Some fields such as the social sciences and life sciences have shown dramatic increases in the numbers of women in recent years with a consequent substantial increase in the percentage of women in the profession. In other fields, such as astronomy, despite increasing numbers of women during the 1960s and 1970s, the percentage of women Ph.D.s in the profession is only half of what it was in the 1920s (Vetter, 1988).

OVERALL STATUS OF
WOMEN IN SCIENCE

In 1980 the Science and Technology Equal Opportunities Act was passed (Public Law 96–516) to provide information that might be used to address issues concerned with full utilization of human resources in science and technology in the United States. Part of this Act mandated that a report on Women and Minorities in Science and Engineering be produced biennially by the National Science Foundation to present information on the participation of women, racial/ethnic minorities, and persons with physical disabilities in science and engineering.

The following excerpt from the Executive Summary of the 1990 Report provides an overall picture of the status of women, including minority women, in science.

Women

• Employment of women scientists and engineers increased by 258 percent (14 percent per year) to 868,000 between 1978 and 1988, compared to an 87 percent (6 percent per year) increase for men. In 1988, women accounted for 16 percent of the S/E workforce, up from 9 percent in 1978. Women continue to constitute a smaller proportion of the S/E workforce than they do of either total U.S. employment (45 percent) or total employment in professional and related occupations (50 percent).

• Representation of women varies substantially by S/E field. In 1988, almost 1 in 3 scientists was a woman compared to only 1 in 25 engineers. Among science fields, the proportion of women ranged from 11 percent of environmental scientists to 48 percent of psychologists.

• Because of their relatively recent influx into science and engineering fields, women generally are younger and have fewer years of professional experience than men. In 1986 (the latest year in which data are available), almost three-fifths of women—but only about one-quarter of men—had fewer than 10 years' experience.

• Annual salaries for women scientists and engineers averaged 75 percent of those for men in 1986 ($29,900 versus $39,800). Women's salaries are lower than men's in essentially all S/E fields and at all levels of professional experience. There were a few exceptions at the entry level, however, where salaries were comparable: for example, salaries for recent bachelor's degree recipients in engineering were virtually identical, regardless of gender.

• The unemployment rate for women was about double that for men in 1986: 2.7 percent versus 1.3 percent. Unemployment rates for both women and men have declined since 1976 when they were 5.4 percent and 3.2 percent, respectively.

• Available data show greater S/E underemployment of women than of men among scientists and engineers. If those working involuntarily in either part-time or non-S/E jobs are considered as a proportion of total employment, about 6 percent of women, compared to 2 percent of men, are underemployed.

Minority Women

• Minorities are more highly represented among women than among men. Of 698,600 employed women scientists and engineers in 1986, roughly 5 percent were black (34,500) and 5 percent were Asian (36,300); less than 1 percent (2,700) were native American. On the other hand, in 1986, about 2 percent of male scientists and engineers were black, 5 percent were Asian, and less than 1 percent were native American.

• Asian women are more highly represented among scientists and engineers than in the general workforce. While they account for about 5 percent of women scientists and engineers, they represent only about 2 percent of all women in the U.S. workforce. Black women account for 11 percent of all employed women and 5 percent of women scientists and engineers.

• In 1986, almost 3 percent (19,600) of women scientists and engineers were Hispanic, compared with 6 percent of all employed women. (NSF, 1990, vii–viii)

The Status of Women in Biology   The Executive Summary indicates that the representation of women in science and engineering varies substantially by field. Almost half of all women scientists and engineers are concentrated in psychology or the life and social sciences. In contrast, a majority of men are in the field of engineering (NSF, 1990).

The field of biology has seen substantial growth in the number of employed women scientists during the decade from 1978 to 1988. In 1978 women constituted 30,000 out of 164,000 (18.29%) of employed biological scientists; in 1988 women numbered 89,200 of the 299,400 (29.79%) employed biological scientists. Although the growth of women employed as biologists was substantial during the decade, it was less than the growth in women employed as psychologists, which increased from 34.51% (42,000/121,700) to 47.84% (132,000/ 275,900) during the same time period. It should be noted, however, that factors such as overall rate of growth of the profession and percentage of women in the profession at the beginning of the decade make comparisons among fields difficult and deceptive. For example, computer specialties was the fastest growing field for both women and men scientists; the field increased from 177,000 to 708,300 in the total number of employed scientists from 1978 to 1988. Although the number of women computer specialists rose from 40,200 to 218,700 (more than a fivefold increase) during this 10-year period, the percentage of employed women went from 22.71% to 30.88% of the profession (NSF, 1990). The percentage increase for employed women computer specialists, which appears smaller than that for employed women biologists, is the result of the enormous growth of computer science and the relatively large percentage of women in the field at the beginning of the decade.

Data from electrical/electronic engineering illustrate the example of a field in which the number of women has increased dramatically, but their percentage of employed scientists still appears small because of the low initial numbers and slower rate of growth of the field. The total number of employed electrical/ electronics engineers increased from 341,500 to 640,900 between 1978 and 1988. The number of employed women electrical/electronics engineers grew from 3,500 to 23,800 (almost a sevenfold increase). However, their percentage of the total number of employed engineers only increased from 1.02% to 3.7% because in 1978 the number of women in the profession was so small.

These examples illustrate how carefully data must be evaluated to assess their true meaning for the status of women in a profession. With this in mind, I excerpt selected data from the NSF 1990 report that reveals the status of women in biology. The percentage of employed women biologists with doctoral degrees increased more rapidly from 1977 to 1987 than the percentage of employed men biologists with doctoral degrees. Women with doctoral degrees constituted 6,700 of 42,100 or 15.9% of employed biologists in 1977; in 1987 women with doctoral degrees numbered 13,500 of 62,000 or 21.8% of employed biologists.

Because the employment of women scientists and engineers increased more rapidly than that of men over the decade from 1978 to 1988, on the whole women are younger and have fewer years experience than men in the profession. In 1986, almost 60% of women scientists and engineers had fewer than 10 years professional work experience; only 15% had more than 20 years of work experience. Comparable respective figures for men were 25% and 46%. Percentages for doctoral-level women scientists and engineers compared to men with the same training demonstrated a similar pattern: 59% of women and 31% of men had fewer than 10 years of work experience; 11% of women and 30% of men had more than 20 years (NSF, 1990).

The NSF data do not separate biologists from life scientists for years of professional experience, so it is only possible to calculate the years of experience for male and female life scientists. Of 102,800 employed women life scientists in 1986, 64,600 (62.8%) have fewer than ten years experience; 13,600 (13.2%) have 20 or more years experience (calculated from Table 9, NSF, 1990, p. 82). Of the 309,000 employed male life scientists in 1986, 99,500 (32.2%) had fewer than ten years experience; 113,000 (36.6%) had 20 or more years experience (calculated from Table 8, NSF, 1990, p. 80). Thus, years of experience for female life scientists were close to the overall averages for employed women scientists and engineers, whereas male life scientists demonstrated somewhat less experience than men overall in science and engineering.

Data on employed doctoral life scientists demonstrate trends similar to those of employed doctoral scientists and engineers in other fields. In 1987 of the 22,100 employed women life scientists, 11,700 (52.9%) had fewer than 10 years experience; 2,100 (9.5%) had 20 or more years of experience (calculated from data, Table 12, NSF, 1990, p. 88). During the same year, of the 85,300 employed men life scientists, 28,600 (33.5%) had less than 10 years experience; 23,400 (27.4%) had 20 years or more of experience (calculated from Table 11, NSF, 1990, p. 86).

In most scientific fields, and particularly in engineering, more men than women report management and research as their primary work activity. The primary work activity of men and women life scientists also differs. Of 102,800 total employed women life scientists in 1986, the percentage breakdowns by primary field were as follows: 31.4% research (32,300); 5.0% development (5,100); 3.9% management of research and development (4,000); 12.6% general management (13,000); 14.3% teaching (14,700); 9.0% production/inspection (9,300); and 4.4% reporting statistical work and computing (4,500) (calculated from data in Table 15, NSF, 1990, pp. 99–100). Of 309,000 total employed men life scientists during that same year, the comparative percentage breakdowns by primary field were as follows: 26.0% research (80,400); 3.4% development (10,600); 8.4% management of research and development (26,100); 21.8% general management (67,200); 15.1% teaching (46,700); 11.2% production/inspection (34,700); and 2.8% reporting, statistical work, and computing (8,800) (calculated from data in Table 14, NSF, 1990, pp. 94–95). More employed women life scientists are in research, whereas many more employed men life scientists are in management. These differences are probably influenced by at least two factors: women's fewer years of work experience, which may account partially for why fewer women are in management, and the fact that grants and other "soft money" often fund positions in research. These "soft money" positions, which are less institutionalized than "regular jobs" in either the public or corporate sector, are held disproportionately by women (Zuckerman, 1987).

Several additional types of data reveal women's poor status overall in the scientific and engineering professions. The position of women life scientists is also exemplary of these trends.

Women scientists and engineers who choose careers in academia hold disproportionately lower ranks than their male counterparts. In 1987 women scientists and engineers in four-year colleges and universities constituted 18% of full professors, 25% of associate professors, 29% of assistant professors, and 28% of other ranks. The comparable statistics for men scientists and engineers demonstrate a reversal of the pyramid: 46% of full professors, 24% of associate professors, 15% of assistant professors, and 15% of other ranks (NSF, 1990, p. 7). Of the 50,600 men life scientists at four-year colleges and universities, 43% (21,800) are full professors, 23% (11,800) are associate professors, and 17% (8,500) are assistant professors; data for the 14,200 women life scientists at comparable institutions are 16% (2,200) full, 24% (3,400) associate, and 27% (3,900) assistant professors.

Not only are women scientists disproportionately represented in the lower ranks, they also hold a predominance of the nontenure track and other "irregular" positions at the four-year colleges and universities. Although 58% of women doctoral scientists and engineers were on the tenure track in 1987, only 36% of them were actually tenured. In contrast, 74% of men doctoral scientists and engineers were on the tenure track and 60% were already tenured in 1987 (NSF,

1990, p. 7). For the 14,200 women doctoral life scientists in 1987 the situation was slightly worse: 51% (7,300) were in the tenure track position and 30% (4,200) had received tenure (data calculated from NSF, 1990, Table 18, p. 106). Of the 50,600 men doctoral life scientists 70% (35,500) were on the tenure track with 55% (28,000) already holding tenure (data calculated from Table 17, NSF, 1990, p. 104). If major research universities rather than four-year institutions had been used as the data base, the disparities would have been even greater between men and women with more men in all ranks and tenure-track positions, and single digit percentages of women in the highest ranks. The largest percentage of women at major research universities are in other ranks and nontenure track positions (Zuckerman, 1987).

In addition to having less experience, differing career patterns, and lower academic rank and tenure status, female scientists and engineers differ from their male counterparts with regard to other labor-market indicators. Although the overall labor-force participation rates were approximately equal (94%–95%) for men and women scientists, the labor-force participation rates varied for women in 1986 by field. For women life scientists, the rate was only 90%, whereas for women computer specialists it was 97%. The primary reason that women scientists (34%) gave for nonparticipation in the labor force was family responsibilities; in contrast the primary reason cited by men scientists (75%) for nonparticipation was retirement (NSF, 1990, p. 8).

Despite the fact that overall labor-force participation rates of men and women scientists are similar, women have more than twice the unemployment rate of men. In 1986, the rate was 2.7% for women and 1.3% for men. For women life scientists, the rate (3.4%) was considerably worse than that for women scientists and engineers (2.7%) and for men life scientists (1.7%) (NSF, 1990, Table 22, p. 114). The underemployment rate for women life scientists (9.6%) is also considerably worse than that for other women scientists and engineers (6.3%), men life scientists (3.1%), and other men scientists and engineers (1.9%) (NSF, 1990, Table 22, p. 114).

In keeping with other negative labor-market indicators for women in 1986, the average annual salaries of women scientists and engineers ($29,900) are lower than those of men ($39,800) scientists and engineers. Although earning only 75% of what male scientists and engineers earn is discouraging for women who are scientists and engineers, it is better than the 67% that all female full-time wage and salary workers over age 24 earn, or the 60% that all women college graduates earned compared to men that year (NSF, 1990, p. 9). The average salary for women life scientists in 1986 was $25,200, which was 71.2% of the $35,400 average salary for men life scientists (NSF, 1990, Table 25, p. 119). Women doctoral life scientists earned $39,600 or 82.5% of the $48,000 earned by men doctoral life scientists in 1987. Although less disparity exists between the salaries of men and women who are recent graduates, even with a bachelor's degree in life science men ($20,000) start out earning $1,000 more than women ($19,000) (NSF, 1990, Table 27, p. 121). With a master's degree men ($25,000) have a slight edge of $900 over women's starting salaries ($24,100) (NSF, 1990, Table 27, p. 121).

MINORITY WOMEN

People of color form a larger proportion of employed female scientists and engineers (11%) than they do of male scientists and engineers (7%) (NSF, 1990, p. 10). As might be expected, proportions of women of color in the science and engineering work force vary by field and their relative proportions in the overall work force. For example, black women constitute 5% of women in the science and engineering work force whereas they constitute 11% of women in the US work force. Only 10% of black women scientists and engineers are life scientists, (NSF, 1990, Table 2, p. 69). Black women make up 2.9% of all doctoral women scientists and engineers. Of the 22,100 (23%) female life scientists 500 are black (NSF, 1990, Table 4, p. 72).

In contrast, Asians were more highly represented among women scientists and engineers (5%) than among women in the general work force. Fifteen percent of Asian women scientists and engineers are life scientists (NSF, 1990, Table 2, p. 69). Asian women constitute 6.6% of all women scientists and engineers with doctorates. Of the women life scientists with doctorates 8.1% (1,800 of 22,100) are Asian (NSF, 1990, Table 4, p. 72).

The overall numbers of Native-American women in the general population and in the science and engineering work force in particular, make generalizations drawn from data collected about them susceptible to inaccuracies. Fewer than 1% (2,700) of all women scientists and engineers were Native American in 1986 and 37% of those were life scientists. Of the female scientists and engineers with Ph.D.s 0.2% (100) were Native American. The number of women life scientists with doctorates who are Native American is .01% (3 of 22,100) (NSF, 1990, Table 4, p. 72).

Although Hispanics constitute a larger proportion of the total population than Native Americans, generalizations based on data from women Hispanic scientists and engineers are also problematic. First, the term "Hispanic" covers diverse ethnic groups of individuals whose Spanish heritage originated in Central or South America, Europe, or Asia. Depending on these origins, much variation with regard to political stance, cultural values, class, and race exists within the grouping of Hispanics (NSF, 1990, p. 12).

About 3% (19,600) of women scientists and engineers were Hispanic; this is approximately half of the representation of Hispanic women in the overall work force (6%). Among doctoral women scientists and engineers Hispanic women accounted for 1.8% (1,200) of the total. Twenty-one percent of Hispanic women scientists and engineers were in the life sciences. Of the women life scientists with doctorates 1.4% (300/22,100) were Hispanic.

Across all racial groups, larger fractions of female than male scientists and engineers have fewer than 10 years experience. Within all racial groups, lower proportions of women than men reported their major work as management, although more black women (24%) and Asian women (22%) were managers than white women (19%).

In 1987, more black women (64%) were in tenure-track positions than white (59%) or Asian (43%) women. However, tenured positions are held in the reverse order: 64% Asian, 62% white, and 50% of black women are tenured. In terms of academic rank, the order again changes: 18% white, 17% Asian, and 13% black women hold full professorships. Black women (39%) were more likely to be assistant professors than white (29%) or Asian women (23%).

Salary differentials among racial groups of women were not large, although white women scientists earned more ($29,400) than Asian ($28,800) or black ($25,400) women scientists. Among engineers, Asian women earned more ($35,000) than white ($34,300) or black ($32,400) women engineers in 1986. At the doctoral level, Asian women held the highest salaries ($44,800) compared to white ($40,200), black ($38,800), and Native-American ($32,700) women.

The major discrepancy in salary, as in career pattern and field, was based on gender rather than race. Regardless of racial group, all women scientists and engineers reported lower annual salaries than those of men in their racial groups: 78% for Blacks, 76% for whites, and 74% for Asians.

In sum, women scientists of all races tend to receive lower salaries, hold lower rank, and face higher unemployment and underemployment than men. These discrepancies represent the culmination of differences in the socialization and educational experiences of boys and girls.

SOCIALIZATION AND EDUCATIONAL FACTORS THAT CONTRIBUTE TO DIFFERENTIAL STATUS

The forces of socialization begin at birth and continue throughout an entire lifetime. The curriculum and methodological approaches used in the education system from preschool through graduate school tend to augment and strengthen the forces found in the family and larger society. Each educational or socialization incident may be minor. Taken by itself it might have little or no effect on career choice or attitudes toward women and feminism. Added together with all the other incidents of a lifetime it may be the final factor that steers many people, particularly women, away from the level of decision-making positions in science and health care.

The studies of Rubin, Provenzano, and Luvia (1974) indicate that baby boys and girls are treated very differently, beginning at birth. What is the first question that most people ask as soon as the baby is born? Is it a boy or girl? Based on the answer to that question, people begin to respond differently to the newborn.

This differential treatment continues, despite the perception of the parents that they are treating their male and female children equally. Will and his colleagues (1974) set up an experiment in which they dressed a six-month-old child in neutral-colored clothing. Eleven mothers were observed to see which of three toys—a train, a doll, or a fish—they would offer the child. Those women who were told that the baby was a girl offered the doll more frequently than the train; those who were told that the baby was a boy, offered the train more frequently than the doll.

Lynn (1966, 1969) and Chodorow (1978) suggest that parents encourage boys to separate from their mothers and become "autonomous and independent" whereas girls are discouraged from separating. The experiments testing these theories (Maccoby & Jacklin, 1974) are somewhat contradictory but the data tend to support the idea that boys are encouraged to be more independent and aggressive. Certainly boys and girls are subjected to different sex-role socialization processes from parents, the media, and institutions in the surrounding society and exhibit some developmental differences during the preschool period.

By the time children reach elementary school, girls are more mature than boys, are ready for verbal and math skills at an earlier age, and have better control of small-motor skills. As Shakeshaft (1986) has pointed out, however, the curriculum, disciplinary system, and environment are all based on male models of development. Thus the grade (or ages) at which various mathematics and verbal skills are introduced fit male needs rather than those of females. The absence of women from most subjects in the curriculum leaves many girls feeling alienated and makes it more difficult for them to see the material as relating to them. The coeducational environment, found in virtually all public schools, favors boys because boys behave better when girls are present. In contrast, girls learn better, show higher self-esteem, and receive more leadership opportunities in single-sex environments.

The work of Sadker and Sadker (1986) documents the fact that boys receive more attention from teachers than girls in co-educational environments. They found that boys in elementary school are eight times as likely as girls to call out and demand attention. Their demands are rewarded, as teachers accept the answers from boys. But when girls exhibited this same behavior teachers corrected them, telling them to raise their hands. Thus the tendency towards aggressive behavior that may have been encouraged by the preschool boy's parents is reinforced in the elementary school environment by the teacher.

The teacher especially may be a crucial figure in helping to develop differential attitudes and skills towards science and mathematics in elementary school-aged boys and girls. Most elementary school teachers are women. The traditional training for elementary school teachers requires minimal competency in basic science and mathematics. This minimal training coupled with the women's own sex-role socialization produces many elementary school teachers who themselves do not feel comfortable with science. Some are very blatant, as was my daughter's first-grade teacher, who stated that she did not like science and did not teach it. She said that she believed in concentrating on the basics, which she defined as reading, writing, and arithmetic. Obviously this teacher represents an extreme that conveys a negative impression of science to both boys and girls. I hope her example is not present in most classrooms throughout the country. However, even blatant behavior such as hers may differentially affect boys and girls. A boy who likes science recognizes that his teacher is female and he can more easily choose not to identify with her attitudes towards science, which he may view as a female feeling about the subject. But a girl who likes science may find it more difficult not to accept the attitude towards science of a teacher with whom she identifies in other respects.

Even when elementary schools are trying to teach science, and use hands-on experiences involving both boys and girls, the teaching methods and subtleties in the way the material is presented may result in a different learning experience for boys and girls in the same classroom. For example, many elementary teachers ask the student to "build a terrarium" to introduce concepts related to ecology, microenvironments, and oxygen supplies. Although the entire class participates in the project, all too frequently the boys go out to gather the soil, plants, and animals, while the girls remain inside to "decorate the terrarium" (Gazzam-Johnson, 1985). Aside from the reinforcement of male-active and female-passive sex role stereotypes that this exercise promotes, the boys have learned much more about fieldwork and plant and animal habitats than have the girls.

A similar lack of learning and reinforcement of passive roles for girls occurs when the teachers do the experiment, solve the math problem, or answer the question for little girls. Research has indicated that these teachers are more likely to provide different feedback for boys who give wrong answers. Boys are told to try harder, whereas girls are praised for simply trying (Stallings, 1980). Data from the 1976–77 NAEP (National Assessment of Educational Progress) indicate that although nine-year-old girls have significantly less experience with scientific observations and the use of science instruments than nine-year-old boys (Kahle & Lakes, 1983), the girls desire to have such experiences. It is particularly unfortunate that our elementary schools are not providing them with the experiences, as girls seem less likely than boys to make up the deficiency in out-of-school experiences (Iliams, 1985). A meta-analysis demonstrated that general experience and specialized training are associated with better performance on spatial skills tasks in both sexes. (Baenninger and Newcombe 1989).

Data from the National Assessment of Educational Progress in 1986 (Educational Testing Service, 1988) indicate the following:

Nine-Year-Olds. A lag in the performance of females, combined with significant changes in the performance of males over the last several years, has opened a large gap between female–male scores in science achievement. In 1986, overall means for females and males were 221.3 and 227.3, respectively. In 1978, however, the score difference was less than 5 points: 217.7 for females versus 222.1 for males.

Differences in proficiency are evident among female and male 9-year-olds. Whereas only about 70 percent of females scored over 200 (understanding of simple principles), 73 percent of males did so. The proportions showing an ability to apply basic information (level 250) were 26 percent for females and 29 percent for males.

Between 1978 and 1986, overall mean scores on the mathematics assessment edged upward for both females and males; progress by males was greater, however. In 1986, mean scores for both females and males were 221.7, up from 219.9 for females and 217.4 for males in 1978.

Levels of proficiency for females and males at this age level are remarkably similar. In 1986, virtually all students (98 percent) scored above 150, indicating a mastery of simple arithmetic facts. Furthermore, 21 percent of both female and male 9-year-olds scored 250 or more, showing they have a basic understanding of simple operations and problem-solving skills. (NSF, 1990, p. 14)

By junior high, girls have lost much of their desire to participate in scientific activities (Kahle & Lakes, 1983). In addition 13-year-old girls have fewer science experiences than boys compared with nine-year-old girls; the disparity in science experiences between boys and girls increases with age. Not too surprisingly this decline parallels a decline in science achievement levels also (Matyas, 1985). Studies reveal that experience with the actual tools and techniques of science in the laboratory are needed to build interest and experience for science achievement (Kahle & Matyas, 1987).

Thirteen-Year-Olds. In this age group, females have made less progress in science than have males. The overall mean for females in 1986 (246.9) was more than 9 points lower than for males (256.1). In 1978, the difference was about 7 points.

Levels of scientific proficiency for females also show lagging performance. About 48 percent of female 13-year-olds, but 58 percent of males, scored above 250 (application of basic knowledge) on the most recent assessment. Likewise, the percentages who scored over 300 (ability to analyze procedures and data) were lower for females: 6 percent versus 13 percent. (NSF, 1990, p. 14)

Although the girls' scores in mathematics achievement decline in junior high school, approximately half of the few gender differences found in mathematics do favor girls at that age (Campbell, 1986).

Thirteen-Year-Olds. Progress of females at this age level begins to lag behind that of males. In 1986, overall means for females and males were 268.0 and 270.0, respectively. Since 1978, however, scores for males have shown a statistically significant (at the 0.05 level) increase from 263.6. Means for females also showed an increase from 264.7, but this change was not statistically significant.

Within this age group, differences begin to emerge at each of the proficiency levels. For instance, almost 72 percent of females, but 74 percent of males, scored above level 250 (basic understanding). The proportions scoring at or above the next highest level, 300—moderately complex procedures and reasoning—were 14 percent (female) and 18 percent (male). (NSF, 1990, p. 14)

Junior high school corresponds with the age at which girls are reaching puberty. Numerous studies have indicated that puberty is the time when sex-role expectations become more rigidly enforced. Parents buy their sons more science- and math-related toys and computers than they buy their daughters (Campbell, 1986). They also have higher expectations of achievement in math and more strongly encourage their sons to take math courses. Boys are also urged to enroll in after-school and outside-of-school science and technology programs (Campbell, 1984). A British study revealed that although boys initially score better on spatial ability tests, the enrollment of girls in one technical craft course eradicates the gender difference (Kelly, Whyte, & Smail, 1984). Teachers may also convey in direct and more subtle ways their differing expectations for boys and girls. For example, in the summer of 1985 a math teacher "assigned a boy who spoke very little English the task of correcting the girls' class work, while she corrected the boys' work and gave them individual feedback" (Campbell, 1986, p. 517). Guidance counselors may routinely discourage girls from the science and math track because they assume that high verbal scores mean they are a "reading and writing" person. (Campbell, 1986). Unfortunately, many guidance counselors reflect their own attitudes regarding traditional careers for men and women in their counseling of students (Remick & Miller, 1978). Girls are not counseled to take the mathematics courses or provided with information on the higher-paying careers that are seen as traditionally male (Kahle & Matyas, 1987).

By high school the subtle and not-so-subtle long-term effects of parents, teachers, counselors, and peers become evident. Girls have fewer science experiences with instruments and materials and score lower on science and mathematical achievement tests than boys.

Throughout high school girls take fewer mathematics courses than boys. Girls also have higher attrition rates than boys from these classes. These higher attrition rates are not due to poor grades, because girls have higher grades in mathematics classes (Remick & Miller, 1978) than boys. Girls who are less confident are more likely to discontinue their math (Sherman, 1982). Girls choosing to continue science and mathematics during high school may be viewed as nonconformists at a developmental period when conformity is highly valued by peers. "Girls taking science courses describe themselves as '. . . less feminine, less attractive, less popular, and less sociable.' That is they appear to see themselves as less socially attractive than their peers" (Kelly, 1981, p. 166). Fox (in Iker, 1980) states that many girls do not enter accelerated math courses because of negative social consequences, especially peer rejection. Because science and math are not seen as part of the female sex role, girls in coeducational classes feel particular pressure not to choose those subjects (Ormerod, 1975).

The curriculum content often reflects little of women's experiences or theories that are relevant to girl's lives. Although this is a major difficulty in the content of all disciplines (McIntosh, 1983), it is a particularly severe problem in the sciences (Rosser, 1986, 1990). Contributions of women to science must be portrayed seriously in narrative as well as in illustrative materials. "The inclusion of women photographed in lab coats was inadequate; their real contributions must be discussed. Our studies suggested that if the repeated message from teacher and text was that scientists were males, adolescent girls, unsure of their femininity would shy away from science or, if enrolled, would perform poorly" (Kahle, 1985, p. 197).

Seventeen-Year-Olds. The biggest difference in means for science was achievement found for this age group. In 1986, the overall mean of 282.3 for females was almost 13 percentage points lower than that for males—294.9. There has been little change in scores for either gender since the late seventies.

Females and males record substantial differences in proficiency levels at this age. For example, the proportions scoring above 300 (analysis of procedures and data) were 34 percent for females and 49 percent for males. The shares scoring at or greater than the highest level, 350 (integration of specialized knowledge), were 5 percent and 10 percent, respectively. (NSF, 1990, p. 14)

The attrition rates coupled with fewer girls enrolling in mathematics courses result in girls entering college with, on the average, one-third less high-school mathematics than boys (Chipman Thomas, 1980; NSF, 1982). In 1988, females reported completing an average of 3.6 years of mathematics course work; the average for males was 3.8 years. The data also reveal that females have slightly fewer years of study (3.1 years) in natural science than do males (3.3 years) (NSF, 1990).

> **Seventeen-Year-Olds**. The largest difference in mean scores occurs at this age level: the mean for females in 1986 was more than 5 points lower than for males (299.4 versus 304.7). Since 1978, changes in scores have not been significant for either group.
>
> Smaller percentages of females than males score above each proficiency level. For example, 48 percent of females compared to more than 54 percent of males scored over 300 (moderately complex procedures and reasoning). A smaller percentage of females also scored above level 350 (multi-problem solving and algebra): 5 percent versus 8 percent (NSF, 1990, p. 14).

An additional result is that girls score lower on the mathematics section of achievement tests for college. Some tests, such as the SAT, on which girls score almost 50 points lower than boys (455 versus 498 in 1988), show more sex-related differences than others such as the American College Test (ACT) (Campbell, 1986). Research by Pallas and Alexander (1983) indicates that the male–female gap shrinks considerably when sex differences in quantitative high-school coursework are controlled.

Furthermore on the mathematics portion of the SAT, females are much less likely (5% compared to 13%) to score in the 650 to 800 range and more likely (31% compared to 27%) to score in the 400 to 499 range than males (NSF, 1990). College-bound girls are less likely to take achievement tests in science and math than boys. However, girls constituted almost half the individuals taking the achievement test in biology, whereas they constituted only one-fifth of those taking the test in physics. Similarly, although girls have scored lower than boys on all science and mathematics achievement tests, girls showed the smallest differential on the biology test (29 points) and the greatest on the physics test (56 points) (NSF, 1990). Although girls represented over half (51%) of individuals taking the advanced placement biology test, they scored slightly lower (2.87) compared to boys (3.23) (NSF, 1990).

Because high-school mathematics is a requirement for many occupations and fields of study, mathematics is often called the ''critical filter'' in the training of future scientists and engineers. Researchers estimate that high-school graduates with fewer than four years of high-school mathematics may be filtered out

TABLE 2.1:   Teaching Behaviors and Techniques Effective for Retaining
              Women in Science

Do	Don't
Use laboratory and discussion activities	Use sexist humor
Provide career information	Use sex-stereotyped examples
Directly involve girls in science activities	Distribute sexist classroom materials
Provide informal academic counseling	Allow boys to dominate discussions or activities
Demonstrate unisex treatment in classrooms	Allow girls to resist passively

of three-fourths of all college majors (Iker, 1980). These majors are usually the ones leading to the higher-paying jobs. Thus girls become the "gender at risk." As Sadker and Sadker (1986) so succinctly sum up the effect of elementary and secondary school on girls: "What other group starts out ahead—in reading, in writing, and even in math—and 12 years later finds itself behind?" (p. 515)

Using case studies of teachers, Kahle (1985, p. 74) has pinpointed teaching behaviors and techniques effective for retaining women in science. These are shown in Table 2.1. "These ten special teaching behaviors and instructional strategies resulted in proportionately more girls in their classes continuing in math and science courses in both high school and college" (Kahle, 1985, p. 74). Few teachers seem to be following these behaviors.

In college the situation for female students does not improve. Studies have demonstrated that throughout the college years women in all majors tend to show a gradual decline in self-esteem. (Astin, 1977). Neither male nor female students who have not passed the critical filter of four years of high-school mathematics are likely to switch to major in science, math, or a technological field while in college. During the college years the potential pool of scientists becomes smaller rather than larger. The female students who did pass the mathematics-critical filter, however, drop out in larger percentages than the men students do. In their report "The Classroom Climate: A Chilly One for Women?" Hall and Sandler (1982, p. 12) point out the factors in student–student and student–teacher interactions that lead to difficulties and lowered self-esteem for all women students. They underline the particular difficulties for women majoring in traditionally masculine fields such as science:

- they comprise a distinct minority in a given class or department;
- they have little contact with other women pursuing the same major because of the vertical progression of required courses;

- they find few female teachers who might serve as role models; and
- they work with many professors who are not accustomed to having women students in their classes.

Hall and Sandler (1982) report that a further deterrent to women staying in science is their own concern over the appropriateness of a nontraditional major. This concern echoes the situation in high school and was voiced again in the study by Baker (1983), which found that both male and female college students held the attitude that women majoring in science were less feminine than women majoring in nonscience. Studies indicate that a critical mass (Byrne, 1985) and unisex or gender-balanced (LeBold, 1987) classroom composition may help to overcome these concerns.

The 1990 NSF *Report on Women and Minorities in Science and Engineering* statistics show 38% of all science and engineering undergraduate degrees being awarded to women, despite the fact that women are earning more than half of the baccalaureate degrees now. These data include some fields such as psychology, which is traditionally considered a social science. The social sciences, psychology, and life sciences account for more than two-thirds of the degrees awarded to women. Of the bachelors degrees awarded in the life sciences 44% are awarded to women. In contrast, only 29.7% of the degrees in physical sciences are awarded to women and only 14.5% of the undergraduate degrees in engineering are awarded to women.

The conflict between perception of lack of femininity and major in science is observed to increase at the graduate level, as many women state the "fear of not being feminine" as a primary reason for not pursuing study in a scientific field. Furthermore the Graduate Record Examination (GRE) scores of women and men are about the same on the verbal component, but men score substantially higher on the quantitative component and slightly higher on the analytical component (NSF, 1990). Those few women who do undertake graduate study usually face more obstacles and receive less support than women in science at the undergraduate level. For example, 43% of women in contrast to 51% of men receive university support. Hornig's (1987) review of the literature suggests that men receive considerably more financial aid from a variety of sources than do women. Sandler and Hall (1986) found that graduate women in science typically faced the following sorts of behaviors:

- Male students and faculty may indirectly or directly disparage women's abilities. ("Everyone knows women are not good in spatial ability.")
- Misperceptions based on stereotypes may be prevalent, such as expecting women in medicine to be more "caring," and steering them to those areas of medicine where "caring" is perceived as being more important (as in pediatrics).

- Faculty may be less willing to work with women students because they see women as having less potential and/or because they may be uncomfortable with women.
- Male peers may intentionally disrupt women's work, as in the case of a woman whose laboratory equipment was repeatedly decalibrated.
- Many students, especially those in engineering, math, economics, and science, report difficulties with foreign male students and faculty who come from cultures where women's role is very circumscribed. They often engage in numerous overt discriminatory behaviors such as sexual harassment, not calling on women students at all, not answering their questions, and openly ridiculing or disparaging women. Students complaining about such treatment often receive no support but are told instead to be "understanding" because that person comes from another culture. (Sandler & Hall, 1986, p. 17)

Other research has documented more subtle behaviors that may superficially appear egalitarian or even helpful to a woman scientist's career goal but which may in fact hurt her career in the long run. The classic example of this type of behavior is the practice of awarding more teaching assistantships to female graduate students (40% female versus 37% male), and more research assistantships to male graduate students (42% female versus 52% male) (NSF, 1990). The women usually like the interaction with students and often request the teaching assistantships. However enjoyable and useful for departmental purposes teaching may be, the current structure of science and career advancement reward research. The male graduate student who has a research assistantship can frequently make use of some if not all of his research data for his own dissertation. At a minimum he will learn to use procedures, equipment, and methods of analysis that will aid him in his dissertation. Furthermore, his assistantship will probably put him in contact with a network of individuals in the laboratory and in the wider scientific community who can serve as sources of information about methods, grants, and even employment opportunities. Although it is not impossible for the female teaching assistant to gather data, learn procedures, and develop a network, she must do so in addition to, rather than as part of, her teaching responsibilities.

The teaching assistantship serves as an example of one of the many factors that may lead to a higher drop-out rate for female compared to male graduate students in science. The data from the 1990 *Report on Women and Minorities in Science and Engineering* demonstrate that 26.6% of the Ph.D.s in science and engineering are awarded to women. Of those, 32.9% are in the life sciences; only 6.8% (286) are in engineering. The National Research Council Doctorate Research File records that the percentage of all physical science and math doctorates awarded to women in the 1980s was 13.8%.

Because scarcity often leads to higher prices one might assume that the starting salaries for women scientists might be higher than those for men scientists. With one exception (engineering) this is not the case. In all scientific fields at all degree levels, women receive lower starting salaries than men with the same degrees (NSF, 1990).

As the data presented earlier in the chapter reveal, the situation for women scientists does not improve with increased time on the job. The NSF *Report on Women and Minorities in Science and Engineering* documents that women scientists have lower salaries, less chance for advancement, and higher unemployment than men scientists (more than twice that of men) in all fields and in all sectors (including government, industry, and academia). The disparities increase with advancing rank. The individuals who prepared this report for the National Science Foundation (1990) applied a series of sophisticated statistical techniques to these data to equalize factors such as length of years of uninterrupted employment from the work force and previous postdoctoral experience. (It is often argued that women have lower rank and salary because they drop out to have children. Similarly some individuals have argued that higher rank and salary for male scientists reflect the higher percentage of male Ph.D.s who have additional years of postdoctoral training.) Even after such factors that might be biasing the data are controlled, much of the disparity could be accounted for by discrimination only.

CONCLUSION

What are the results of a process that begins at birth, actively and passively discouraging girls and women at every step of the way from entering fields in science and technology? One obvious result of the process is that there are very few women in most fields. Another result of the process is that very few US citizens of either gender and any race are being attracted to science. The Office of Technology Assessment (OTA) and the National Science foundation (NSF) predict a severe shortage of American-trained scientists for the mid-1990s. Demographic trends predict a significant drop in the number of white males of college age (Widnall, 1988) who have been the majority of the students in science and engineering.

Based on current participation rates, the future pool of science and engineering baccalaureates is projected to show a significant drop (NSF, 1987). The peak of U.S. graduate students available from traditional pools has passed; a 26% decrease in the pool is predicted by the late 1990s. Hidden in these statistics is the fact that the percentage of minority students in this age cohort will increase substantially. Because this group is currently underrepresented in science and engineering graduate programs, a projection based on the current participation of various groups would show an even more severe drop in the production of scientifically trained personnel at the Ph.D. level.

The percentage of B.S. degree holders in science and engineering who attain the Ph.D. degree has also fallen, from about 12% to 6% over the past 20 years (NSF, 1987). In engineering, the number of Ph.D.s obtained by U.S. citizens per year fell by more than 50% between 1970 and 1984 (NRC, 1986); currently more than 50% of the doctorates awarded in engineering each year go to foreign nationals (NSF, 1987). In science, the actual number of doctoral degrees awarded to male U.S. citizens has continued a downward trend since 1970. In engineering, increased competition is already evident, constituting a major reason for the significant decrease in U.S. students attaining the Ph.D. in engineering.

The OTA report (1985) describes the pipeline (see Preface) for students in the natural sciences and engineering in which the attrition of women is dramatic relative to that of men. It points out that beginning with 2,000 male and 2,000 female students at the ninth-grade level five men and one woman will earn a Ph.D. degree in some field of the natural sciences or engineering.

It appears that many of the obstacles and barriers are not only discouraging men of color and most women, but that they are also discouraging many white men. This current dearth of scientists and the panic over its projected increasing severity have had a direct impact on feminism and biology. Because of the shortage, the leaders of the scientific establishment and the mainstream scientists feel forced to listen to critiques of their current teaching and research practices to determine why they are not attracting others to the profession.

White women and people of color are seen statistically as the most likely groups from which the shortage may be filled. Critiques of scientific theory, research, and teaching advanced by scholars in women's studies and ethnic studies during the last decade are beginning to be of interest to mainstream scientists. Because biology is the area within the sciences outside the social sciences that has the most women, the feminist critiques of biology serve as the more developed model for the other natural and physical sciences.

REFERENCES

Altekruse, J. M., & McDermott, S. W. (1988). Contemporary concerns of women in medicine. In S. V. Rosser (Ed.), *Feminism within the science and health care professions: Overcoming resistance*. Elmsford, NY: Pergamon Press.

Astin, A. (1977). *Four critical years: Effects of college on beliefs, attitudes, and knowledge*. San Francisco: Jossey-Bass.

Baker, Dale. (1983, November). Can the difference between male and female science majors account for the low number of women at the doctoral level in science? *Journal of College Science Teaching*, 102–107.

Baenninger, M. & Newcombe, N. (1989). The role of experience in spatial test performance: A meta-analysis. *Sex Roles, 20,* 327–44.

Briscoe, A., & Pfafflin, S. M. (Eds.). (1979). *Expanding the role of women in the sciences.* New York: New York Academy of Sciences.

Byrne, E. M. (1985). *Women and engineering: A comparative overview of new initiatives.* Bureau of Labour Market Research Monograph Series No. 11. Sydney: Australian Government Publishing Service.

Campbell, P. (1984). The computer revolution: Guess who's left out? *Interracial Books for Children Bulletin, 15,* 3–6.

Campbell, P. B. (1986). What's a nice girl like you doing in a math class? *Phi Delta Kappan,* March, 516–520.

Chipman, S. F., & Thomas, V. G. (1980). *Women's participation in mathematics: Outlining the problem.* Washington, DC: Report to the National Institute of Education, Teaching and Learning Division.

Chodorow, N. (1978). *The reproduction of mothering.* Berkeley: University of California Press.

Dix, L. S. (1987). *Women: Their underrepresentation and career differentials in science and engineering: Proceedings of a workshop.* Washington, DC: National Academy Press.

Educational Testing Service. (1988). *The science report card: Elements of risk and recovery, trends and achievement based on the 1986 national assessment* (Report No. 17-5-01). Princeton: Educational Testing Service.

Gazzam-Johnson, V. (1985). Personal communication.

Haas, V. B., & Perucci, C. C. (Eds.). (1984). *Women in the scientific and engineering professions.* Ann Arbor: University of Michigan Press.

Hall, R., & Sandler, B. (1982). *The classroom climate: A chilly one for women.* Washington, DC: Project on the Status and Education of Women, AAC.

Hornig, L. (1987). Women graduate students: A literature review and synthesis. In L. S. Dix (Ed.), *Women: Their underrepresentation of career differentials in science and engineering. Proceedings of a workshop* (pp 103–122). Washington, DC: National Academy Press.

Iker, S. (1980). A math answer for women. *MOSAIC, 11,* 39–45.

Iliams, C. (1985). Early school experiences may limit participation of women in science. In *Contributions to the Third GASAT Conference.* London: Chelsea College.

Kahle, J. B. (1985). *Women in science.* Philadelphia: Falmer Press.

Kahle, J. B., & Lakes, M. K. (1983). The myth of equality in science classrooms. *Journal of Research in Science Teaching, 20,* 131–140.

Kahle, J. B., & Matyas, M. L. (1987). Equitable science and mathematics education: A discrepancy model. In L. S. Dix (Ed.), *Women: Their underrepresentation and career differentials in science and engineering* (pp. 5–42). Washington, DC: National Academy Press.

Kelly, A. (1981). *The missing half.* Manchester, England: Manchester University Press.

Kelly, A., Whyte, J., & Smail, B. (1984). *Final report of the GIST Project.* Manchester, England: University of Manchester, Dept. of Sociology.

LeBold, W. K. (1987). Women in engineering and science: An undergraduate research perspective. In L. S. Dix (Ed.), *Women: Their underrepresentation and career differentials in science and engineering. Proceedings of a workshop* (pp. 49–98). Washington, DC: National Academy Press.

Lynn, D. (1966). The process of learning parental and sex-role identification. *Journal of Marriage and the Family, 28*, 466–470.

Lynn, D. (1969). *Parental and sex-role identification: A theoretical formulation.* Berkeley, CA: McCutchan.

Maccoby, E., & Jacklin, C. (1974). *The psychology of sex differences.* Stanford, CA: Stanford University Press.

McIntosh, P. (1983). Interactive phases of curricular revision: A feminist perspective (Working Paper No. 124). Wellesley, MA: Wellesley College, Center for Research on Women.

Mattfield, J. A., & C. G. Van Aken (Eds.). (1979). *Expanding the role of women in the sciences.* New York: New York Academy of Sciences.

Matyas, M. L. (1985). Obstacles and constraints on women in science. In J. B. Kahle (Ed.), *Women in science.* Philadelphia: Falmer Press.

National Assessment of Educational Progress (NAEP). (1978, December). *Science achievement in the schools* (Science Report No. 08-5-01). Denver, CO: Education Commission of the States.

National Research Council. (1986). *Summary report, 1985 doctorate recipients from United States universities.* Washington, DC: U.S. Government Printing Office.

National Science Foundation. (1982). *Science and engineering education: Data and information* (NSF 82-30). Washington, DC: Author.

National Science Foundation. (1987). *A guide to NSF science/engineering resources data* (NSF 87-308). Washington, DC: Author.

National Science Foundation. (1990). *Women and minorities in science and engineering* (NSF 90-301). Washington, DC: Author.

Ormerod, M. B. (1975). Subject preference and choice in coeducational and single-sex secondary schools. *British Journal of Educational Psychology, 45*, 257–67.

Pallas, A. M., & Alexander, K. L. (1983). Sex differences in quantitative SAT performance: New evidence on the differential course work hypothesis. *American Educational Research Journal, 20*: 165–182.

Remick, H., & Miller, K. (1978). Participation rates in high school mathematics and science courses. *The Physics Teacher*, May, 280–282.

Rosser, S. V. (1986). *Teaching science and health from a feminist perspective: A practical guide.* New York: Pergamon Press.

Rosser, S. V. (1990). *Female friendly science.* New York: Pergamon Press.

Rubin, Z., Provenzano, J., & Luria, Z. (1974). The eye of the beholder: Parents views on sex and newborns. *American Journal of Orthopsychiatry, 44*, 512–519.

Sadker, M., & Sadker, Z. (1986). Sexism in the classroom: From grade school to graduate school. *Phi Delta Kappan*, March, 512–515.

Sandler, B., & Hall, R. (1986). *The campus climate revisited: Chilly for women faculty, administrators, and graduate students.* Washington, DC: Project on the Status and Education of Women, AAC.

Shakeshaft, C. (1986). A gender at risk. *Phi Delta Kappan*, March, 499–503.

Sherman, J. (1982): "Continuing in mathematics: A longitudinal study of the attitudes of high school girls." *Psychology of Women Quarterly, 7*, 132–140.

Stallings, J. (1980). Comparisons of men's and women's behaviors in high school math classes. Washington, DC: National Institute of Education.

Vetter, B. (1988). Where are the women in the physical sciences? In S. V. Rosser (Ed.), *Feminism within the science and health care professions: Overcoming resistance.* Elmsford, NY: Pergamon Press.

Widnall, S. (1988). American association for the advancement of science presidential lecture: Voices from the pipeline. *Science, 241*, 1740–1745.

Will, C. Self, P., and Datan, N. (1974). Unpublished paper presented at 82nd annual meeting of the American Psychological Association.

Zuckerman, H. (1987). Persistence and change in the careers of men and women scientists and engineers: A review of current research. In L. S. Dix (Ed.), *Women: Their underrepresentation and career differentials in science and engineering. Proceedings of a workshop* (pp. 123–156). Washington, DC: National Academy Press.

EFFECTS OF FEMINISM ON THEORIES AND METHODS

3.

CRITIQUES OF RESEARCH IN ORGANISMAL BIOLOGY

The women who become biologists overcome the obstacles of socialization and survive the perils of scientific education and training. For most of them this means that they are trained in and believe in the power of the scientific method. Few biologists trained in American universities have taken courses in the history or philosophy of science. Like most scientists, the majority of women biologists are unaware of the historical and philosophical roots of logical positivism and objectivity that form the foundation of the scientific method.

Positivism implies that "all knowledge is constructed by inference from immediate sensory experiences" (Jaggar, 1983, pp. 355–356). It is premised on the assumption that human beings are highly individualistic and obtain knowledge in a rational manner that may be separated from their social conditions. This is the cornerstone of the scientific method: the possibility of obtaining knowledge that is both objective and value-free. The notion of objectivity arises from the assumption that similar sensory experiences or circumstances would stimulate similar perceptions in individuals with normal sensory perception even when those individuals perceptions occur at different times or places. In order for these separate individuals to perceive these sensations in the same way, the individuals must rely only on their empirical observations and control their own values, interests, and emotions. Objectivity is thus contingent upon value neutrality—

freedom from values, interests, and emotions associated with a particular class, race, or sex.

Scientists, like all scholars, hold, either explicitly or implicitly, certain beliefs concerning their enterprise. Most scientists believe, for example, that the laws and facts gathered by scientists are constant, providing that experiments have been done correctly. As Hilary and Steven Rose put it, scientists seem to feel that "Science is the pursuit of natural laws, laws which are valid irrespective of nation, race, politics, religion, or class position of their discoverer" (1980, p. 17). If the observations of science reflect natural law, they stand outside historical context. Both the facts and the theories based on them are, according to this kind of view, affect- and effect-free, having come from sheer attentiveness to the outside world unshackled by opinion or desire and leading only to applications that others might wish to make of them.

Historians of science are making us aware that, quite to the contrary, the individuals who make observations and create theories are people who live in a particular country during a certain time in a definable socioeconomic condition, and that their situations and mentalities inevitably impinge on their discoveries. Even their "facts" may be contingent on these conditions. Aristotle "counted" fewer teeth in the mouths of women than in those of men—adding this dentitional inferiority to all the others (Arditti, 1980). Galen, having read the book of Genesis, "discovered" that men had one less rib on one side than women did (Webster & Webster, 1974). Clearly, observation of what would appear by today's standards to be easily verifiable facts can vary depending on the theory or paradigm, to use the terminology of Thomas S. Kuhn, under which the scientist is operating (1970).

Although each scientist strives to be as objective and value free as possible, most scientists, feminists, and philosophers of science recognize that no individual can be neutral or value free. Instead "objectivity is defined to mean independence from the value judgments of any particular individual" (Jaggar, 1983, p. 357). The paradigms themselves, however, also are far from value free. The values of the culture, historical past, and present society heavily influence the ordering of observable phenomena into theory. The world view of a particular society, time, and person limits the questions that can be asked and thereby the answers that can be given. Kuhn has demonstrated that the very acceptance of a particular paradigm that may appear to cause a "scientific revolution" within a society depends in fact on the congruence of that theory with the institutions and beliefs of the society.

Longino (1990) has explored the extent to which methods employed by scientists can be objective and lead to repeatable, verifiable results while contributing to hypotheses or theories that are congruent with nonobjective institutions and ideologies of the society.

> Background assumptions are the means by which contextual values and ideology are incorporated into scientific inquiry . . . The background assumptions that determine evidential reasoning are those that emerge from the transformative interrogation by the scientific community (or a sufficient part of it). This means that community values may well remain embedded in scientific reasoning and research programs. Social interactions determine what values remain encoded in inquiry and which are eliminated, and thus which values remain encoded in the theories and propositions taken as expressing scientific knowledge at any given time. Values are not incompatible with objectivity, but objectivity is analyzed as a function of community practices rather than as an attitude of individual researchers towards their material or a relation between representation and represented. (Longino, 1990, p. 216)

The institutions and beliefs of our society reflect the fact that the society is patriarchal. Female scientists, just as their male counterparts, have until recently been unaware of the influence of patriarchal bias in the paradigms of science.

Over the past two decades feminist historians and philosophers of science (Fee, 1981, 1982; Harding, 1986; Haraway, 1978, 1989; Longino, 1990) and feminist scientists (Bleier, 1984, 1986; Fausto Sterling, 1985; Birke, 1986; Keller, 1983, 1985; Rosser, 1988) have pointed out a source of bias and absence of value neutrality in science, particularly biology. By excluding females as experimental subjects, focusing on problems of primary interest to males, using faulty experimental designs, and interpretations of data based in language or ideas constricted by patriarchal parameters, experimental results in several areas of biology are biased or flawed. These flaws and biases were permitted to become part of the mainstream of scientific thought and were perpetuated in the scientific literature for decades, because most scientists were men. Because most, if not all, scientists were men, values held by them as males were not distinguished as biasing. Values held by male scientists were congruent with the values of all scientists and became synonymous with the "objective" view of the world (Keller, 1982, 1985).

A first step of feminist scientists was recognition of the possibility of androcentric bias that resulted from having virtually all theoretical and decision-making positions in science held by men (Keller, 1982). As suggested in the preface to this volume, it was not until a critical mass of women existed in the profession (Rosser, 1986) that the bias of androcentrism might emerge. As long as only a few women were scientists, they had to demonstrate or conform to the male view of the world in order to be successful and have their research meet the criteria for "objectivity."

Once the possibility for androcentric bias was discovered, feminist scientists set out to explore the extent to which it had distorted science. They recognized potential distortion on a variety of levels of research and theory: the choice and definition of problems to be studied, exclusion of females as experimental subjects, bias in methodology used to collect and interpret data, and bias in theories and conclusions drawn from the data. The bulk of work done by feminists in biology up to the time this volume goes to press has centered on critique of biological research and theories that have been flawed because of androcentric bias. For the remainder of this chapter, I will focus on the critiques of the biological subdisciplines on the organismal level including evolutionary biology, animal behavior (especially sociobiology and primatology), and ecology.

EVOLUTIONARY BIOLOGY

Modern evolutionary biology is based on and has its roots in the nineteenth-century theory proposed by Charles Darwin ([1859] 1967). Although this theory seemed revolutionary at the time, scholars have suggested that natural selection, as described by Darwin, was ultimately accepted by his contemporaries because it was a paradigm laden with the values of nineteenth-century England. Rose and Rose (1980) underline the congruence between the values expressed in Darwin's theory and those of the upper classes of Victorian England. "Its central metaphors drawn from society and in their turn interacting with society were of the competition of species, the struggle for existence, the ecological niche, and the survival of the fittest" (Rose & Rose, 1980, p. 28). These metaphors reflect Victorian society and were acceptable to it because they, and the "social Darwinism" quickly derived from it, seemed to ground its norms solidly in a biological foundation. When Darwin depicts the fittest as the individuals who pass on their genes to the greatest number of offspring, one thinks of the importance of passing on property in this society. One can hardly overlook an upper-class perspective and appeal when, in the *Descent of Man*, Darwin implores that "both sexes ought to refrain from marriage if they are in any marked degree inferior in body or mind; . . . All ought to refrain from marriage who cannot avoid abject poverty for their children, for poverty is . . . a great evil" (1871, p. 618). The upper class of Victorian England had self-serving reasons for finding Darwin's theory attractive: it gave biological rationale for their position in society. Nor was Darwin's own position a matter unrelated to the acceptability of his theory. Even though Darwin himself was not aggressive in advancing it, he had wealthy and influential friends such as Thomas Henry Huxley, Sir Charles Lyell, and Sir Joseph Dalton Hooker who championed the theory for him. One wonders if

Alfred Russel Wallace might not have fared better in receiving credit and publicity for his contributions had he had such friends and been from an equally prominent social class.

Aside from noting its statement in terms of upper-class Victorian values and decrying the misuse of his theory of natural selection by social Darwinists, feminist scientists by and large have not critiqued the theory of natural selection. As scientists, they have recognized the significance of the theory for the foundations of modern biology. Given the strong attacks on natural selection by creationists and other groups not known for their profeminist stances, most feminist scientists who might have critiqued some minor points have been reluctant to provide creationists with evidence that they might misuse. One notable exception is Ruth Hubbard's (1990) suggestion, related to the work of Lewontin, Rose and Kamin (1984), that the reductionism and gradualism implied by the theory of natural selection led to over reliance on the Master Molecule and central dogma for DNA structure and protein synthesis proposed by Watson and Crick (Watson, 1969) as the models to explain change in species. The fascination with these models led people to reject more complex, interactive models such as those of McClintock (Keller, 1983), which might also explain more rapid, punctuated change (Lewontin et al., 1984) in evolution.

In contrast to accepting his theory of natural selection, many feminist scientists have critiqued Darwin's theory of sexual selection for its androcentric bias. The theory of sexual selection reflected and reinforced Victorian social norms regarding the sexes. By this theory Darwin set out to explain a phenomenon still not fully understood, that of the existence of secondary sex characteristics. He claimed that "when the males and females of any animal have the same general habits of life, but differ in structure, color, or ornament, such differences have been mainly caused by sexual selection" (Darwin, 1967, p. 89). Expanding considerably on the theory first presented in the *Origin*, Darwin specified, in the *Descent of Man*, how the process functions and what roles males and females play in it: "The sexual struggle is of two kinds: in the one it is between the individuals of the same sex, generally the males, in order to drive away or kill their rivals, the females remaining passive; whilst in the other, the struggle is likewise between the individuals of the same sex, in order to excite or charm those of the opposite sex, generally the females, which no longer remain passive, but select the more agreeable partners" (Darwin, 1871, p. 64). According to the theory, the males who triumph over their rivals will win the more desirable females and will leave the most progeny, thereby perpetuating and increasing, over numerous generations, those qualities that afforded them victory. The females who succeed, by the seductive means they employ, in being chosen will also procreate best and pass on their characteristics. As a result, by the time

evolution has produced modern man and modern woman, the two are considerably different, men being superior to women both physically and mentally. Not
only are they "taller, heavier, and stronger than women, with squarer shoulders
and more plainly pronounced muscles," but also they attain to a "higher emi-
nence" in whatever they take up (Darwin, 1871, p. 564). The theory reflects the
Victorian age, with its depiction of active males competing and struggling with
each other for passive females. That depiction of male–female interaction would
have seemed quite obvious to most segments of Victorian society and its ground-
ing in scientific fact most reassuring.

However the process of selection involved in the theory encountered much
resistance. Biologists of Darwin's time came up with numerous counterexamples.
Alfred Wallace, who independently had arrived at the theory of natural selection,
fundamentally disagreed with the theory of sexual selection. Even Darwin himself
gives proof, in *Descent of Man*, of considerable difficulty with many of the
assumptions and necessities of his theory and admits that, especially as applied
to the history of man, it "wants scientific precision" (1871, p. 605). Antoinette
Blackwell attacked his theory on a number of points ([1875] 1976). In her
understanding that a central problem of the theory was Darwin's limited perspective as a male observer, she may be said to have made the first feminist criticism
of it.

Why, then, one wonders, did Darwin insist on the theory so much? What
role did it play in his total conception of change in nature? Initially, in the *Origin*,
Darwin used the theory as a secondary agent to explain the means by which
evolution takes place: "Amongst many animals, sexual selection will give its
aid to ordinary selection, by assuring to the most vigorous and best adapted males
the greatest number of offspring" (1967, p. 127). The reader understands readily
that sexual selection is a minor support to natural selection. But the reader may
be surprised to see that males only are mentioned as the bearers of the desirable
characteristics that are sexually selected. At this point in the text Darwin adds a
second benefit of sexual selection: "Sexual selection will also give characters
useful to the males alone, in their struggles with other males." Again, the focus
is entirely on the male half of the species. The only activity envisioned in this
expression is bound up in a masculine world.

Later in *Origin* Darwin stresses the variability of secondary sexual characteristics. He wonders why there is more variability in these characters than in those
of other parts of the organism. Sexual selection has "wide scope for action."
At this point, Darwin expands on the possible benefits of sexual selection:
"Variations of this part would, it is highly probable, be taken advantage of by
natural and sexual selection, in order to fit the several species to their several
places in the economy of nature, and likewise to fit the two sexes of the same

species to each other, or to fit the males and females to different habits of life or the males to struggle with other males for the possession of the females'' (1967, pp. 157–58). The verb ''to fit'' is used three times in this society-oriented view. Darwin speaks as if places have been somehow previously marked out for the species and the sexes. As the sentence continues, he increasingly stresses the differences between the sexes and again depicts a world in which the males actively struggle for passive females who become the property of the winning males.

What seems to have struck Darwin most when he observed males and females of species throughout the natural world was the tremendous difference between them: ''How enormously these sometimes differ in the most important characters is known to every naturalist'' (Darwin, 1967, p. 424). What amazed him was the fact that such different beings belong to the same species. When viewing the human world in the light of other natural realms, he was even surprised to note that even greater differences still had not been evolved. ''It is, indeed, fortunate that the law of the equal transmission of characters to both sexes prevails with mammals; otherwise it is probable that man would have become as superior in mental endowment to woman, as the peacock is in ornamental plumage to the peahen'' (Darwin, 1871, p. 565).

At first view it may seem strange that Darwin stresses the differences between the sexes. In the *Origin* he depicts the struggle for existence as a mainly intraspecific conflict, claiming that competition is fiercest among those closest in the scale of nature (Darwin, 1967, p. 76). Yet when he comes to those beings most closely related, namely the males and females of a given species, he does not speak of competition at all but rather of an entirely masculine struggle for females. Indeed, as he depicts male–female interaction it seems that the males constitute something like a separate group, interacting mainly with each other in relation to another quite separate group, the members of which have relatively fewer secondary sex characteristics. In order to make the differentiation between males and females as strong as possible, the theory of sexual selection is needed. The theory is the agent of differentiation, that which assures an ever-increasing separation between the sexes and their operation in two quite distinct realms that touch only for the purpose of procreation.

ANIMAL BEHAVIOR

Just as Darwin observed the behavior of lower animals to develop his theories of natural and sexual selection, current animal behavior research is based on Darwin's work. Much research in animal behavior has been reviewed by feminist scientists and found not to be flawed by androcentric bias. However, some researchers have observed behavior in lower animals in a search for "universal" behavior patterns that occur in males of all species or in all males of a particular order or class such as primates or mammals. This behavior is then extrapolated to humans in an attempt to demonstrate a biological or innate basis for the behavior.

Some sociobiologists, such as Barash (1977), Dawkins (1976), and Wilson (1975) have based their new discipline on biological determinism in stating that behavior is genetically determined and that differences between males and females in role, status, and performance are biologically based. Sociobiology is the study of the biological basis of behavior. It attempts to show that human social institutions and social behavior are the results of biological forces acting through prehuman and human evolution. The theory is based on Darwin's theory of evolution through natural selection, which sociobiologists claim to extend and amplify (Lowe & Hubbard, 1979). Sociobiologists describe human sex roles and behaviors as innate and programmed into the genes. They base these roles and behaviors on examples of social interaction in lower animals, which, not coincidentally, remind us in their turn of the human world: "aggression," "selfishness," "male dominance" (Wilson, 1975).

Feminist critiques of sociobiology have centered around criticisms of the assumption that behaviors such as aggression, homosexuality, promiscuity, selfishness, and altruism are biologically determined and the problems involved with anthropomorphism in animal behavior studies. The anthropomorphism occurs in at least two forms: (1) the use of human language and frameworks to describe animal behavior that is then used to "prove" that certain human behaviors are innate as they are also found in animals; and (2) the selective choice of species for study that mirror human society. The data from those selected species is then assumed to be the universal behavior of all species. Some scientists have suggested that these feminist critiques are obvious. However, the most renowned sociobiologists (Dawkins, 1976; Trivers, 1972; Wilson, 1978) have continued to assume that genes do determine behavior and that the behaviors described as aggression, homosexuality, rape, selfishness, and altruism in animals are equivalent to those behaviors in humans, even though more than one decade of criticism by feminists (Bleier, 1976; Hubbard, 1990 Lowe, 1978; Lowe & Hubbard, 1979) has been leveled against the "obvious" flaws in the sociobiological theories and assumptions.

Similarly, it was clear in the early primatology work (Yerkes, 1943) that particular primate species, such as the baboon and chimpanzee, were chosen for study primarily because their social organization was seen by the observers as closely resembling that of human primates. However, subsequent researchers forgot the "obvious" limitations imposed by such selection of species and proceeded to generalize the data to universal behavior patterns for all primates. It was not until a significant number of women entered primatology that the concepts of the universality and male leadership of dominance hierarchies among primates (Lancaster, 1975; Leavitt, 1975; Leibowitz, 1975; Rowell, 1974) were questioned and shown to be inaccurate for many primate species. The "evident" problems discussed by feminist critics (Bleier, 1984) of studying nonhuman primates in an attempt to discover what the true nature of humans would be without the overlay of culture, have been largely ignored by many of the sociobiologists and scientists studying animal behavior.

Feminist critiques of animal behavior and sociobiology attack the assumption of biological determinism: that biology (genes) determines behavior and that those biological effects may be measured separately from those of culture. Hubbard (1985) in reviewing *Not In Our Genes: Biology, Ideology, and Human Nature* by Lewontin, Rose, and Kamin (1984) presents an excellent critique of the problems with the nature/nurture dichotomy:

> Reductionist thinking about organisms would have us believe that an organism can be looked at in isolation, untouched by what we, for convenience, separate off as its environment. But organisms and their environments are quite literally part of each other. We continuously incorporate portions of what we call our environment and continuously change it by breathing, excreting, and other activities. Similarly, our biological functions and the ways society affects us are inseparable: Their conjunction makes us who we are. Antireductionists, myself included, have sometimes proposed "interactive" models to describe the relationships between organism and environment, biology and society. Lewontin, Rose and Kamin object that this does not go far enough because the notion of interaction implies the existence of separate units that "interact". Far better, they say, to insist on the essential oneness of the organism-in-its-environment. I agree. (Hubbard, 1985, pp. 7–8)

In addition to the problems of selective use of species, anthropomorphic and vague language, and universalizing and extrapolating beyond limits of the data, feminist scientists revealed another obvious flaw in much animal behavior research: failure to study females. When females were studied, it was usually only in their interaction (usually reaction) to males or infants. Presumably the fact that until recently most animal behavior researchers were male resulted in an androcentric bias in the conceptualization of design for observation of animal behavior. Because male researchers had only *experienced* male–male and male–female interactions themselves, their male world view prohibited them from realizing that female–female interaction might be *observed* in their own and other species. Female primatologists (Goodall, 1971; Fossey, 1983) and sociobiologists (Hrdy, 1977, 1979, 1981, 1984, 1986) revealed new information that led to the overthrow of previously held theories regarding dominance hierarchies, mate selection (Hrdy, 1984), and female–female competition (Hrdy & Williams, 1983) by focusing on female–female interactions. Some claim to be feminist sociobiologists (Hrdy, 1981, 1986) because they believe that genes determine behavior and have revealed the central role that females in many species play. These few feminist sociobiologists have pointed out the flaws of their male colleagues extrapolating from insect and bird species to human beings that go beyond the limits of the data. They have also pointed out to their feminist colleagues who are not sociobiologists that rejecting all sociobiology research because of unwarranted extrapolations by some extremists (Barash, 1977; Dawkins, 1976; Trivers, 1972; Wilson, 1975, 1978) who have been given considerable media attention for political reasons may constitute an example of throwing out the baby with the bath water.

ECOLOGY

Recognizing their link with females of other species led women in animal behavior to reveal the androcentric blinders that had limited observation in other species. This revelation in turn led to new information that reversed theories and revolutionized basic concepts within the subdiscipline. Women who identify as feminists in ecology are expressing an even broader relationship with all species. "While we can describe what is meant by ecofeminism, perhaps there can be no precise intellectual definition because ecofeminism is fundamentally a feeling experienced by many women that they are somehow intimately connected to and part of the earth" (Davies, 1988, p. 6).

Beginning in the mid-1970s ecofeminists have explored the similarities and overlaps in the ways in which women, other animal and plant species, and the physical environment are controlled, exploited, and dominated by white, middle-upper-class men in Western society. Griffin (1978) and Merchant (1979) traced the historical roots, beginning in the seventeenth century, of the shift from an organic, hermetic approach to science (in which men revered and saw themselves as part of the environment and nature, and women as identified with nature) to a mechanistic, objective approach. This resulting distance justified men's domination and exploitation of the environment (and women).

Individuals have elaborated, from a variety of perspectives, the origins of the links between women and nature in opposition to men. Merchant (1979) documents the role of industrialization in supporting a science and technology that exploit women and nature. Stone (1976) and Gary (1979) suggest that the Judeo–Christian tradition legitimated the divine right of patriarchy, which endorsed men to dominate both women and nature. Chodorow (1978) and Dinnerstein (1976) propose that the opposition has its roots in differential psychological development in males and females. Because in modern Western culture most child care is done by women, male psychology is based on autonomy and separation, whereas female psychology is based on identification with others. The science and technology created by men tends to perpetuate distance and domination.

Feminists suggest critiques of science (Birke, 1986; Bleier, 1984; Keller, 1985; 1987) and use of feminist interdisciplinary (Rosser, 1989), holistic (Hubbard, 1985), and qualitative methods (Harding, 1986) as more humane approaches to science and the environment. Keller (1983) and Goodfield (1981) discuss the ways in which female scientists shorten the distance between themselves as observers and their object of study, suggesting that their relationship with their experimental subject makes them less likely to exploit or harm that subject.

Feminists have delineated the extent to which interdisciplinary approaches and combinations of qualitative and quantitative methods are more appropriate when studying important questions in women's health in areas such as childbirth, pregnancy, and menopause (Hamilton, 1985; Rosser, 1989). These interdisciplinary approaches and combinations of qualitative and quantitative methods often provide fruitful information for solutions to environmental problems. As Hynes (1985) points out, many of the classic tests used in ecology were developed by women: Ellen Swallow Richards developed the evaporation tests for volatile oils that became the world standard; the Normal Chlorine Map used to discern incipient pollution caused by human, municipal, and industrial waste leading to the first Water Purity Tables; and tests leading to the first pure food laws in the United States. Rachel Carson combined data from the effects of agricultural pesticides, particularly DDT, correctly extrapolating beyond the available data to underline the fact that pesticides might be carcinogenic and cause chromosomal damage and to alert the world to the dangers of pesticides as biocides harmful to people, plants, and animals (Hynes, 1989). Her work led to the establishment of the Environmental Protection Agency (EPA) and the promulgation of some of the most rigorous environmental legislation in the world. Lois Gibbs, a high-school graduate and housewife, devised a scheme that demonstrated that illness possibly caused by toxic waste in her neighborhood followed the pattern of former stream beds and swales. Her data combined with protests and lobbies eventually forced the state of New York to acknowledge the accuracy of her swale theory and to purchase with federal help all the homes in the Love Canal area (Hynes, 1985).

Feminists who critique science call for a consideration of the potential use of the research and its possible social and environmental effects as part of the determination of whether or not the research should be undertaken (Birke, 1986; Bleier, 1984; Fausto-Sterling, 1985; Hubbard, 1983; Rosser 1988). These writers claim that the division between basic and applied should be blurred and research that is militaristic, destructive, and exploitative of the environment and certain groups of people, should not be undertaken. As Bleier states, "it would aim to eliminate research that leads to the exploitation and destruction of nature, the destruction of the human race and other species, and that justifies the oppression of people because of race, gender, class, sexuality, or nationality" (1986, p. 16). In this sense both ecologists and feminists share the same commitment to political and social action based on their principles.

In their critique of science, its theories, methods, and uses, feminists have delineated an improved science that would result from less androcentrism (Keller, 1982). Ecofeminists have made explicit the connection between the domination of both women and the environment through the androcentrism of modern science (King, 1983, 1989; Harding, 1986). They propose that science, including ecology, has much to learn from feminism.

CONCLUSION

Critiques by biologists writing during the first part of the twentieth-century wave of feminism (Bleier, 1984; Fausto-Sterling, 1985; Rosser & Hogsett, 1984; Hubbard, 1979; Lowe, 1978) refuted claims of biological determinism. Just as Darwin's work had been used by social Darwinists in the nineteenth century to provide a biological justification for the social inequalities between classes, biological determinism in anthropology (Ardrey, 1971, 1976; Fox, 1967; Tiger, 1970; Tiger & Fox, 1974) and sociobiology (Barash, 1977; Dawkins, 1976; Trivers, 1972; Wilson, 1975, 1978) provided a biological basis for the inequalities in political power, social prestige, and professional opportunities between the sexes.

Feminist scientists writing in the 1970s and early 1980s exposed the flaws in logic and the androcentric bias in biological determinism and emphasized social construction of gender as the basis for inequalities between the sexes. Specifically their critiques revealed the following: androcentric assumptions in Darwin's theory of sexual selection about the passivity of females in mate selection (Rosser & Hogsett, 1984; Hrdy, 1986); reduction of complex behaviors that include social and cultural learning to simple genetic determinants (Bleier, 1984; Fausto-Sterling, 1985; Hubbard, 1979); failure to observe or study females (Goodall, 1971; Hrdy, 1981) extrapolating and universalizing beyond limited data collected on males of a particular species to females and other species (Bleier, 1984; Merchant, 1979; Rosser, 1988); and the historical origins and current detrimental effects (Hynes, 1989) of the view that men should use science and technology to dominate and exploit women, other species, and the ecosystem.

These feminist biologists recognized that biological determinism and reductionism united aspects of research in evolutionary biology, animal behavior, especially sociobiology, and ecology that were often used to provide a biological justification for women's inferior position in society. They critiqued this research not only because it was flawed scientifically but also because they recognized the danger of using biology to justify social and political inequality for women, men of color, gays, and lesbians. As long as inequality is biologically caused, there is little need for new laws, educational programs, or money to be used to try to achieve equality. Biological bases for differences and behavior may be used to justify a conservative political agenda (Gould, 1981; Hubbard, 1990). Not surprisingly, the time in which these critiques of biological determinism were made coincided with a time that was more politically liberal. It included attempts towards affirmative action, passage of the ERA, the gay and lesbian rights movements, and changing divorce and custody laws.

Beginning in the mid-1980s, feminists in most disciplines began to reexamine differences—differences among women and differences between men and women. Some feminists in biology have also begun to examine whether biological differences between the sexes, when coupled with gender socialization, may result in behavioral differences between men and women and boys and girls. The work of feminist sociobiologists such as Hrdy (1977, 1979, 1981, 1984) emphasizes genetic contributions to behavior. Some work on aggression and the link between women and peace (Rosoff, 1991; Wishnia, 1991) suggests that hormonal differences coupled with the biological fact that women give birth and physically nourish offspring makes them more peace seeking. Some lesbian and gay rights activists, such as members of Queer Nation, favor genetic and biological explanations for homosexuality implying that sexual orientation cannot be changed by choice, counseling, or religious conversion. Some ecofeminists (Williams, 1991) also emphasize that in addition to parturition and lactation, the cyclical nature of women's menstrual cycles makes them more harmonious with the earth and other living beings.

Emphasis on biological difference between the sexes may be used to justify diverse political causes and be related to diverse theoretical roots in feminism. Minimizing biological difference in deference to social construction of gender fits a liberal political agenda. Its roots are in liberal feminism, which seeks equality and assumes objectivity and the possibility of a value-free, neutral standpoint. Not surprisingly, the feminist critiques in the 1970s and 1980s revealed an androcentric bias in evolutionary biology, sociobiology, and ecology. They used the scientific method itself to demonstrate "bad" science as biased by androcentrism; they left the notions of objectivity and the scientific method itself intact.

In contrast, the more recent writing on biological difference may be used to support either a fairly conservative or a radical political position. Emphasis on biological difference is usually linked with essentialist feminism. Some individuals interpret essentialism as suggesting that differences between the sexes and women's inferior position in society are subject to little or no influence from social forces (a conservative political agenda). Alternatively, some feminists, particularly ecofeminists, have used biological difference to justify women's superiority to men in their connection to the earth and other species. Essentialist feminism and the emphasis on difference implicitly challenge the notions of value neutrality and objectivity. Essentialism implies that men and women would construct a different science. Challenging the notions of value neutrality and objectivity inherent in logical positivism implies acceptance of the social construction of knowledge, including scientific knowledge. In accepting the possibility of the social construction of scientific knowledge, feminists must still be wary of androcentric bias. In a patriarchal society in which theoretical and decision-making positions in the scientific hierarchy are held by men, the potential for androcentric bias is substantial.

REFERENCES

Arditti, R. (1980). Feminism and science. In R. Arditti, P. Brennan, & S. Cavrak (Eds.), *Science and liberation*. Boston: South End Press.

Ardrey, R. (1971). *The territorial imperative*. New York: Dell.

Ardrey, R. (1976). *The hunting hypothesis*. New York: Atheneum.

Barash, D. (1977). *Sociobiology and behavior*. New York: Elsevier.

Birke, L. (1986). *Women, feminism, and biology: The feminist challenge*. New York: Methuen.

Blackwell, A. (1976). *The sexes throughout nature*. Westport, CT: Hyperion Press. (Original work published 1875).

Bleier, R. (1976). Myths of the biological inferiority of women: An exploration of the sociology of biological research. *University of Michigan Papers in Women's Studies, 2*, 39–63.

Bleier, R. (1984). *Science and gender: A critique of biology and its theories on women*. Elmsford, NY: Pergamon Press.

Bleier, R. (1986). Sex differences research: Science or belief? In R. Bleier (Ed.), *Feminist approaches to science* (pp. 147–164). Elmsford, NY: Pergamon Press.

Chodorow, N. (1978). *The reproduction of mothering: Psychoanalysis and the sociology of gender*. Berkeley and Los Angeles: The University of California Press.

Darwin, C. (1967). *On the origin of species: A facsimile of the first edition*. New York: Atheneum. (Original work published 1859)

Darwin, C. (1871). *The descent of man and selection in relation to sex*. London: John Murray.

Davies, K. (1988). What is ecofeminism? *Women and Environments, 10*, 4–6.

Dawkins, R. (1976). *The selfish gene*. New York: Oxford University Press.

Dinnerstein, D. (1976). *The mermaid and the minotaur*. New York: Harper & Row.

Fausto-Sterling, A. (1985). *Myths of gender*. New York: Basic Books.

Fee, E. (1981). Is feminism a threat to scientific objectivity? *International Journal of Women's Studies, 4* (4), 213–233.

Fee, E. (1982). A feminist critique of scientific objectivity. *Science for the People, 14* (4), 8.

Fossey, D. (1983). *Gorillas in the mist*. Boston: Houghton Mifflin.

Fox, R. (1967). *Kinship and marriage*. Baltimore: Penguin.

Goodall, J. (1971). *In the shadow of man*. Boston: Houghton Mifflin.

Goodfield, J. (1981). *An imagined world*. New York: Penguin Books.

Gould, S. J. (1981). *The mismeasure of man*. New York: W. W. Norton.

Gray, E. D. (1979). *Green paradise lost*. Wellesley, MA: Roundtable Press.

Griffin, S. (1978). *Women and nature: The roaring inside her*. New York: Harper & Row.

Hamilton, J. (1985). Avoiding methodological biases in gender-related health research. In *Women's health report of the Public Health Service Task Force on women's health issues*. Washington, DC: U.S. Department of Health and Human Services Public Health Service.

Haraway, D. (1978). Animal sociology and a natural economy of the body politic, Part I: A political physiology of dominance; Animal sociology and a natural economy of the body politic, Part II: The past is the contested zone: Human nature and theories of production and reproduction in primate behavior studies. *Signs: Journal of Women in Culture and Society, 4* (1), 21–60.

Haraway, D. (1989). Monkeys, aliens, and women: Love, science, and politics at the intersection of feminist theory and colonial discourse. *Women's Studies International Forum, 12* (3), 295–312.

Harding, S. (1986). *The science question in feminism*. Ithaca, NY: Cornell University Press.

Hrdy, S. B. (1977). *The langurs of Abu: Female and male strategies of reproduction*. Cambridge: Harvard University Press.

Hrdy, S. B. (1979). Infanticide among animals: A review, classification and examination of the implications for the reproductive strategies of females. *Ethology and Sociobiology, 1*, 3–40.

Hrdy, S. B. (1981). *The woman that never evolved*. Cambridge: Harvard University Press.

Hrdy, S. B. (1984). Introduction: Female reproductive strategies. In M. Small (Ed.), *Female primates: Studies by women primatologists*. New York: Alan Liss.

Hrdy, S. (1986). Empathy, polyandry, and the myth of the coy female. In R. Bleier (Ed.), *Feminist approaches to science*. Elmsford, NY: Pergamon Press.

Hrdy, S. B., & Williams, G. C. (1983). Behavioral biology and the double standard. In S. K. Wasser (Ed.), *Social behavior of female vertebrates*. New York: Academic Press.

Hubbard, R. (1979). Have only men evolved? In R. Hubbard, M. S. Henifin, & B. Fried (Eds.), *Women look at biology looking at women*. Cambridge, MA: Schenkman.

Hubbard, R. (1983). Social effects of some contemporary myths about women. In M.

Lowe & R. Hubbard (Eds.), *Women's nature: Rationalizations of inequality*. Elmsford, NY: Pergamon Press.

Hubbard, R. (1985). Putting genes in their place. *The Women's Review of Books, 2* (4), 7–8.

Hubbard, R. (1990). *Politics of women's biology*. New Brunswick, NJ: Rutgers University Press.

Hubbard, R. & Lowe, M. (1979). Introduction. In R. Hubbard & M. Lowe (Eds.), *Genes and gender II: Pitfalls in research on sex and gender*. New York: Gordian Press.

Hynes, H. P. (1985). "Ellen Swallow, Lois Gibbs, and Rachel Carson: Catalysts of the American Environmental Movement." *Women's Studies International Forum*, 8 (4): 291–298.

Hynes, H. P. (1989). *The recurring silent spring*. Elmsford, NY: Pergamon Press.

Jaggar, A. M. (1983). *Feminist politics and human nature*. Totowa, NJ: Rowman & Allanheld.

Keller, E. F. (1982). Feminism and science. *Signs: Journal of Women in Culture and Society, 7* (3), 589–602.

Keller, E. F. (1983). *A feeling for the organism: The life and work of Barbara McClintock*. New York: W. H. Freeman.

Keller, E. F. (1985). *Reflections on gender and science*. New Haven, CT: Yale University Press.

Keller, E. F. (1987). Women scientists and feminist critics of science. *Daedalus*, 77–91.

King, Y. (1983). Toward an ecological feminism and a feminist ecology. In J. Rothschild (Ed.), *Machina ex dea: Feminist perspectives on technology*. New York: Pergamon Press.

King, Y. (1989). The ecology of feminism and the feminism of ecology. In J. Plant (Ed.), *Healing the wounds: The promise of ecofeminism* (pp. 18–28). Philadelphia, PA and Santa Cruz, CA: New Society Publishers.

Kuhn, T. S. (1970). *The structure of scientific revolution* (2nd ed.). Chicago: The University of Chicago Press.

Lancaster, J. (1975). *Primate behavior and the emergence of human culture*. New York: Holt, Rinehart & Winston.

Leavitt, R. R. (1975). *Peaceable primates and gentle people: Anthropological approaches to women's studies*. New York: Harper & Row.

Leibowitz, L. (1975). Perspectives in the evolution of sex differences. In R. R. Reiter (Ed.), *Toward an anthropology of women*. New York: Monthly Review Press.

Lewontin, R. C., Rose, S., & Kamin, L. J. (1984). *Not in our genes: Biology, ideology, and human nature*. New York: Pantheon.

Longino, Helen. (1990). *Science as social knowledge: Values and objectivity in scientific inquiry*. Princeton, NJ: Princeton University Press.

Lowe, M. (1978). Sociobiology and sex differences. *Signs: Journal of Women in Culture and Society, 4* (1), 118–125.

Lowe, M. and R. Hubbard. (1979) Sociobiology and Biosociology: Can Science Prove the Biological Basis of Sex Differences in Behavior? in *Genes and Gender* II, ed. Ruth Hubbard and Marion Lowe. New York: Gordian Press, 91–111.

Merchant, C. (1979). *The death of nature: Women, ecology and the scientific revolution*. New York: Harper & Row.

Rose, H., & Rose, S. (1980). The myth of the neutrality of science. In R. Arditti, P. Brennan, & S. Carak (Eds.), *Science and liberation*. Boston: South End Press.

Rosoff, B. (1991). Genes, hormones, and war. In A. E. Hunter (Ed.), *Genes and gender IV: On peace, war, and gender* (pp. 39–49). New York: Feminist Press.

Rosser, S. V. (1986). *Teaching science and health from a feminist perspective: A practical guide*. Elmsford, NY: Pergamon Press.

Rosser, S. V. (1988). Women in science and health care: A gender at risk. In S. V. Rosser (Ed.), *Feminism within the science and health care professions: Overcoming resistance*. Elmsford, NY: Pergamon Press.

Rosser, S. V. (1989). Teaching techniques to attract women to science. *Women's Studies International Forum, 12*, 363–278.

Rosser, S. V. & Hogsett, A. C. (1984). Darwin and sexism: Victorian causes, contemporary effects. In D. L. Fowlkes & C. S. McClure (Eds.), *Feminist visions: Toward a transformation of the liberal arts curriculum* (pp 42–45). Tuscaloosa: University of Alabama Press.

Rowell, T. (1974). The concept of social dominance. *Behavioral Biology, 11*, 131–154.

Stone, M. (1976). *When God was a woman*. New York: Harcourt, Brace, Jovanovich.

Tiger, L. (1977). The possible biological origins of sexual discrimination. In D. W. Brothwell (Ed.), *Biosocial man*. London: Eugenics Society.

Tiger. L., & Fox, R. (1974). *The imperial animal*. New York: Dell.

Trivers, R. L. (1972). Parental investment and sexual selection. In B. Campbell (Ed.), *Sexual selection and the descent of man*. Chicago, IL: Aldine.

Watson, J. D. (1969). *The double helix*. New York: Atheneum Publishers.

Webster, D., & Webster, M. (1974). *Comparative vertebrate morphology*. New York: Academic Press.

Williams, R. E. (1991). Mothermilk. In A. E. Hunter (Ed.), *Genes and Gender IV: On peace, war, and gender*. New York: Feminist Press.

Wilson, E. O. (1975). *Sociobiology: The new synthesis*. Cambridge, MA: Harvard University Press.

Wilson, E. O. (1978). *On human nature*. Cambridge, MA: Harvard University Press.

Wishnia, J. (1991). Pacifism and feminism in historical perspective. In A. E. Hunter (Ed.), *Genes and gender IV: On peace, war, and gender*. New York: Feminist Press.

Yerkes, R. M. (1943). *Chimpanzees*. New Haven, CT: Yale University Press.

4.

CRITIQUES OF RESEARCH IN CELLULAR AND MOLECULAR BIOLOGY

Perhaps it will come as no surprise that the same thread—androcentric bias in research that can support biological determinism as a basis for the social status quo—unites the feminist critiques of biology at the cellular and molecular level with critiques at the organismal level. Several single-authored books, including *Science and Gender* (Bleier, 1984), *Reflections on Gender and Science* (Keller, 1985), *Myths of Gender* (Fausto-Sterling, 1985), *Women, Feminism and Biology* (Birke, 1986), *The Politics of Women's Biology* (Hubbard, 1990), and collections of essays, among them *Feminism and Science* (Tuana, 1989) and *Feminism and Science* (Rosser, 1989), include explorations of androcentric bias on both levels by feminist scientists whose outstanding training and research qualifies them to critique one subdiscipline particularly well. They conclude that faulty research design, overextension of data, and general "bad" science may be more acceptable in some areas of research that may provide scientific bases for the social status quo.

The strands of feminist critiques of evolutionary biology, animal behavior, and ecology also form the fabric for critiques in the neurosciences, endocrinology, and developmental and cell biology. Patriarchal language and values of scientists and society inform the problems chosen for study and theoretical concepts of the subdisciplines that examine cellular and molecular processes that

70

occur below the organismal level. Because reductionism is inherent in each of these subdisciplines, problems of extrapolation from the simple to the complex within an organism and from one species to another are further exacerbated. Studying neurons, hormones, cells, and molecules also tends to reduce complex biological/environmental interactions to structures and chemicals. Stripping off the environmental context in which these structures and chemicals function may also occur with the use of sophisticated technological equipment to study the chemicals and structures. This context stripping further clouds the role such structures and chemicals play in the entire organism and particularly in complicated behavioral and social interactions with organisms of the same and other species. Feminist critiques of cellular and molecular biology have helped to reveal the points at which androcentric bias has crippled the foundations of biological research.

NEUROSCIENCES

In the neurosciences, a substantial amount of work has been done relating to sex differences in the brains of men and women. As Birke (1986) and Bleier (1984) have stressed, the voluminous research on sex differences that is well funded by federal and foundation sources and attracts considerable attention, clearly plays a significant role in our society. Numerous studies have documented (Maccoby & Jacklin, 1974) that similarities and overlappings rather than differences and clear separation between the sexes are the reality for most abilities and behaviors studied. Even in the four areas of aggression, verbal, visuo-spatial, and mathematical ability in which studies have found differences between the sexes (Maccoby & Jacklin, 1974), those differences were statistically significant only when very large numbers were used for the sample size. The ranges between the two sexes for even these four areas overlap so much that thousands of people must be sampled in one study to show a significant difference between the means for males and females for those abilities and behaviors.

For nonbiological factors such as pay inequities, child-care responsibilities, and single-parent-headed households there are clear separations between the sexes and statistically significant mean differences can be easily established even when small sample sizes are used. The difference between the average female worker earning $0.74 for every dollar earned by a male worker is significant and clear cut. Does the search for biologically based sex differences (sexual orientation and racial differences) represent an attempt to find biological bases for the social inequality between the sexes? One can imagine that a society free from inequality between the sexes would not view sex differences research as a valid scientific endeavor. For example, how much money and emphasis are placed on research studying eye color or hair color differences? The fact that our society supports research on sex, race, and sexual orientation differences indicates the extent to which the values of the society and the scientists influence the choice of topics chosen for study and the "objectivity" with which such research is likely to be approached.

Bleier (1979), Star (1979), and Sayers (1982) have critiqued the studies on brain lateralization, hormones, and brain anatomy (Bleier, 1984) that attempt to link differences in male and female brains with behavioral traits such as visuo-spatial ability, verbal ability, and aggression. These feminists have demonstrated flaws in experimental design, assumptions based on limited experimental data, unwarranted extrapolation of data from rodents to humans, and problems with biochemical conversion of hormones from estrogens to androgens within the body (Bleier, 1984). Fennema and Sherman (1977), Sherman (1980), Haven (1972), and Kelly, Whyte, and Smail (1984) have documented the importance of social factors such as number of mathematics courses taken, familiarity with games that develop visuo-spatial skills (Caplan, MacPherson, & Tobin, 1985), and peer pressure as extremely important factors affecting the differential performance of adolescent males and females on tests of mathematical ability. New techniques such as meta-analysis (Hyde and Linn, 1986) for analyzing groups of studies reveal that sex differences in performance of spatial-visualization tasks vary depending upon the age of the individual and complexity of the task. For example, beginning in elementary school and increasing with age, boys perform better than girls on some (but not all) tasks of mental rotation. On more complex spatial-visualization tasks requiring both mental rotation and spatial perception, there are no gender-related differences at any age (Linn and Petersen, 1985). Feminists (Hubbard & Lowe, 1979) as well as other scientists (Lewontin, Rose, & Kamin 1984; Halpern, 1986) have pointed out the cultural and gender biases in the I.Q. test.

Feminist critiques have revealed that in their search for biological differences that may correlate well or be used to explain differences in social, political, or economic positions between the sexes, some researchers have allowed flaws to infect their research. One flaw is having weaker criteria for acceptance of studies that provide biological evidence that can be interpreted to support the social status quo. Bleier (1988) recounts her dealings with *Science*, a very reputable journal, over refutation of a study published by *Science* (Utamsing & Holloway, 1982) based on the autopsy of 14 human brains (9 male, 5 female). The study purported to demonstrate a sex difference in the size of the splenium of the corpus callosum between male and female brains that would support the theory of less lateralization of the human female brain. Bleier's letters to the editor questioning the small sample size, the use of selected brains from autopsied patients without specifying age, cause of death, or mode of selection, and assumption without evidence that size of splenium reflects number of axons and degree of hemispheric lateralization were not published. Bleier's own study to refute Utamsing and Holloway of 39 subjects (22 female; 17 male) was not even sent out for review by the editor of *Science*. It was ultimately published in another journal (Bleier, Houston, & Byne, 1986).

Ironically, in their eagerness to explore sex differences, many researchers have overlooked another flaw, failure to consider *species* differences. Bleier (1984) describes the differences between the nervous system and developmental stages in the rodent and human. Just as it is not appropriate for sociobiologists to extrapolate from one species to another and generalize beyond the limits of the data on the organismal level, such extrapolations and generalizations are equally inappropriate when discussing the development of the nervous system. Although the exposure to fetal androgens in the male rat prevents cyclic release of luteinizing hormones (LH) in response to estrogens and progestins (the so-called organizing effect), it does not have a similar effect in guinea pigs or primates, including humans (Bleier, 1984). Estrogens will elicit an LH surge in men similar to women (Kulin & Reiter, 1976) and androgens do *not* suppress cyclicity, ovulation, menstruation, or pregnancy in women (or nonhuman primates) exposed to fetal androgens (Bleier, 1984). Is it valid to overlook species differences in an attempt to find sex differences within a species?

Perhaps the most pervasive flaw in the neurosciences research is excessive reductionism with its corollary assumption that neuroanatomy or neurosecretions can be separated from their environment. Feminist critiques of the neurosciences again rest on the same basis: genetic, hormonal, and structural effects of the brain on behavior cannot be separated from the effects of learning and socialization in the environment on behavior. Indeed, the two are so interrelated that the environment may actually affect the prenatal structure of the brain, which may then affect learning abilities. As Bleier (1984) states:

> Even though genes are involved in the embryonic differentiation of the various nerve cell types and in the spatial organization of nerve cells (neurons) within the fetal brain, the final form, size, and connections between different neurons and therefore the brain's proper functioning also depend on maternal environment milieu and on input from the external world. . . . It has been found that malnutrition throughout the period of postnatal development of rat pups results in a decrease in both the number and the size of neurons in the brain. If the pups were also malnourished in utero, they can suffer as much as a 60 percent reduction in brain cell number, as compared with controls, by the time of

weaning. Human infants dying of malnutrition during the first year of life also
have smaller than normal brains with a reduced number and size of neurons.
(Winick, 1975 as cited in Bleier, 1984, p. 44)

ENDOCRINOLOGY

In endocrinological research, much effort has also supported searches for differences between the sexes. The terminology of male hormone (commonly used to
describe testosterone and its derivatives) and female hormones (frequently used
for both the estrogen-related hormones and the progestins) is a telling example
of the emphasis on sex differences. In fact both of the so-called male hormones
and female hormones are found in both males and females. The major difference
is in the levels or amounts produced in the two sexes, not in their presence in
one sex or absence in the other. There are also differences in their major anatomical sources in the adults of the two sexes (ovaries in the female, testes in the
male, and adrenal glands in both males and females) and their cyclicity of
production. Furthermore, there are many different forms of estrogens, progestins,
and androgens, all closely related to each other in chemical structure. They all
have as their basic structure the four carbon rings of cholesterol (which is the
common characteristic of hormones in the class known as steroids), with the
main difference among them being in one or two of the side chains having oxygen
(O) or hydrogen (H). In various body tissues of both sexes, cholesterol is normally
metabolized to progesterone, which is metabolized to testosterone, the major
androgen, which is metabolized to estradiol, the major estrogen. There are
many other circulating metabolic forms of the three steroids, each with unique
physiological effects, present all of the time in varying levels in females and
males, with constant conversions from some forms to others. However, use of
the terms "male" and "female" hormones obscures these true differences in
amount and cycle of production and suggests incorrectly to the layperson that
men produce only "male hormones" and that women produce only "female
hormones."

    Although presumably aware of these biological subtleties regarding "male
and female" hormones, researchers in endocrinology have produced work that
suggests some fuzziness and flaws in their understanding of the relationship
between hormones and sex.

1. Some of the work in endocrinology has assumed that the cyclical nature of
    the female reproductive pattern made female rodents and primates unsuitable
    as experimental subjects for tests of hormones or other chemicals. Feminists
    in science have pointed out the problems of hormonal and drug tests, includ-

ing those for human consumption (Wheeler, 1990) run only on male subjects who may yield "cleaner" but limited data.

This cyclicity has also led most researchers to reject the female as a model system for hormone action. The work of Hoffman (1982) however, suggests that the female body because of its cyclic reproductive hormone levels may provide a more accurate model for most hormones.

Using the male as the experimental subject not only ignores the fact that females may respond differently to the variable tested, it may also lead to less accurate models even in the male. Models that more accurately simulate the functioning of complex biological systems may be derived from using female rats as subjects in experiments. Women scientists such as Joan Hoffman have questioned the tradition of using male rats or primates as subjects. With the exception of insulin and the hormones of the female reproductive cycle, traditional endocrinological theory assumed that most of the 20-odd human hormones are kept at constant levels in both males and females. Thus, the male of the species, whether rodent or primate, was chosen as the experimental subject because of his noncyclicity. However, new techniques of measuring blood hormone levels have demonstrated episodic, rather than steady, patterns of secretion of virtually all hormones in both males and females. As Hoffman points out, the rhythmic cycle of hormone secretion as also portrayed in the cycling female rat appears to be a more accurate model for the secretion of most hormones (Hoffman, 1982).

2. Because "male hormones" and "female hormones" occur in both sexes and are closely related biochemically, biochemical conversions between hormones may occur within the body. An injection of testosterone may be converted to estrogen or another derivative before it reaches the brain (Bleier, 1979). Therefore, research that purports to demonstrate that testosterone makes males more aggressive or faster at running mazes may be flawed because the testosterone injected may or may not have been converted to other derivatives before it reaches the operative organs.

3. In addition to problems with biochemical conversions of hormones after injection, behavioral effects induced in one species do not insure similar effects in a different species. Bleier (1979), Hubbard (1983), Lowe (1983), and Fausto Sterling (1985) have warned repeatedly against extrapolating from one species to another in biochemical traits. They also warn against the assumption that changes in hormone levels necessarily are the cause of behavioral or performance differences between the sexes.

4. In endocrinology, feminists have stressed the importance of the inseparability of biological and behavioral factors. Environmental physical or psychological stress factors such as position in the dominance hierarchy have been shown to be both the cause and the effect of higher or lower levels of testosterone in primates (Rose, Holaday, & Bernstein, 1971). In addition, Hrdy (1981) discusses the interrelationships between hormone levels, reproductive inhibition, and dominance in female primates.

Feminist scientists (Bleier, 1984; Birke, 1986; Fausto-Sterling, 1985) have been in the vanguard to warn against confounding correlation of changing hormone levels and behavioral manifestations with cause and effect. This confounding is particularly likely to occur when the biological results correlate well with the social status quo.

DEVELOPMENT

Emphasis on sex differences has also dominated developmental biology. This emphasis is revealed in the repeated attempts to understand the differences and separation rather than similarities and interaction between the sperm and egg, the nucleus and cytoplasm, and the developing male and female. Androcentric notions regarding masculine and feminine gender roles also dominate the language and conceptualization of the theories used to describe reproduction and development.

Historians and philosophers of science (Fee, 1981, 1982; Haraway, 1978, 1989; Keller, 1985; Merchant, 1979) have examined the ways in which the modern mechanistic notion of science has come to represent a masculine approach to the world by which men are given the authority to dominate and control both women and nature. In her provocative essay, "The Weaker Seed: The Sexist Bias of Reproductive Theory," Nancy Tuana (1989) traces the roots of the bias of women's inferiority on theories of human reproduction back through the preformationists to Aristotle. She argues that "adherence to a belief in the inferiority of the female creative principle biased scientific perception of the nature of woman's role in human generation" (Tuana, 1989, p. 147) thereby illustrating ways in which the gender/science system informs the process of scientific investigation.

Of course scientists today recognize numerous flaws in Aristotle's biology. Certainly his ideas that women are colder than men and therefore less developed and that women are "not the parent, just a nurse to a seed" (Aeschylus, 1975, pp. 666–669) are not acceptable to modern biologists. His ideas about woman's inferiority and man's providing the form and motion of the fetus were not only perpetuated in one form or another until the eleventh century, they also influenced the notion of preformation. While looking at "systematic animalcules" under the microscope, Van Leeuwenhoek claimed to observe two kinds of spermatozoa, one from which the male developed and the other from which the female developed (Tuana, 1989, p. 165). Clearly an example of androcentric bias influencing observation, Van Leeuwenhoek's "seeing" the preformed homunculus in the sperm makes sense in light of the basic belief in the primacy of the male and his active role in reproduction, which fit with social stereotypes regarding the passivity and inferiority of women for the previous 2000 years.

Feminist developmental biologists writing today (Biology and Gender Study Group, 1989; Fausto-Sterling, 1986) suggest that these same stereotypes of female inferiority and passivity may influence current reproductive and developmental theories. As early as 1948, Ruth Herschberger wrote a most amusing account of fertilization. By reversing the sexes she drew attention to the extreme activity and importance assigned to the sperm as contrasted with passivity and insignificance given to the role of the egg in fertilization. Emily Martin (1991) reviews the language that science has used to describe fertilization in ''The Egg and the Sperm: How Science Has Constructed A Romance Based on Stereotypical Male–Female Roles.''

The Biology and Gender Study Group (1989, pp. 174–175) describe the courtship narratives with the role of the sperm as a heroic victor used to describe fertilization.

> Courtship is only one of the narrative structures used to describe fertilization. Indeed, ''sperm tales'' make a fascinating subgenre of science fiction. One of the major classes of sperm stories portrays the sperm as a heroic victor. In these narratives, the egg doesn't choose a suitor. Rather the egg is the passive prize awarded to the victor. This epic of heroic sperm struggling against the hostile uterus is the account of fertilization usually seen in contemporary introductory biology texts. The following is from one of this decade's best introductory textbooks. ''Immediately, the question of the fertile life of the sperm in the reproductive tract becomes apparent. We have said that one ejaculation releases about 100 million sperm into the vagina. Conditions in the vagina are very inhospitable to sperm, and vast numbers are killed before they have a chance to pass into the cervix. Millions of others die or become infertile in the uterus or oviducts, and millions more go up the wrong oviduct or never find their way into an oviduct at all. The journey to the upper portion of the oviducts is an extremely long and hazardous one for objects so tiny. . . . Only one of the millions of sperm cells released into the vagina actually penetrates the egg cell and fertilizes it. As soon as that one cell has fertilized the egg, the [egg] cell membrane becomes impenetrable to other sperm cells, which soon die.'' (Keeton, 1976, p. 394)

Countering the stereotype of the passive egg, Gerald and Heide Schatten (1983) have reevaluated old data and uncovered new data demonstrating a much more active role for the egg:

> In the past years, investigations of the curious cone that Wilson recorded have led to a new view of the roles that sperm and egg play in their dramatic meeting. The classic account, current for centuries, has emphasized the sperm's performance and relegated to the egg the supporting role of Sleeping Beauty— a dormant bride awaiting her mate's magic kiss, which instills the spirit that brings her to life. The egg is central to this drama, to be sure, but it is as passive

a character as the Grimm brothers' princess. Now, it is becoming clear that the egg is not merely a large yolk-filled sphere into which the sperm burrow to endow new life. Rather, recent research suggest the almost heretical view that sperm and egg are mutually active partners. (Schatten & Schatten, 1983, p. 29)

The work of the Schattens (1983) and other investigators (Biology & Gender Study Group, 1989) has also demonstrated that the female reproductive tract is more than a passive tube through which the sperm passes in its quest for the egg. Instead, new research reveals that secretions of the female reproductive tract capacitate the sperm, thus making them capable of fertilizing the egg, and activate sperm enzymes, which then permit the sperm to reach the egg nucleus. This new research documents a much more active and mutual role for the female in fertilization.

Androcentrism in the form of dominance, control, and male activity pervade other aspects of developmental biology theory besides fertilization. Traditional theories of mammalian sex determination have assigned a passive role to the development of the female body condition. Using the experiments by Jost (1947, 1958) on the rabbit as the prototype, they assumed that a female body type would develop in the absence of active production of testosterone in the male. It should be noted that not only did this theory suffer from extrapolation from one species to others but also from extrapolation from the generation of accessory and secondary characteristics (the experiments performed by Jost) back to primary sex determination (differentiation into ovaries or testes). This theory also *assumed* passivity in female development rather than *testing* for it. Because the development of both the male and female fetus occurs inside a pregnant females' body, it was impossible to distinguish the potential effects of the hormones from the fetal ovaries from the effects of maternal hormones produced during pregnancy.

Scientists have also critiqued more recent research on the H–Y antigen model that explains the development of testes by proposing that males synthesize a factor absent in female cells.

Some investigators have over-emphasized the hypothesis that the Y chromosome is involved in testis determination by presenting the induction of testicular tissue as an active (gene directed, dominant) event while presenting the induction of ovarian tissue as a passive (automatic) event. Certainly, the induction of ovarian tissue is as much an active, genetically directed developmental process as is the induction of testicular tissue or, for that matter, the induction of any cellular differentiation process. Almost nothing has been written about genes involved in the induction of ovarian tissue from the undifferentiated gonad. The genetics of testis determination is easier to study because human individuals with a Y chromosome and no testicular tissue or with no Y chromosome and testicular tissue, are relatively easy to identify. Nevertheless, speculation on the kind of gonadal tissue that would develop in an XX individual if ovarian tissue induction fails could provide criteria for identifying affected individuals and thus lead to the discovery of ovarian determination genes. (Eicher & Washburn, 1986, p. 328)

Masculine and feminine social roles may have subtly pervaded other theories of developmental biology. The Biology and Gender Study Group (1989) reveal the patterning of theories about the relationship between the nucleus and the cytoplasm within the cell on husband–wife interactions within the nuclear family. The issue was who had control—the husband (nucleus) or wife (cytoplasm)— or was mutual interaction possible? ''The nucleus came to be seen as the masculine ruler of the cell, the stable yet dynamic inheritance from former generations, the unmoved mover, the mind of the cell. The cytoplasm became the feminine body of the cell, the fluid, changeable, changing partner of the marriage'' (Biology and Gender Study Group, 1989, p. 179). Not only does the nucleus/husband and cytoplasm/wife analogy demonstrate the influence of gender on scientific theories, it also illustrates the search for reductionism to a simpler or single part that controls and directs other differentiation.

These same themes of reductionism and control have dominated other aspects of developmental biology research. In her brilliant essay ''The Force of the Pacemaker Concept in Theories of Aggregation in Cellular Slime Mold,'' Keller (1985) points out the fascination of generations of developmental biologists with the search for a single, central governor or ''pacemaker'' substance, responsible for organizing development of the organism. She suggests that the pacemaker theory was appealing, despite contradictory data because it was simpler to comprehend than an interactive model. The search for a pacemaker or ''special'' cells that organized development was also carried out in progressively simpler species. A particular favorite was the slime mold. The reasoning behind using a simple organism was that the organizer would be more easily discovered in a simpler organism in which fewer complex interactions occurred. Thus, reductionism in the form of a simple control mechanism for differentiation was compounded by reductionism in the organism as subject of study.

CELL BIOLOGY

Reductionism and control have also been the themes dominating the study of cellular structure, physiology, and molecular interactions. In the earlier part of the twentieth century, various species ranging from the simple (bacteria) to more complex (corn, drosophila, mice) were used to study complexities of the cell. Both interactive and organizer models were proposed to explain development and functioning.

During the latter half of the century, control mechanisms in simpler organ-isms began to dominate the research funded and accepted as theoretically valid. One obvious influence on the direction of the research was the phenomenal increase in technologically sophisticated equipment that made it possible to see increasingly smaller structures in simple organisms. Evelyn Fox Keller (1983) also points out the profound influence of the large number of physicists who entered the field of molecular biology, particularly after World War II. Trained as physicists, they transferred some of the tenets of physics—the emphasis on simplicity, deductive reasoning, and search for universal laws that control—to molecular biology. In short, as Ruth Hubbard suggests, the physicists sought the answer to the question "what is life," by reducing living organisms to the smaller and smaller units of chemistry and physics.

> I emphasize this reductionism because Watson has written that, long before they knew each other, he and Crick acquired their keen interest in genes and DNA by reading Erwin Schrödinger's (1944) *What Is Life?* Written by one of the great physicists, this little book drew the attention of physicists to biology at the end of World War II, when many of them were becoming disillusioned with physics. After all, by 1945, the proud physics of relativity and quantum theory and of the principles of complementarity and uncertainty had generated the atomic bombs that destroyed Hiroshima and Nagasaki. Intellectually as well, physics was beginning to degenerate into queuing up in front of bigger and bigger machines so as to produce smaller and smaller particles. Many physicists had begun to look for more interesting problems and responded to Schrödinger's challenge of the gene as the new frontier. (Hubbard, 1990, p. 53)

Substantial critiques have been written by feminist scientists (Birke, 1986; Bleier, 1984; Fausto-Sterling, 1985; Hubbard, 1990; Keller, 1983) about the Watson–Crick model of DNA as the "master molecule" as an androcentric view of the cell. The masculine world view that surrounded Watson and Crick's "discovery" of the double helix as the control mechanism in the cell is well documented in Watson's (1969) own account of the discovery. Sayre (1975) revealed their exclusion and shameful treatment of Rosalind Franklin and their failure to acknowledge her substantial contribution as one facet of their andro-centrism. Feminist philosophers of science (Haraway, 1978) and feminist scien-tists (Hubbard, 1990; Keller, 1983) have demonstrated the androcentrism of reductionism and control inherent in the idea that life can be reduced to the DNA on the genes in the nucleus. (They also note that this gives the father equal status as the father contributes DNA to the developing cell in amounts equal to that contributed by the mother). They also point out that the hierarchical nature of the "central dogma" of DNA—RNA—protein parallels the hierarchical organi-zational charts of corporate structures (Keller, 1985) with unidirectional informa-tion flow from the top down.

The congruence of this hierarchical, reductionistic model, which centers unidirectional control for all life processes in the DNA found in the nucleus of the cell with other social institutions such as corporations, the Catholic church, and the patriarchal family, led scientists to accept this model despite increasing contradictory evidence. Alternative models that emphasize interaction between the nucleus and cytoplasm and the importance of interrelationships and process (Nanney, 1957; Thomas, 1974) were proposed by scientists who represented a minority view during the "central dogma" era. Individuals who worked with more complex organisms (McClintock, 1950) warned that the Watson–Crick model did not explain the functioning of complex organisms. The views of these scientists were and continue to be largely rejected, misunderstood, or ignored. Partially due to the biography of Barbara McClintock written by Evelyn Fox Keller (1983) more interactive models contradicting DNA as the master molecule are slowly being accepted.

Barbara McClintock is an achieving scientist who is not a feminist. However, in her approach towards studying maize, she indicates a shortening of the distance between the observer and the object being studied and a consideration of the complex interaction between the organism and its environment. Her statement upon receiving the Nobel Prize was that "it might seem unfair to reward a person for having so much pleasure over the years, asking the maize plant to solve specific problems and then watching its responses" (Keller, 1983). This statement suggests a closer, more intimate relationship with the subject of her research than typically is expressed by the male "objective" scientist. One does not normally associate words such as "a feeling for the organism" (Keller, 1983) with the rational, masculine approach to science. McClintock also did not accept the predominant hierarchical theory of genetic DNA as the "master molecule" that controls gene action but focused on the interaction between the organism and its environment as the locus of control.

Despite some growing recognition of the oversimplicity of DNA as the master molecule and its failure to explain data from complex organisms, it continues to dominate the direction of much research in molecular biology. Most recently Watson has received billions of dollars, a large percentage of the budget of the National Institutes of Health, plus additional funding from other foundations for the Human Genome Project. The Human Genome Project is an attempt to sequence (find the chemical structure in terms of base pairs of DNA) all 23 pairs of human chromosomes. Not surprisingly, reductionism and control in the form of DNA as the master molecule underlay the foundations of this project. The premise undergirding the project is that defects in genes cause diseases and syndromes. Knowing the exact location of each gene on the chromosome and its molecular structure (which can be discovered through gene sequencing) is the first step toward being able to correct the gene and therefore cure the disease or defect.

In a time of tight fiscal constraints, spending billions of federal dollars for the Human Genome Project is a questionable use of resources for many reasons. It is reductionistic and controlling in that it isolates the gene (not even the gene interaction with the environment) as the focus for disease. This is problematic in that genetic defects are responsible for only a small percentage of diseases. Even for those diseases such as cancer and cardiovascular disease that have a genetic component, it is interaction of those genetic components with environmental factors that determines who gets the disease. Most disease and death in our society are not due to genetic defects. Poverty, malnutrition, lack of education about prevention, lack of access to existing medical care such as vaccination and prenatal care are the major causes of disease and death. By focusing on sequencing DNA in the chromosomes, the Human Genome Project diverts money from known cures for disease. It suggests a simple biological basis for problems that have complex social and economic causes in our society.

Conclusion   In her recent work, *The Science Question in Feminism*, the philosopher of science Sandra Harding (1986) discusses five effects that the feminist critique has had on science. "First of all, equity studies have documented the massive historical resistance to women's getting the education, credentials, and jobs available to similarly talented men; they have also identified the psychological and social mechanisms through which discrimination is informally maintained even when the formal barriers have been eliminated" (Harding, 1986, p. 21). Second, the critique has revealed the use of science to support "sexist, racist, homophobic, and classist social projects." Third, the critiques question the extent to which all science must be value laden and biased towards men's perspective both in selection and definition of research problems and in the design and interpretation of research. Fourth, the feminist critique has used techniques from other disciplines such as psychoanalysis, literary criticism, and historical interpretation to reveal "the hidden symbolic and structural agendas—of purportedly value neutral claims and practices" (Harding, 1986, p. 23) of science. Finally, feminist epistemologies provide an alternative understanding for what kinds of social experience "should ground the beliefs we honor as knowledge" (Harding, 1986, p. 24).

After discussing the evidence for each of these effects, Harding concludes that the feminist critiques that point out the androcentrism, and therefore "bad science," raise a paradox. "Clearly, more scientifically rigorous and objective inquiry has produced the evidence supporting specific charges of androcentrism—but that same inquiry suggests that this kind of rigor and objectivity is androcentric'' (Harding, 1986, p. 110). This paradox in turn raises the question of the potential for a nonandrocentric, gender neutral or even gynocentric science.

Feminist critiques can serve as a correction for this androcentrism. The Biology and Gender Study Group (1989) expresses the potential for correction.

> We have come to look at feminist critique as we would any other experimental control. Whenever one performs an experiment, one sets up all the controls one can think of in order to make as certain as possible that the result obtained does not come from any other source. One asks oneself what assumptions one is making. Have I assumed the temperature to be constant? Have I assumed that the pH doesn't change over the time of the reaction? Feminist critiques asks if there may be some assumptions that we haven't checked concerning gender bias. In this way feminist critique should be part of normative science. Like any control, it seeks to provide critical rigor, and to ignore this critique is to ignore a possible source of error. (pp. 172–173)

REFERENCES

Aeschylus. (1975). *The oresteia* (R. Fagles; Trans.). New York: Viking Press.

Biology and Gender Study Group. (1989). The importance of feminist critique for contemporary cell biology. In N. Tuana (Ed.), *Feminism and science*. Bloomington and Indianapolis: Indiana University Press.

Birke, L. (1986). *Women, feminism, and biology: The feminist challenge*. New York: Methuen.

Bleier, R. (1979). Social and political bias in science: An examination of animal studies and their generalizations to human behavior and evolution. In R. Hubbard & M. Lowe (Eds.), *Genes and gender II: Pitfalls in research on sex and gender* (pp. 49–70). New York: Gordian Press.

Bleier, R. (1984). *Science and gender: A critique of biology and its theories on women*. Elmsford, NY: Pergamon Press.

Bleier, R. (1988). *Science* and the construction of meanings in the neurosciences. In S. Rosser (Ed.), *Feminism within the science and health care professions: Overcoming resistance*. Elmsford, NY: Pergamon Press.

Bleier, R., Houston, L., & Byne, W. (1986). Can the corpus callosum predict gender, age, handedness, or cognitive differences? *Trends in Neurosciences, 9*, 391–394.

Caplan, P. J., MacPherson, G. M., & Tobin, P. (1985). Do sex-related differences in spatial abilities exist? *American Psychologist, 40*, 786–799.

Eicher, E. M., & Washburn, L. (1986). Genetic control of primary sex determination in mice. *Annual Review of Genetics, 20*, 327–360.

Fausto-Sterling, A. (1985). *Myths of gender*. New York: Basic Books.

Fee, E. (1981). Is feminism a threat to scientific objectivity? *International Journal of Women's Studies, 4*(4), 213–233.

Fee, E. (1982). A feminist critique of scientific objectivity. *Science for the people, 14*(4), 8.

Fennema, E., & Sherman, J. (1977). Sex related differences in mathematics achievement, spatial visualization and affective factors. *American Educational Journal, 14*, 51–71.

Halpern, D. F. (1986). *Sex differences in cognitive abilities.* Hillsdale, NJ: Erlbaum.

Haraway, D. (1978). Animal sociology and a natural economy of the body politic, Part I: A political physiology of dominance; Animal sociology and a natural economy of the body politic, Part II: The past is the contested zone: Human nature and theories of production and reproduction in primate behavior studies. *Signs: Journal of Women in Culture and Society, 4,* (1), 21–60.

Haraway, D. (1989). Monkeys, aliens, and women: Love, science, and politics at the intersection of feminist theory and colonial discourse. *Women's Studies International Forum 12* (3), 295–312.

Harding, S. (1986). *The science question in feminism.* Ithaca, NY: Cornell University Press.

Haven, E. W. (1972). Factors associated with the selection of advanced academic mathematical courses by girls in high school. *Research Bulletin, 72,* 12. Princeton, NJ: Educational Testing Service.

Herschberger, R. (1970). *Adam's rib.* New York: Harper & Row. (Original work published 1948)

Hoffman, J. C. (1982). Biorhythms in human reproduction: The not-so-steady states. *Signs: Journal of Women in Culture and Society, 7* (4), 829–844.

Hrdy, S. (1981). *The woman that never evolved.* Cambridge, MA: Harvard University Press.

Hubbard, R. (1983). Social effects of some contemporary myths about women. In M. Lowe & R. Hubbard (Eds.), *Woman's nature: Rationalizations of inequality.* Elmsford, NY: Pergamon Press.

Hubbard, R. (1990). *Politics of women's biology.* New Brunswick, NJ: Rutgers University Press.

Hubbard, R., & Lowe, M. (1979). Introduction. In R. Hubbard & M. Lowe (Eds.), *Genes and gender II: Pitfalls in research on sex and gender.* New York: Gordian Press.

Hyde, J. S. and Linn, M. C. (Eds.) (1986). *The psychology of gender: Advances through meta-analysis.* Baltimore: Johns Hopkins.

Jost, A. (1947). Recherches sur la differenciation sexuelle de l'embryon de Lapin. I. Introduction et embryologie genitale normale. *Archives d'Anatomie Microscopique et de Morphologie Experimentale* 36; 151–200.

Jost, A. (1958). Embryonic sexual differentiation. In H. W. Jones & W. W. Scott (Eds.), *Hermaphroditism, genital anomalies and related endocrine disorders.* Baltimore: Williams and Wilkins.

Keeton, W. C. (1976). *Biological science* (3rd ed.). New York: W. W. Norton.

Keller, E. F. (1982). Feminism and science. *Signs: Journal of Women in Culture and Society, 7* (3), 589–602.

Keller, E. (1983). *A feeling for the organism: The life and work of Barbara McClintock.* New York: W. H. Freeman & Co.

Keller, E. (1984, November). Women and basic research: Respecting the unexpected. *Technology Review,* 44–47.

Keller, E. F. (1985). *Reflections on gender and science.* New Haven, CT: Yale University Press.

Kelly, A., Whyte, J., & Smail, B. (1984). *Final Report of the GIST Project.* Manchester, England: University of Manchester, Department of Sociology.

Kulin, H., & Reiter, E. O. (1976). Gonadotropin and testosterone measurement after estrogen administration to adult men, prepubertal and pubertal boys, and men with hypogonadotropism. *Pediatric Research, 10,* 46–51.

Lewontin, R. C., Rose, S., & Kamin, L. J. (1984). *Not in our genes: Biology, ideology, and human nature.* New York: Pantheon.

Linn, M. C. & Petersen, A. C. (1985). Emergence and characterization of sex difference in spatial ability: A meta-analysis. *Child Development, 56,* 1479–1498.

Lowe, M. (1983). The dialectic of biology and culture. In M. Lowe & R. Hubbard (Eds.), *Woman's nature: Rationalizations of inequality.* Elmsford, NY: Pergamon Press.

McClintock, B. (1950). The origin and behavior of mutable loci in maize. *Proceedings of the National Academy of Sciences, 36,* 344–355.

Maccoby, E., & Jacklin, C. (1974). *The psychology of sex differences.* Stanford, CA: Stanford University Press.

Martin, E. (1991). The egg and the sperm: How *Science* has constructed a romance based on stereotypical male-female roles. *Signs, 16* (3), 485–501.

Merchant, C. (1979). *The death of nature: Women, ecology and the scientific revolution.* New York: Harper & Row.

Nanney, D. L. (1957). The role of cytoplasm is heredity. In W. E. McElroy & H. B. Glenn (Eds.), *The chemical basis of heredity* (pp. 134–166). Baltimore: Johns Hopkins University Press.

Rose, R. M., Holaday, J. W., & Bernstein, I. S. (1971). Plasma testosterone, dominance rank, and aggressive behavior in male rhesus monkeys. *Nature, 231,* 366–368.

Rosser, S. V. (Ed.). (1989). Feminism and science special issue in memory of Ruth Bleier [Special issue]. *Women's Studies International Forum, 12* (3).

Sayers, J. (1982). *Biological politics: Feminist and anti-feminist perspectives.* London and New York: Tavistock Publications.

Sayre, A. (1975). *Rosalind Franklin and DNA.* New York: W. W. Norton.

Schatten, G., & Schatten, H. (1983). The energetic egg. *The Sciences, 23*(5), 28–34.

Schrödinger, E. (1944). *What is Life?* London: Cambridge University Press.

Sherman, J. (1980). Mathematics, spatial visualization, and related factors: Changes in girls and boys, grades 8–11. *Journal of Educational Psychology, 72,* 476–482.

Star, S. L. (1979). Sex differences and the dichotomization of the brain: Methods, limits and problems in research on consciousness. In R. Hubbard & M. Lowe (Eds.), *Genes and gender II.* New York: Gordian Press.

Thomas, L. (1974). *The lives of a cell.* New York: Viking.

Tuana, N. (1989). The weaker seed: The sexist bias of reproductive theory. In N. Tuana (Ed.), *Feminism and science.* Bloomington: Indiana University Press.

Utamsing, C., & Holloway, R. L. (1982). Sexual dimorphism in the human corpus callosum. *Science, 216,* 1431–1432.

Watson, J. D. (1969). *The double helix.* New York: Atheneum.

Wheeler, D. L. (1990). NIH to require researchers to include women in studies. *The Chronicle of Higher Education,* XXXVII(3), pp. A32–33.

Winick, M. (1975). Nutritional disorders during brain development. In D. B. Tower (Ed.), *The clinical neurosciences.* New York: Raven Press.

5.

FEMINIST METHODOLOGIES FOR THE NATURAL SCIENCES

The debates surrounding feminist methodology (Alcoff, 1989; Christ, 1987; Harding, 1987; MacKinnon, 1987;) constitute a major focus for discussion in many of the disciplines such as anthropology, literature, history, and psychology in which the feminist critique has had a profound impact on the knowledge base and theoretical framework of the field. In Women's Studies the debates serve as yet another issue that crosses disciplinary lines and demonstrates the strengths and uniqueness of this interdisciplinary field.

These debates raise basic and fundamental questions for all disciplines: is there a feminist methodology or methodologies? If there is, what is it and how does it differ from other non-mainstream or non-positivist methodologies? What kinds of new and different questions might be explored using feminist methodologies that have not been explored with previous methodologies? How would results of research done with feminist methodologies look compared to results obtained using more traditional methodologies?

For the sciences, the debates reveal the significant diversity among the disciplines and the values and status accorded by most of Western society to results derived from the traditional methodologies. Researchers in the social sciences have been the individuals most actively challenging the traditional methods by feminist critiques and development of feminist methodologies. In the early 1970s women social scientists began to recognize that women were often excluded as subjects and that androcentric experimental designs sought to uncover data to answer questions of importance to men based on male experience. Sociologists (Bert, 1971, Oakley, 1981; Roberts, 1981;), psychologists (Chodorow, 1974; Wallston, 1981; Weisstein, 1971), and anthropologists (Collier & Rosaldo, 1981; Leacock, 1981; Linton, 1974; Ortner, 1974) began to evolve methodologies that centered on women's experience and that might answer questions of interest to women.

In the physical sciences, virtually no attempts have been made to explore feminist methodologies. In fact, very few feminist critiques of the traditional methodologies exist; the two or three existing critiques take a historical approach. Griffin (1978) and Merchant (1979) explore the historical roots of twentieth-century mechanistic science, which becomes the rational, objective approach to problem-solving men use to dominate both women and nature. Keller (1985) in her work on Bacon also examines the extent to which the scientific method becomes an androcentric approach to the world that might be used not only to dominate women but to exclude women and women's experience. Although not the major focus of her work, to my knowledge Keller (1985) is the only one who has begun to extend the critique to an examination of the influence on the methodologies in physics in her one essay "Cognitive Repression in Contemporary Physics."

That further explorations of feminist methodologies in the physical sciences do not exist is not surprising given the dearth of women physical scientists. In 1988, 14.9% of all physical scientists employed were women (NSF, 1990) and 16.8% of those receiving doctorates were women. The status of the physical sciences and the scientific method as a paradigm of the objective approach to problem solving in our current society provide other barriers to the evolution of feminist methodologies in the physical sciences.

The natural sciences, and biology in particular, represent a field in which women form a growing segment of the scientists—36.56% of the Ph.D.s and 29.79% of employed biologists in 1988 (NSF, 1990). Despite their lower wages, documented discrimination that prevents advancement (NSF, 1990), and the overwhelming pressure they face to adopt mainstream theories, approaches, and practices in order to achieve success, a considerable volume of feminist critique has been produced by courageous feminist biologists (Birke, 1986; Bleier, 1984; Fausto-Sterling, 1985; Hubbard, 1990; Rosser, 1990) and philosophers of science (Fee, 1982; Haraway, 1990; Harding, 1986). Building on these critiques, some feminists in science (Birke, 1986; Keller, 1985; Rosser, 1990) and philosophy (Haraway, 1990; Harding, 1987) have begun to raise the parameters for feminist methodologies in biology: Are the critiques raised by feminists simply examples of bad science? Is good science gender free? Would feminist methodologies lead to better practice of the scientific method or do they imply that the scientific method as we know it is inadequate or unacceptable? What are these feminist methodologies? If they exist, would these feminist methodologies result in major differences in the types of problems that might be solved or just minor variations in the types of problems currently explored in science? Could men develop and use feminist methodologies? What might be the practical results or applications of feminist methodologies?

Definition of Terminology   Before exploring these and other issues regarding feminist methodologies in biology, it is necessary to distinguish several terms that are frequently confused with each other and sometimes used differently or mistakenly by biologists and individuals from other disciplines. These terms are epistemology, methods, and methodology.

Lengthy discourses, and in fact, entire books have been written about each of these terms. It might be desirable for an individual who is shocked to learn that the scientific method is really a methodology to read a more lengthy, complex discussion of each term. The brief definitions I will give here are based on the work of Harding (1987). An *epistemology* is a theory of knowledge that considers what kinds of things can be known, who can be a knower, and how (through what tests) beliefs are legitimated as knowledge. The epistemology associated with traditional biology suggests that the physiological, chemical, and anatomical characteristics of living beings can be known by observers trained as scientists who test their observations by validation through the scientific method. Feminist critiques of the epistemology of biology (Fee, 1981, 1982, 1983; Harding, 1986; Keller, 1985, 1987) have suggested that its theory of knowledge constitutes a masculine view of the world. To be trained to be a scientist is to be trained to observe the characteristics of living beings of interest to men in an objective, distant, autonomous fashion that resonates with an androcentric perspective on the world.

Methods are techniques for gathering evidence or data. Most biological methods fall under the broad category of observation, including observation of animals, plants, and chemical behavior either directly or indirectly on the organic, structural, and microscopic level. Some biological methods involve examining historical traces and records, particularly in the study of paleontology and evolution. Although feminists use these same methods, what they choose to observe and examine may differ quite markedly from the choices of a traditional scientist with a masculine world view. For example, female primatologists (Fedigan, 1982; Hrdy, 1979, 1981, 1986; Lancaster, 1975; Small, 1984) discovered many new insights regarding primate social behavior simply by observing female–female primate interaction. Because of their masculine world view, male primatologists had virtually ignored female–female lower primate interactions. Presumably this oversight came from the fact that as human males they had only experienced male–male and male–female interactions, so their masculine world view led them to fail to observe female–female interaction in other primate species.

Methodology constitutes a theory and analysis of how research proceeds or should proceed; it examines how "the general structure of theory finds its application in particular scientific disciplines" (Caws, 1967). The discussion of the scientific method using the example of the number of legs an insect has as given in most introductory biology texts provides an example of methodology. Application of the scientific method to explore problems such as the length of exposure to video display terminals (VDTs) that cause possible cluster miscarriages or birth defects are examples that shift the focus from problems traditionally explored to women's experience and concerns.

Epistemology, methods, and methodology are related concepts and are usually connected during the process of research. As Harding states: "Epistemological issues certainly have crucial implications for how general theoretical structures can and should be applied in particular disciplines and for the choice of methods of research" (1987, p. 3). In talking about feminist methodology in biology I will attempt to describe how research does or should proceed when feminist theory and analysis are applied to the discipline of biology.

FEMINIST THEORIES

Individuals unfamiliar with feminism or Women's Studies might assume that feminist theory provides a singular and unified framework for analysis. In one sense this is correct; all feminist theory posits gender as a significant characteristic that interacts with other characteristics such as race and class to structure relationships between individuals, within groups, and within society as a whole. However, using the lens of gender to view the world results in diverse images or theories: liberal feminism, Marxist feminism, socialist feminism, African-American feminism, lesbian separatist feminism, conservative or essentialist feminism, existential feminism, psychoanalytic feminism, and radical feminism. The variety and complexity of these various feminist theories provide a framework through which to explore interesting methodology issues raised in biology.

Liberal Feminism

Beginning in the eighteenth century, political scientists, philosophers, and feminists (Friedan, 1974; Jaggar, 1983; Mill, 1970; Wollstonecraft, 1975) have described the parameters of liberal feminism. The differences between nineteenth-century and twentieth-century liberal feminists have varied from libertarian to egalitarian, and numerous complexities exist among definitions of liberal feminists today. A general definition of liberal feminism is the belief that women are suppressed in contemporary society because they suffer unjust discrimination (Jaggar, 1983). Liberal feminists seek no special privileges for women and simply demand that everyone receive equal consideration without discrimination on the basis of sex.

Most scientists would assume that the implications of liberal feminism for biology and other disciplines within the sciences are that scientists should work to remove the documented overt and covert barriers (NSF, 1990; Rosser, 1990; Rossiter, 1982; Vetter, 1988) that have prevented women from entering and succeeding in science. Although they might hold individual opinions as to whether or not women deserve equal pay for equal work, access to research resources, and equal opportunities for advancement, most scientists, even those who are brave enough to call themselves feminists, assume that the implications of liberal feminism extend only to employment, access, and discrimination issues.

In fact, the implications of liberal feminism extend beyond this. Liberal feminism shares two fundamental assumptions with the foundations of the traditional method for scientific discovery: (1) both assume that human beings are highly individualistic and obtain knowledge in a rational manner that may be separated from their social conditions; and (2) both accept positivism as the theory of knowledge. These two assumptions lead to the belief in the possibilities of obtaining knowledge that is both objective and value free, concepts that form the cornerstones of the scientific method. Although each scientist strives to be as objective and value free as possible, most scientists, feminists, and philosophers of science recognize that no individual can be neutral or value free. Instead "objectivity is defined to mean independence from the value judgments of any particular individual" (Jaggar, 1983, p. 357).

In the past two decades feminist historians and philosophers of science (Fee, 1982; Haraway, 1990; Harding, 1986) and feminist scientists (Birke, 1986; Bleier, 1984, 1986; Fausto-Sterling, 1985; Keller, 1983, 1985; Rosser, 1988; Spanier, 1982) have pointed out a source of bias and absence of value neutrality in science, particularly biology. By excluding females as experimental subjects, focusing on problems of primary interest to males, using faulty experimental designs, and interpretations of data based in language or ideas constricted by patriarchal parameters, experimental results in several areas in biology have been demonstrated to be biased or flawed. Feminist critiques (Harding, 1986; Keller,

1985) suggest that these flaws and biases were permitted to become part of the mainstream of scientific thought and were perpetuated in the scientific literature for decades, in some cases (Sayers, 1982) for more than a century, because virtually all of the individuals who were scientists were men. Because most, or all scientists, were male, values held by most males were not distinguishable as biasing; they became synonymous with the "objective" view of the world.

Three examples from within three different areas in biology illustrate the flawed research resulting from male bias in the discipline. Feminist critiques of sociobiology have centered around criticisms of the assumption that behaviors such as aggression, homosexuality, promiscuity, selfishness, and altruism are biologically determined. Critiques also underline problems involved with anthropomorphosis in animal behavior studies: (a) the use of human language and frameworks to describe animal behavior that is then used to "prove" that certain human behavior are innate as they are also found in animals; (b) the selective choice of species for study that mirror human society. The data from those selected species is then assumed to be the universal behavior of all species (see chapter 3).

Although the baboon and chimpanzee were chosen for study primarily because their social organization was seen by the observers as closely resembling that of human primates (Yerkes, 1943), female primatologists had to point out the "obvious" limitations imposed by such selection of species. It was also not until a significant number of women entered primatology that concepts of the universality and male leadership of dominance hierarchies among primates (Lancaster, 1975; Leavitt, 1975; Leibowitz, 1975; Rowell, 1974) were questioned and shown to be inaccurate for many primate species. Feminist critics (Bleier, 1984) revealed the "evident" problems of studying nonhuman primates in an attempt to discover what the true nature of humans would be without the overlay of culture.

In the neurosciences, a substantial amount of work has been done relating to sex differences in the brains of men and women. The studies on brain lateralization, genes, brain structure, and effects of prenatal and postpubertal androgens and estrogens on the nervous system have been carried out in an attempt to discern biological bases for differences between males and females in behavioral or performance characteristics such as aggression, or verbal, visuo-spatial, and mathematical ability. Excellent critiques have been made by feminists of the faulty experimental designs and unfounded extrapolations beyond the data of the work in brain lateralization (Star, 1979), hormones (Bleier, 1984), genes (Fennema & Sherman, 1977), and brain structure (Bleier, 1986). Although most scientists accept the validity of the critiques, reputable scientific journals (see

Bleier, 1988, for an account of her encounters with *Science* over this matter), textbooks, and the popular press continue to publish studies biased by similar methodological inconsistencies, extrapolations in data from one species to another, and over generalizations of data.

These examples of flawed research and other examples resulting from the critiques of feminists have raised fundamental questions regarding gender and good science: Do these examples simply represent "bad science"? Is good science really gender free or does the scientific method, when properly used, permit research that is objective and unbiased?

A liberal feminist answer to these questions is that good science can be gender free. Liberal feminists suggest that now that the bias of gender has been revealed by the feminist critique, scientists can take this into account and correct for this bias that had not been previously uncovered. A liberal feminist position has two significant implications.

1. It does not question the integrity of the scientific method itself or of its supporting corollaries of objectivity and value neutrality. Liberal feminism reaffirms the idea that it is possible to find a perspective from which to observe that is truly impartial, rational, and detached. Lack of objectivity and presence of bias occur because of human failure to properly follow the scientific method and avoid bias due to situation or condition. Liberal feminists argue that it was through attempts to become more value neutral that the possible androcentrism in previous scientific research has been revealed.

2. Liberal feminism also implies that good scientific research is not conducted differently by men and women and that in principle men can be just as good feminists as women. Now that feminist critiques have revealed flaws in research caused by gender bias, both men and women will use this revelation to design experiments, gather and interpret data, and draw conclusions and theories that are more objective and free from bias, including gender bias (Biology and Gender Study Group, 1989).

In contrast to liberal feminism all other feminist theories call into question the fundamental assumptions underlying the scientific method, its corollaries of objectivity and value neutrality, or its implications. They reject individualism for a social construction of knowledge and question positivism and the possibility of objectivity obtained by value neutrality. Many also imply that men and women may conduct scientific research differently, although each theory posits a different cause for the gender distinction. Just as an examination of liberal feminism uncovered interesting information about methodology in biology, exploration of other feminist theories reveals fruitful points.

Marxist Feminism

Marxist feminism serves as the clearest example of a feminist theory that contrasts with liberal feminism in its rejection of individualism and positivism as approaches to knowledge. Marxist critiques of science, the historical precursors and foundation for Marxist-feminist critiques, view all knowledge as socially constructed and emerging from practical human involvement in production that takes a definite historic form. According to Marxism, knowledge, including scientific knowledge, cannot be solely individualistic. Because the pursuit of knowledge is a productive activity engaged in by human beings, it cannot be objective and value free because the basic categories of knowledge are shaped by human purposes and values. Marxism proposes that the form of knowledge is determined by the prevailing mode of production. In the twentieth-century United States, according to Marxism, scientific knowledge would be determined by capitalism and reflect the interests of the dominant class. In strict Marxist-feminism, in which class is emphasized over gender, only bourgeois (liberal) feminism or proletarian feminism can exist. A bourgeois woman scientist would be expected to produce scientific knowledge that would be the same as that produced by a bourgeois male scientist, but would be different from that produced by a proletarian female scientist.

Although feminists have critiqued Marxism for decades (Flax, 1981; Foreman, 1977; Goldman, 1931; Vogel, 1983) about its shortcomings on the woman question, the Marxist critique of science opened the door for three insights shared by feminist theories and methodologies.

1. It proposed that scientific knowledge was socially constructed and could not be dichotomized from other human values the scientist holds. Beginning with the work of Thomas Kuhn (1970) and his followers, historians and philosophers of science have pointed out that scientific theories and practice may not be dichotomized from other human values held by the scientist. The scientific paradigms that are acceptable to the mainstream of the practicing scientists are convincing precisely because they reinforce or support the historical, economic, and social, racial, political, and gender policies of the majority of scientists at that particular time. Rose and Rose (1980 p. 28) underscore the fact that the reason Darwin's theory of natural selection was acceptable to nineteenth-century England, was that it was laden with the values of the upper classes of that Victorian period—competition of the species, the struggle for existence, and survival of the fittest. These metaphors reflected Victorian society and were acceptable to it because they, and the social Darwinism quickly derived from it, seemed to ground its norms solidly in a biological foundation. The use of craniometry provides a nine-

teenth-century example of the acceptance of incorrect biological measurements and false conclusions drawn from accurate measurements because the biological "facts" permitted a justification for the inferior social position of colonials (especially blacks) and women (Gould, 1981).

Feminist critics today (Bleier, 1984, 1986; Fee, 1982; Haraway, 1978; Hein, 1981; Hubbard, 1979) have discussed the extent to which the emphasis on research pointing out the differences between the sexes (when in fact for most traits there are no differences or only very small mean differences characterized by a large range of overlap between the sexes) in the neurosciences and endocrinology and on the search for genetic bases to justify sex-role specialization and the division of labor come from the desire to find a biological basis for the social inequality between the sexes. The measurement of hormone levels in homosexuals compared to heterosexuals and the search for a "gene" for homosexuality provide other examples of an attempt to separate biological from environmental determinants and to seek biological bases for the discriminatory treatment against homosexuals (Birke, 1986). One can imagine that a society free from inequality between the sexes and lacking homophobia would not view research that points out sex differences and sexual-preferences differences as valid scientific endeavors. The fact that our society supports such research indicates the extent to which the values of the society and the scientists influence scientific inequity and "objectivity."

2. By emphasizing the social construction of knowledge, Marxism implies that dichotomies such as nature/culture, subjective/objective might not be the only or even appropriate ways to categorize knowledge.

3. It also suggests that methods that distance the observer from the object of study and/or place the experimenter in a different plane from the subject are seen as more scientific only when the social construction of knowledge is not recognized.

African-American Critique

African-American or black feminism also rejects individualism and positivism for social construction as an approach to knowledge. It is based on the African-American critique of a Eurocentric approach to knowledge. In addition to the rejection of objectivity and value neutrality associated with the positivist approach accepted by liberal feminism, the African-American approach critiques dichotomization of knowledge or at least the identification of science with the first half and African-American with the latter half of the following dichotomies: culture/nature; rational/feeling; objective/subjective; quantitative/qualitative; active/passive; focused/diffuse; independent/dependent; mind/body; self/others; knowing/being. Like Marxism, African-American critiques question methods that distance the observer from the object of study, thereby denying a facet of the social construction of knowledge.

Whereas Marxism posits class as the organizing principle around which the struggle for power exists, African-American critiques maintain that race is the primary oppression. Neo-Marxists view the entire scientific enterprise as a function of context and class-specific interests with scientific methodology itself constituted by these interests. African-Americans critical of the scientific enterprise may view it as a function of white Eurocentric interests with the methodology a reflection of those interests. Just as Marxists view class oppression as primary and superseding gender oppression, African-American critiques place race above gender as an oppression. A strict, traditional interpretation of African-American critiques would suggest that scientific knowledge produced by African-American women would more closely resemble scientific knowledge produced by African-American men than that produced by white women.

Many feminists were attracted by certain tenets—particularly the ideas of the social construction of knowledge, rejection of objectivity and other dualisms, and locating the observer in the same plane as the object of study—of both Marxist and African-American critiques. However, as feminists they had experienced and recognized the oppression of gender and found it unacceptable to have it ignored or subsumed as a secondary oppression under class or race. Both Socialist feminism and African-American feminism have examined the respective intersection of class and gender or race and gender in an attempt to provide a more complex and comprehensive view of reality.

Socialist Feminism and African-American Feminism

The addition of Socialist feminism and African-American feminism to classical Marxist and African-American critiques is the assertion that the special position of women within (or as) a class or race gives them a special standpoint that provides them with a particular world view. From the standpoint of women, this world view is supposed to be more reliable and less distorted than that of men from the same class or race. Implicit in the acceptance of the social construction of knowledge is the rejection of the standpoint of the neutral, disinterested observer of liberal feminism; Marxist and African-American critiques posit differing standpoints. They suggest that the prevailing knowledge and science reflect the interests and values of the dominant race and class. Because the dominant race and class have an interest in concealing, and may not in fact recognize the way they dominate, the science and picture of reality they present will be distorted. Classical Marxist and African-American critiques suggest that individuals oppressed by class (Marxist) and/or race (African-American) have an advantageous and more comprehensive view of reality. Because of their oppression, they have an interest in perceiving problems with the status quo and the science and knowledge produced by the dominant class and race. Simultaneously, their position requires them to understand the science and condition of the dominant group in order to survive. Thus, the standpoint of the oppressed comprehends and includes that of the dominant group, so it is superior.

Socialist-feminist (Hartmann, 1981; Jaggar, 1983; Mitchell, 1971; 1974; Young, 1980; 1981) and African-American feminist critiques assert that in contemporary society, women suffer oppression because of their gender. Women oppressed by both class and gender (Socialist-feminist) or both race and gender (African-American feminists) have a more comprehensive, inclusive standpoint than that of working-class men or black men. Socialist-feminist and African-American feminist theory imply that women scientists, through a collective process of political and scientific struggle (Jaggar, 1983) might produce a science and knowledge different from that produced by men of any race or class.

Other feminist theories also maintain that women, because they are women, possess a different perspective or standpoint, than men. Common to these other feminist theories is the assumption that diversity among women due to race, class, religion, ethnic background, sexual orientation, age, and other factors exists. However, gender is a predominant factor that provides women with a sufficiently unique and unified perspective that their knowledge, science, and view of reality are likely to differ from that of men. The primary difference among these other feminist theories is their position on the source of gender differences between men and women. Because the theories differ on the source of gender differences, some variation exists among them about its effects on methodology.

Essentialist Feminism

Essentialist feminist theory posits that women are different from men because of their biology, specifically their secondary-sex characteristics and their reproduction systems. Frequently, essentialist feminism may extend to include gender differences in visuo-spatial and verbal ability, aggression and other behavior, and other physical and mental traits based on prenatal or pubertal hormone exposure. Nineteenth-century essentialist feminists (Blackwell, [1885] 1976; Calkins, 1896; Tanner, 1896) often accepted the ideas of male essentialist scientists such as Freud [anatomy is destiny (1924)] or Darwin as interpreted by the social Darwinists that there are innate differences between men and women. These nineteenth-century essentialist feminists proposed that the biologically based gender differences meant that women were inferior to men in some physical

(Blackwell, 1976; Smith-Rosenberg, 1975) and mental (Hollingsworth, 1914; Tanner, 1896) traits, but that they were superior in others. Biological essentialism formed the basis for the supposed moral superiority of women that nineteenth-century suffragettes (Dubois, 1978; Hartmann & Banner, 1974) used as a persuasive argument for giving women the vote.

In the earlier phases of the current wave of feminism, most feminist scientists (Bleier, 1979; Fausto-Sterling, 1985; Hubbard, 1979; Rosser, 1982) fought against some sociobiological research such as that by Wilson (1975), Trivers (1972), and Dawkins (1976) and some hormone and brain lateralization research (Buffery & Gray, 1972; Gorski, Harlan, Jacobson, Shryne & Southam, 1980; Goy & Phoenix, 1971; Sperry, 1974) that seemed to provide biological evidence for differences in mental and behavioral characteristics between males and females. Essentialism was seen as a tool for conservatives who wished to keep women in the home and out of the work place. More recently, feminists have reexamined essentialism from perspectives ranging from conservative to radical (Corea, 1985; Dworkin, 1983; MacKinnon, 1982; 1987; O'Brien, 1981; Rich, 1979) with a recognition that biologically based differences between the sexes might imply superiority and power for women in some arenas.

Essentialist feminism would imply that because of their biology, differential hormonal effects on the brain, the physical experiences of menstrual cycles, pregnancy, childbirth, lactation, and menopause, and/or other differing anatomical or physiological characteristics, female scientists would produce a different science from that of men. It seems logical and understandable that due to their biological experiences women might be interested in different problems than men. However, essentialism would imply that these differences would lead them to different methods in approaching these problems, that is, experiencing menstruation might lead women to different methods than those used by men for studying menstruation.

A contradiction within essentialist feminism would seem to be that although it rejects the positivist "neutral observer" standpoint of liberal feminism, its relationship with the social construction of knowledge seems somewhat different from that of other feminist theories. Liberal feminism is usually equated not only with the positivist neutral observer but also with nonessentialism or at least the assumption of equality between the sexes. Essentialism is based on biological differences between men and women rather than the social construction of gender posited by other feminist theories, including liberal feminism. Yet, essentialist feminism, in its suggestion that male and female scientists might approach problems differently because of their gender, implies a social construction of knowledge and science.

Existentialist feminism

Existentialist feminism, first described by Simone de Beauvoir (1974), suggests that women's "otherness" and the social construction of gender rest on society's interpretation of biological differences. "The enslavement of the female to the species and the limitations of her various powers are extremely important facts; the body of woman is one of the essential elements in her situation in the world. But that body is not enough to define her as woman; there is no true living reality except as manifested by the conscious individual through activities and in the bosom of a society. Biology is not enough to give an answer to the question that is before us: why is woman the Other?" (de Beauvoir, 1974, p. 51). In other words, it is the value that society assigns to biological differences between males and females that has led woman to play the role of the Other (Tong, 1989); it is not the biological differences themselves. It is possible to imagine a society without gender differences.

The methodological implications which flow from existentialist feminism are that a society that emphasizes gender differences would produce a science that emphasizes sex differences. In such a society, men and women might be expected to create very different sciences because of the social construction of both gender and science. The possibility of a gender-free or gender-neutral (positivist) science evolving in such a society is virtually nil. Elizabeth Fee (1982) summed up the situation very well: she states that a sexist society should be expected to develop a sexist science. Conceptualizing a feminist science from within our society is "like asking a medieval peasant to imagine the theory of genetics or the production of a space capsule" (Fee, 1982, p 31). Existentialist feminists would suggest that this is why we can point to no or very limited examples of feminist methodologies in science.

Psychoanalytic feminism

In many ways, psychoanalytic feminism takes a stance similar to that of existentialist feminism. Derived from Freudian theory, psychoanalysis posits that girls and boys develop contrasting gender roles because they experience their sexuality differently and deal differently with the stages of psychosexual development. Based on the Freudian prejudice that anatomy is destiny, psychoanalytic theory assumes that biological sex will lead to different ways for boys and girls to resolve the Oedipus and castration complexes that arise during the phallic stage of normal sexual development. As was the situation with existentialism, psychoanalysis recognizes that gender construction is not biologically essential; in "normal" gender construction the biological sex of the child–caretaker interaction differs depending on the sex of the child (and possibly that of the primary caretaker). However, psychoanalytic theory is not strictly biologically deterministic as cases of "abnormal" sexuality may result when gender construction is opposite or not congruent with biological sex.

Simone de Beauvoir admired Freud for advancing the idea that sexuality is the ultimate explanation for the form of civilization and gender relations (Tong, 1989). However, she rejected Freud's interpretation as overly simplistic. She particularly rejected his theory of women's castration complex as a psychological explanation for their inferior social status. De Beauvoir suggested that the reason women may suffer from so-called penis envy is that they desire the material and psychological privileges permitted men in our society rather than the anatomical organ itself.

Numerous feminists (Firestone, 1970; Friedan, 1974; Millett, 1970) in the 1960s and 1970s attacked Freud and the successor psychoanalytic theories because of their negative view of women and the considerable damage that application of those theories had done to women's sexuality. They also read his statement "anatomy is destiny" as a major obstacle blocking reforms allowing women to work outside the home and to assume other prominent roles in public life. Changes in social structures will not change gender relationships if the root of the problem is biological rather than social.

In recent years, a number of feminists have again become interested in Freud's theories. Rejecting the biological determinism in Freud, Dinnerstein (1977) and Chodorow (1978) in particular have used an aspect of psychoanalytic theory known as object relations theory to examine the construction of gender and sexuality. Chodorow and Dinnerstein examine the Oedipal stage of psychosexual development to determine why the construction of gender and sexuality in this stage usually results in male dominance. They conclude that the gender differences resulting in male dominance can be traced to the fact that in our society, women are the primary caretakers for most infants and children.

Accepting most Freudian ideas about the Oedipus complex, Chodorow and Dinnerstein conclude that boys are pushed to be independent, distant, and autonomous from their female caretakers, whereas girls are permitted to be more dependent, intimate, and less individuated from their mothers or female caretakers. Building on the work of Chodorow and Dinnerstein, feminists (Keller, 1982; Harding, 1986; Hein, 1981) have explored how the gender identity proposed by object relations theory with women as caretakers might lead to more men choosing careers in science. Keller (1982; 1985) in particular applied the work of Chodorow and Dinnerstein to suggest how science has become a masculine province that excludes women and causes women to exclude themselves. Science is a masculine province not only because it is populated mostly by men but also because of their choice of experimental topics, use of male subjects for experimentation, interpretation and theorizing from data, as well as the practice and applications of science undertaken by the scientists. Keller suggests (1982; 1985) that since the scientific method stresses objectivity, rationality, distance, and autonomy of the observer from the object of study (i.e., the positivist neutral observer), individuals who feel comfortable with independence, autonomy, and distance will be most likely to become scientists. Because most caretakers during the Oedipal phase are female, most individuals in our culture who will be comfortable as scientists will be male. The type of science they create will also be reflective of those same characteristics of independence, distance, and autonomy. It is on this basis that feminists have suggested that the objectivity and rationality of science are synonymous with a male approach to the physical, natural world.

According to psychoanalytic feminism, female scientists might be more likely to use approaches that shorten the distance between them as observer and their object of study; they might develop a relationship with their object of study, and therefore appear to be less objective. The biography of Barbara McClintock, *A Feeling For the Organism*, written by Evelyn Fox Keller (1983) demonstrates this. Works by Goodfield (1981) and Hynes (1989) have also discussed this more "feminine" approach taken by women scientists.

Psychoanalytic feminism does not necessarily imply that biological males will take a masculine approach and that biological females will take a feminine approach. In most cases, due to the resolution of the Oedipal complex with a female caretaker, this will be the case. Proponents of psychoanalytic feminism (Keller, 1985) suggest that this is why so many more males than females are attracted to science. However, many of the biological females who are currently scientists probably take a more masculine approach, due not only to resolution of psychosexual developmental phases but also to training by male scientists. Psychoanalytic feminism also suggests that biological males could take a "feminine" approach.

Psychoanalytic feminism also opens the door for "gender-neutral" or "gender-free" (Keller, 1984) science. Chodorow (1978) and Dinnerstein (1977) find the solution to gender differences that result in male dominance to be the father's or other male's having a much more active role in the child's caretaking. They suggest that the active involvement of both women and men in caretaking will lead children to recognize that both men and women have strengths and weaknesses. It would also presumably result in less polarization in gender roles and the possibility of a gender-free science. Although the gender-free potential of psychoanalytic feminism seems similar to the neutral, detached observer of liberal feminism, psychoanalytic feminism is premised on a type of social construction of knowledge—knowledge of sexuality and gender.

Radical Feminism

Radical feminism, in contrast to psychoanalytic feminism and liberal feminism, rejects the possibility of a gender-free science or a science developed from a neutral, objective perspective. Radical feminism maintains that women's oppression is the first, most widespread, and deepest oppression (Jaggar & Rothenberg, 1984). Because men dominate and control most institutions, politics, and knowledge in our society, they reflect a male perspective and are effective in oppressing women. Scientific institutions, practice, and knowledge are particularly male-dominated and have been documented by many feminists (Bleier, 1984; Fee, 1982; Griffin, 1978; Haraway, 1978; Hubbard, 1990; Keller, 1985; Merchant, 1979; Rosser, 1990) to be especially effective patriarchal tools to control and harm women. Radical feminism rejects most scientific theories, data, and experiments precisely because they not only exclude women but also because they are not women centered.

The theory that radical feminism proposes is evolving (Tong, 1989) and is not as well developed as some of the other feminist theories previously discussed. The reasons that its theory is less developed spring fairly directly from the nature of radical feminism itself. First, it is radical. That means that it rejects most currently accepted ideas about scientific epistemology—what kinds of things can be known, who can be a knower, and how beliefs are legitimated as knowledge. Radical feminism also rejects current methodology—the general structure of how theory finds its application in particular scientific disciplines. Second, unlike the feminisms previously discussed, radical feminism does not have its basis in a theory such as Marxism, positivism, psychoanalysis, or existentialism, already developed for decades by men. Because radical feminism is based in women's experience, it rejects feminisms rooted in theories developed by men based on their experience and world view. Third, the theory of radical feminism must be developed by women and based in women's experience (MacKinnon, 1987). Because radical feminism maintains that the oppression of women is the deepest, most widespread, and historically first oppression, women have had few opportunities to come together, understand their experiences collectively, and develop theories based on those experiences.

Not surprisingly, the implications of radical feminism for science and the scientific method are much more far reaching than those of other feminist theories. Radical feminism implies rejection of much of the standard epistemology of science. It perceives reality as an inseparable whole, always alive and in motion, both spiritual and material (Capra, 1973) so that connections between humans and other parts of the natural and physical world constitute part of what can be known (Jaggar, 1983) and should be investigated. Radical feminism posits that it is women, not men, who can be the knowers. Because women have been oppressed, they know more than men. They must see the world from the male perspective in order to survive, but their double vision from their experience as an oppressed group allows them to see more than men. In this respect radical feminism parallels Marxist-feminist and African-American feminist critiques of who has the most accurate view of reality.

However, radical feminism deviates considerably from other feminisms in its view of how beliefs are legitimated as knowledge. A successful strategy that women use to obtain reliable knowledge and correct the distortions of patriarchal ideology is the consciousness-raising group (Jaggar, 1983). Using their personal experiences as a basis, women meet together in communal, nonhierarchical groups to examine their experiences to determine what counts as knowledge (MacKinnon, 1987).

Because radical feminists believe in a connection with and a conception of the world as an organic whole, they reject dualistic and hierarchical approaches. Dichotomies such as rational/feeling, objective/subjective, mind/body, culture/nature, and theory/practice are viewed as patriarchal conceptions that fragment the organic whole of reality. Linear conceptions of time and what is considered to be "logical" thinking in the Western traditions are frequently rejected by radical feminists. Cyclicity as a conception of time and thinking as an upward spiral seem more appropriate approaches to studying a world in which everything is connected in a process of constant change (Daly, 1978; 1984).

Radical feminists view all human beings, and most particularly, themselves as connected to the living and nonliving world. Consequently radical feminists view themselves as "participators" (Jaggar, 1983) connected in the same plane with rather than distanced from their object of study. Many radical feminists also believe that because of this connection, women can know things by relying on intuition and/or spiritual powers. Radical feminists vary in their belief as to whether women's special ways of knowing are caused by their biology (Daly, 1978; Griffin, 1978) or their common social experiences as an oppressed group (Belenky, Clinchy, Goldberger, & Tarule; 1986) or both.

Lesbian Separatism

By its very nature, radical feminism emphasizes a connection among the diverse beliefs held by women about ways to obtain knowledge and rejects the examination of a constantly changing, complex whole by looking at one of its parts. However, lesbian separatism, usually viewed as a subgroup theory within radical feminism, has some interesting implications for feminist methodology in science. To the tenets of radical feminist theory and their methodological implications for a feminist science, lesbian separatism provides one major addition. Lesbian separatists suggest that daily interaction with the patriarchal world and compulsory heterosexuality (Rich, 1976) make it impossible for women to completely understand their oppression and its distortion of their experience of reality. Therefore, in order to connect with other women and nature to understand reality, women must separate themselves from men. Only when freed from male oppression and patriarchy for a considerable period of time will women be able to understand their experiences and ways of knowing. Although based on separation from one part of reality—men—lesbian separatists presumably seek separation in order to enhance connection with the rest of reality. Radical feminism in general, and lesbian separatism in particular, suggest that their methods, arising from an extremely different view of reality, would result in a very different science and scientific method. Given the current oppression of women and a male-dominated scientific hierarchy that controls the scientific problems considered worthy of funding for study and the acceptable approaches that might be used to study those problems, the results of a radical feminist science and especially of lesbian separatism are unimaginable.

CONCLUSION

A reexamination of the questions raised about feminist methodologies in the introduction to this chapter reveals that answers are complex and dependent upon the feminist theory from which the methodology springs. There is certainly not just one feminist methodology just as there is not one feminist theory. The jumble of descriptors for feminist methodology—that it rejects dualisms, is based on women's experience, shortens the distance between the observer and object of study, rejects unicausal, hierarchical approaches, unites application with problem—seem contradictory when portrayed as feminist methodology. They become much more understandable when viewed as a lumping together of possible methodological implications for science resulting from different feminist theories. This lumping together explains why some feminist theories (liberal and psychoanalytic) posit that feminist methodologies would lead to a gender-free or gender-neutral science that could be carried out by male or female scientists. Meanwhile other feminist theories (essentialist and radical) suggest that only women could develop feminist methodologies. Most feminist theories, with the exception of liberal feminism, reject the neutral objective observer for a social construction of scientific knowledge based on the standpoint of the observer, which is influenced by gender, as well as other factors such as race or class. Radical feminism, and particularly lesbian separatism, suggests strong reasons for why we are not able to see the results of a feminist methodology. As long as oppression of women and patriarchy continue, it is unlikely that the effects of feminist methodologies derived from the feminist theories that present some challenge to the status quo will be felt. Certainly the biology and its accompanying feminist methodologies that would evolve under radical feminism are impossible to imagine under current circumstances.

REFERENCES

Alcoff, L. (1989). Justifying feminist social science. In N. Tuana (Ed.), *Feminism and science*. Bloomington, IN: Indiana University Press.

Bart, P. (1971). Sexism and social science: From the gilded cage to the iron cage, or, perils of Pauline. *Journal of Marriage and the Family*, 33(4): 734–745.

Beauvoir, de, S. (1974). *The second sex*. (H. M. Parshley, Trans., Ed.) New York: Vintage Books.

Belenky, M. F., Clinchy, B. M., Goldberger, N. R., & Tarule, J. M. (1986). *Women's ways of knowing*. New York: Basic Books.

Biology and Gender Study Group. (1989). The importance of feminist critique for contemporary cell biology. In N. Tuana (Ed.), *Feminism and science*. Bloomington, IN: Indiana University Press.

Birke, L. (1986). *Women, feminism, and biology: The feminist challenge*. New York: Methuen.

Blackwell, A. (1976). *The sexes throughout nature*. Westport, CT: Hyperion Press. (Original work published 1875).

Bleier, R. (1979). Social and political bias in science: An examination of animal studies and their generalizations to human behavior and evolution. In R. Hubbard & M. Lowe (Eds.), *Genes and gender II: Pitfalls in research on sex and gender* (pp. 49–70). New York: Gordian Press.

Bleier, R. (1984). *Science and gender: A critique of biology and its theories on women*. Elmsford, NY: Pergamon Press.

Bleier, R. (1986). Sex differences research: Science or belief? In R. Bleier (Ed.), *Feminist approaches to science* (pp. 147–164). Elmsford, NY: Pergamon Press.

Buffery, W., & Gray, J. (1972). Sex differences in the development of spatial and linguistic skills. In C. Ounsted & D. C. Taylor (Eds.), *Gender differences: Their ontogeny and significance*. Edinburg: Churchill Livingstone.

Calkins, M. W. (1896). Community of ideas of men and women. *Psychological Review* 3(4), 426–430.

Capra, F. (1973). *The Tao of physics*. New York: Bantam Books.

Caws, P. (1967). Scientific method. In P. Edwards (Ed.), *The Encyclopedia of Philosophy* (p. 339). New York: MacMillan.

Chodorow, N. (1974). Family structure and feminine personality. In M. Z. Rosaldo & L. Lamphere (Eds.), *Women, culture, and society*. Stanford, CA: Stanford University Press.

Chodorow, N. (1978). *The reproduction of mothering: Psychoanalysis and the sociology of gender*. Berkeley and Los Angeles: The University of California Press.

Christ, C. P. (1987). Toward a paradigm shift in the academy and in religious studies. In C. Farnham (Ed.), *The impact of feminist research in the academy*. Bloomington, IN: Indiana University Press.

Collier, J., & M. Z. Rosaldo. (1981). Politics and gender in simple societies. In S. Ortner and H. Whitehead (Eds.), *Sexual meanings*. New York: Cambridge University Press.

Corea, G. (1985). *The mother machine: Reproductive technologies from artificial insemination to artificial wombs*. New York: Harper & Row.

Daly, M. (1978). *Gyn/Ecology: The metaethics of radical feminism*. Boston: Beacon Press.

Daly, M. (1984). *Pure lust: Elemental feminist philosophy*. Boston: Beacon Press.

Dawkins, R. (1976). *The selfish gene*. New York: Oxford University Press.

Dinnerstein, D. (1977). *The Mermaid and the Minotaur: Sexual arrangements and human malaise*. New York: Harper Colophon Books.

Dubois, E. Kelly, G. P. Kennedy, E. L., Korsmeyer, C. W., and Robinson, L. S. (1985). *Feminist scholarship: Kindling in the groves of academe*. Urbana, IL: University of Illinois Press.

Dworkin, A. (1983). *Right-wing women*. New York: Coward-McCann.

Fausto-Sterling, A. (1985). *Myths of gender*. New York: Basic Books.

Fedigan, L. M. (1982). *Primate paradigms: Sex roles and social bonds*. Montreal: Eden Press.

Fee, E. (1981). Is feminism a threat to scientific objectivity? *International Journal of Women's Studies, 4*(4), 213–233.

Fee, E. (1982). A feminist critique of scientific objectivity. *Science for the People, 14*(4), 8.

Fee, E. (1983). Women's nature and scientific objectivity. In M. Lowe & R. Hubbard (Eds.), *Women's nature: Rationalizations of inequality*. Elmsford, NY: Pergamon Press.

Fennema, E., & Sherman, J. (1977). Sex related differences in mathematics achievement, spatial visualization and affective factors. *American Educational Research Journal, 14*, 51–71.

Firestone, S. (1970). *The dialectic of sex*. New York: Bantam Books.

Flax, J. (1981). Do feminists need Marxism? *Building feminist theory: Essays from "Quest," A Feminist Quarterly* (pp. 174–185). New York: Longmen.

Foreman, A. (1977). *Femininity as alienation: Women and the family in Marxism and psychoanalysis*. London: Pluto Press.

Friedan, B. (1974). *The feminine mystique*. New York: Dell.

Freud, S. (1924). The dissolution of the Oedipus complex. *Standard edition of the complete psychological works of Sigmund Freud, 19*. London: Hogarth Press and the Institute of Psychoanalysis.

Goldman, E. (1970). *Living my life*. (2 vol.) New York: Dover Publications. (Original work published 1931).

Goodfield, J. (1981). *An imagined world*. New York: Penguin Books.

Gorski, R., Harlan, R. E., Jacobson, C. D., Shryne, J. E. & Soutam, A. M. (1980). Evidence for the existence of a sexually dimorphic nucleus in the preoptic area of the rat. *Journal of Comparative Neurology. 193*, 529–539.

Gould, S. J. (1981). *The mismeasure of man*. New York: W. W. Norton.

Goy, R. & Phoenix, C. H. (1971). The effects of testosterone propionate administered before birth on the development of behavior in genetic female rhesus monkeys. In C. H. Sawyer & R. A. Gorski (Eds.), *Steroid hormones and brain function.* Berkeley: University of California Press.

Griffin, S. (1978). *Women and nature: The roaring inside her.* New York: Harper & Row.

Haraway, D. (1978). Animal sociology and a natural economy of the body politic, Part I: A political physiology of dominance; Animal sociology and a natural economy of the body politic, Part II: The past is the contested zone: Human nature and theories of production and reproduction in primate behavior studies. *Signs: Journal of Women in Culture and Society, 4*(1), 21–60.

Haraway, D. (1990). *Primate visions.* New York: Routledge.

Harding, S. (1986). *The science question in feminism.* Ithaca, NY: Cornell University Press.

Harding, S. (1987). *Feminism and methodology.* Bloomington and Indianapolis: Indiana University Press.

Hartmann, H. (1981). The unhappy marriage of Marxism and feminism: Towards a more progressive union. In L. Sargent (Ed.), *Women and revolution: A discussion of the unhappy marriage of Marxism and feminism* (pp. 1–41). Boston: South End Press.

Hartman, M., & Banner, L. (Eds.) (1974). *Clio's consciousness raised.* New York: Harper and Row.

Hein, H. (1981). Women and science: Fitting men to think about nature. *International Journal of Women's Studies, 4,* 369–377.

Hollingsworth, L. S. (1914). Variability as related to sex differences in achievement. *American Journal of Sociology, 19*(4), 510–530.

Hrdy, S. B. (1979). Infanticide among animals: A review, classification and examination of the implications for the reproductive strategies of females. *Ethology and Sociobiology, 1,* 3–40.

Hrdy, S. B. (1981). *The woman that never evolved.* Cambridge, MA: Harvard University Press.

Hrdy, S. B. (1986). Empathy, polyandry, and the myth of the coy female. In R. Bleier (Ed.), *Feminist approaches to science.* Elmsford, NY: Pergamon Press.

Hubbard, R. (1979). Have only men evolved? In R. Hubbard, M. S. Henifin, & B. Fried (Eds.), *Women look at biology looking at women.* Cambridge, MA: Schenkman.

Hubbard, R. (1990). *Politics of women's biology.* New Brunswick, NJ: Rutgers University Press.

Hynes, H. P. (1989). *The recurring silent spring.* Elmsford, NY: Pergamon Press.

Jaggar, A. M. (1983). *Feminist politics and human nature.* Totowa, NJ: Rowman & Allanheld.

Jaggar, A., & Rothenberg, P. (Eds.). (1984). *Feminist frameworks.* New York: McGraw-Hill.

Keller, E. F. (1982, Spring). "Feminism and science." *Signs. 7*(3): 589–602.

Keller, E. F. (1983). *A feeling for the organism: The life and work of Barbara McClintock.* New York: W. H. Freeman.

Keller, E. F. (1984, November/December). Women and basic research: Respecting the unexpected. *Technology Review, 87:* 44–47.

Keller, E. F. (1985). *Reflections on gender and science.* New Haven, CT: Yale University Press.

Keller, E. F. (1987). Women scientists and feminist critics of science. *Daedalus, 116* (4): 77–91.

Kuhn, T. S. (1970). *The structure of scientific revolutions* (2e.). Chicago: The University of Chicago Press.

Lancaster, J. (1975). *Primate behavior and the emergence of human culture*. New York: Holt, Rinehart & Winston.

Leacock, E. (1981). *Myths of male dominance*. New York: Monthly Review Press.

Leavitt, R. R. (1975). *Peaceable primates and gentle people: Anthropological approaches to women's studies*. New York: Harper & Row.

Leibowitz, L. (1975). Perspectives in the evolution of sex differences. In R. R. Reiter (Ed.), *Toward an anthropology of women*. New York: Monthly Review Press.

Linton, S. (1974). Woman the gatherer. In R. Reiter, (Ed.). *Toward an anthropology of women*. New York: Monthly Review Press.

MacKinnon, C. (1982). Feminism, Marxism, method and the state: An agenda for theory. *Signs: Journal of Women in Culture and Society, 7*(3), 515–544.

MacKinnon, C. A. (1987). *Feminism unmodified: Discourses on life and law*. Cambridge, MA and London: Harvard University Press.

Merchant, C. (1979). *The death of nature: Women, ecology and the scientific revolution*. New York: Harper & Row.

Mill, H. T. (1970). Enfranchisement of Women. In Alice S. Rossi (Ed.), *Essays on sex equality*. Chicago: University of Chicago Press.

Mill, J. S. (1970). The subjection of women. Mill, & A. S. Rossi (Eds.). *Essays on sex equality* (pp. 123–242). Chicago: University of Chicago Press.

Millett, K. (1970). *Sexual politics*. Garden City, NY: Doubleday.

Mitchell, J. (1971). *Woman's estate*. New York: Pantheon Books.

Mitchell, J. (1974). *Psychoanalysis and feminism*. New York: Vintage Books.

National Science Foundation. (1990). *Women and minorities in science and engineering*. (NSF 90–301). Washington, DC: Author.

O'Brien, M. (1981). *The politics of reproduction*. Boston: Routledge and Kegan Paul.

Ortner, S. (1974). Is female to male as nature to culture? In M. Rosaldo & L. Lamphere (Eds.), *Woman, culture, and society*. Stanford: Stanford University Press.

Rich, A. (1976). *Of woman born: Motherhood as experience*. New York: W. W. Norton.

Roberts, H. (1981). *Doing feminist research*. London & Boston: Routledge and Kegan Paul.

Rose, H., & Rose, S. (1980). The myth of the neutrality of science. *Science and liberation*. Boston: South End Press.

Rosser, S. V. (1982). Androgyny and sociobiology. *International Journal of Women's Studies, 5*(5), 435–444.

Rosser, S. V. (1990). *Female-friendly science*. Elmsford, NY: Pergamon Press.

Rossiter, M. W. (1982). *Women scientists in America: Struggles and strategies to 1940*. Baltimore, MD: The Johns Hopkins University Press.

Rowell, T. (1974). ''The concept of social dominance.'' *Behavioral Biology, 11*, 131–154.

Sayers, J. (1982). *Biological politics: Feminist and anti-feminist perspectives*. London: Tavistock.

Small, M. (1984). *Female primates*. New York: Alan R. Liss.

Smith-Rosenberg, C. (1975; Autumn). The female world of love and ritual: Relations between women in nineteenth century America. *Signs 1*, 1–29.

Spanier, B. (1982, April). Toward a balanced curriculum: The study of women at Wheaton College. *Change, 14*, 31–34.

Sperry, R. W. (1974). Lateral specialization in the surgically separated hemisphres. In F. O. Schmitt & R. T. Wardon (Eds.), *The neurosciences: Third study program*. Cambridge: MIT Press.

Star, S. L. (1979). Sex differences and the dichotomization of the brain: Methods, limits and problems in research on consciousness. In R. Hubbard & M. Lowe (Eds.), *Genes and gender II: Pitfalls in research on sex and gender*. New York: Gordian Press.

Tanner, A. (1896). The community of ideas of men and women. *Psychological Review* 3(5), 548–550.

Trivers, R. L. (1972). Parental investment and sexual selection. In B. Campbell (Ed.), *Sexual selection and the descent of man*. Chicago, IL: Aldine.

Tong, R. (1989). *Feminist thought: A comprehensive introduction*. Boulder, CO: Westview Press.

Vogel, L. (1983). *Marxism and the oppression of women: Towards a unitary theory*. New Brunswick, NJ: Rutgers University Press.

Wallston, B. S. (1981). What are the questions in the psychology of women? A feminist approach to research. *Psychology of Women Quarterly 5*, 597–617.

Weisstein, N. (1971). Psychology constructs the female, or the fantasy life of the male psychologist. In M. H. Garskof (Ed.), *Roles women play: Readings toward women's liberation*. Belmont, CA: Brooks/Cole Publishing Co.

Wilson, E. O. (1975). *Sociobiology: The new synthesis*. Cambridge, MA: Harvard University Press.

Wollstonecraft, M. (1975). C. H. Poston, (Ed.), *A vindication of the rights of woman*. New York: W. W. Norton.

Yerkes, R. M. (1943). *Chimpanzees*. New Haven: Yale University Press.

Young, I. (1980). Socialist feminism and the limits of dual systems theory. *Socialist Review 10* (2–3); 174.

Young, I. (1981). Beyond the unhappy marriage: A critique of the dual systems theory. In L. Sargent (Ed.), *Women and revolution: A discussion of the unhappy marriage of Marxism and feminism*. Boston: South End Press.

APPLICATIONS
OF FEMINISM
TO BIOLOGY

6.

TRANSFORMING THE BIOLOGY CURRICULUM

The previous section of this book examined the impact of feminism on research methods, theories, and conclusions drawn from the data. As increasing numbers of women have entered the biological sciences they have made substantial critiques of research done at the organismal level as well as that undertaken at the cellular and molecular level. They have also begun to explore diverse approaches, including feminist methodologies.

At the same time that feminist critiques and methodologies began to evolve, other feminists in biology sought to transform the biology curriculum. The impetus for many of the first "biology of women" courses was the recognition by activists in the women's movement that women not only lacked control over their bodies but also were woefully ignorant about their bodies' functioning. Most of the first biologically oriented, Women's Studies courses were "know your body" courses that originated in an attempt to fill this knowledge gap. Because many of the teachers of these first classes were the same individuals, or at least were friends and colleagues of the people beginning feminist critiques of biology, they began to develop upper-level courses such as "gender and science" and the "history of women in science" to include these critiques.

As more evidence from research on feminist critiques and methodologies accumulated in disciplines within the humanities and social sciences, projects were undertaken to mainstream this evidence into introductory and traditional disciplinary courses. Inspired by the models for curriculum transformation developed in other disciplines, and in some cases even pushed by women's studies directors to apply those models, biologists have more recently sought to integrate feminist critiques into introductory and upper-level specialized courses in biology. The shortage of American-trained scientists currently predicted to reach epidemic proportions by the twenty-first century has forced mainstream scientists to be more open to considering feminist critiques and women's studies pedagogical techniques in an attempt to attract more women to biology.

BIOLOGY IN WOMEN'S STUDIES COURSES

In 1985 I published an article called "Science and Health-Related Women's Studies Courses: A Report After Ten Years in the Academy" (Rosser, 1985) in *The Feminist Teacher*. The article was based on responses to a questionnaire sent to chairs of all 434 Women's Studies programs in the country. The results were analyzed on the basis of 36 courses taught at 28 institutions who returned completed questionnaires, including syllabi (Rosser, 1985, p. 32).

The results of this questionnaire gave a picture of the types of science and health-related women's studies courses that had emerged throughout the country after a decade of women's studies in the academy. Most of these courses were related to women's health and biology and were taught by faculty whose primary affiliations were with women's studies, health, and/or biology departments. This finding is not surprising when one considers that two major issues of the current women's movement are women's health and reproductive rights. The influence of self-health clinics, political action, and women's taking responsibility for learning about their bodies in collective efforts outside the academy have been extensive. These courses may represent the academy's response to the desire for knowledge in these two areas.

The second largest number of courses fell in the categories of the history of women in science, health, and/or medicine. Whereas the roots for the health/biology courses may lie in the women's movement outside the academy, I think that the stimulus for the history of women in science, health, and/or medicine courses and research might come from inside the academy. The progress made by Women's Studies scholars in the history departments in uncovering the lost women of history and their concepts of new ways to look at the role of women in history may have provided the outlines for the Women's Studies scholars interested in the history of women in science, health, and/or medicine (Lerner, 1975).

These courses in women's health, biology, and the history of women in science and medicine are extremely important. They provide a fundamental basis of knowledge that we must have about ourselves before we may begin to think about more theoretical issues regarding women and science. However, the other two categories in which there was more than one course were the theories of the relationship between women and science, and women and technology. In many respects I find these to be the most exciting courses. From the syllabi and course descriptions, it is evident that these courses focus on the complex interdependence and interaction between women and science and our complicated technological society. In these courses, the instructors and students explore what it is about the nature of science and technology as it is currently practiced in our Western androcentric society that excludes women at all but the most menial levels while allowing it to control us through computers, medical technologies, and engineering designs. Students and instructors in these courses begin to consider the ways in which science might be different—less hierarchical, less dualistic, less separate from human values and relationships—if women could and did participate in science and technology at the controlling, decision-making levels.

Courses in women's health and/or sexuality were usually the first science-related courses to appear in most women's studies programs. In many institutions they appeared later in the decade, well after the first wave of women's studies courses; they often represent the only science courses that a program offers today. Few colleges and universities offer higher level courses in science such as Biology and Gender (University of Wisconsin–Madison and Colgate University) or Women and Science (Hunter College), which explore feminism and science at a theoretical level. A survey of a small nonrandom sample of colleges that offer certificates in women's studies revealed that there are more programs that do not have a distribution requirement that includes a science or women's health course for the certificate in women's studies than programs that do make such a demand. There is also a dearth of scientists on or affiliated with the faculties of most women's studies programs (Rosser, 1986).

INTEGRATION OF FEMINISM INTO THE BIOLOGY CURRICULUM

Despite the dearth of scientists affiliated with most Women's Studies programs, transformation of the science curriculum has been included in the goals of most projects seeking to incorporate feminist scholarship into the curriculum. Most feminist scholars accepted the stages for Women's Studies articulated by Florence Howe (1984). Stage I includes the development of Women's Studies courses and research centers. Stage II integrates the information developed in Stage I into traditional courses in the disciplines. It is understood that Stage II must occur only while maintaining separate Women's Studies programs, courses, and research centers as a resource for the materials needed for Stage II.

The few scientists involved with Women's Studies tend to be biologists rather than physical scientists; this has resulted in biology representing the area within the physical and natural sciences in which feminist critiques are most evolved. Feminists in biology have been encouraged by their colleagues in Women's Studies to attempt curriculum transformation in traditional biology courses. The shortage of scientists has also caused their colleagues in biology to view their attempts at curriculum integration as a positive mechanism for attracting women to science.

Two decades of Women's Studies scholarship and experience with curriculum transformation projects have enabled faculty involved with numerous projects at diverse institutions of higher education to chart the developmental phases through which integration occurs in a variety of disciplines. McIntosh (1984), Schuster and Van Dyne (1984), and Tetreault (1985) have published schemes documenting these phases. Although the schemes vary in the number of phases and complexity, the initial phase of each is one in which the absence of women has not been noted; the final phase represents a transformed curriculum.

The scheme I present is unique in two ways. First, although it borrows heavily from other schemes, particularly the Schuster–Van Dyne scheme, it is based on my experience with the natural sciences. Second, this scheme was developed for biology and includes examples particularly appropriate for the biology curriculum. Biology is not only the discipline within the natural sciences in which the most women are receiving undergraduate degrees and doctorates (NSF, 1990), but the discipline in which I hold a Ph.D. and have taught for many years.

Phase I—Absence of Women is not Noted   Most biology curricula are in phase I. In this phase, faculty and students are not aware of the absence of women scientists in theoretical and decision-making positions in the scientific establishment or the absence of women's health issues or a focus on women in the curriculum. They assume that because science is "objective," gender does not influence either who becomes a scientist or the science produced by those scientists. Many scientists would suggest that science is "manless" as well as "womanless"; they are unaware or would openly reject the notion that gender might influence the theories, data collection, subjects chosen for experimentation, or questions asked.

Phase II—Recognition that Scientists are Male and that Science May Reflect a Masculine Perspective   Recent publicity from the federal government and various professional societies has made most scientists aware that women are underrepresented in all fields of natural science, particularly in the theoretical and decision-making levels of that profession. Some scientists, influenced by scholarship in women's studies, the philosophy and history of science, and psychology have begun to recognize that gender may influence science. Thomas Kuhn (1970) and his followers have suggested that all scientific theories are the products of individuals living in a particular historical and social milieu. As such, they are biased by the perspective and paradigms of those individuals. Fee (1981) and Keller (1982) have suggested that the absence of women from the decision-making levels of science has produced a science that views the world from a male perspective and is, therefore, womanless. The failure of scientists to recognize this bias has perpetuated the idea of the "objectivity" of science.

Phase III—Identification of Barriers that Prevent Women from Entering Science   Acceptance of the possibility that a preponderance of male scientists may have led to the production of a science that reflects a masculine approach to the world constitutes the first step towards recognition of barriers to women becoming scientists.

An aspect of this phase shows up in current studies that attempt to attract more women into science and math, the traditionally "male" disciplines. The National Science Foundation (1990), the Rockefeller Foundation (Berryman 1983), the American Association of Colleges under the auspices of the Carnegie Corporation and the Ford Foundation (Hall & Sandler, 1982), the Office of Technology Assessment (1987), and the American Chemical Society (1983), along with other foundations and professional societies, have each issued studies and reports with statistics documenting the lack of women in science and possible "causes and cures."

Other evidence of the obstacles faced surfaces in article titles written by and about women in science:

- "Adventures of a Woman in Science" (Weisstein, 1979)
- "Rosalind Franklin and DNA: A Vivid View of What It Is Like to be a Gifted Woman in an Especially Male Profession" (Sayre, 1975)
- "Sex Discrimination in the Halls of Science" (Vetter, 1980)
- "Women in Academic Chemistry Find Rise to Full Status Difficult" (Rawls & Fox Jeffrey, 1978)
- "The Anomaly of a Woman in Physics" (Keller, 1977)

- "The Disadvantaged Majority: Science Education for Women" (Kahle, 1983)
- "Can the Difference Between Male and Female Science Majors Account for the Low Number of Women at the Doctoral Level in Science?" (Baker, 1983)
- "Obstacles and Contraints on Women in Science" (Matyas, 1985)
- "Where are the Women in the Physical Sciences?" (Vetter, 1988)

These titles suggest that women who do become scientists are frequently viewed as anomalies or face numerous problems and difficulties because of their gender.

The dearth of women scientists and the marginalization of the few women who do exist as anomalies have led to questions about a source of bias and absence of value neutrality in science. Because most, if not all, scientists are men, values held by male scientists are congruent with values of all scientists and became synonymous with the "objective" view of the world (Keller, 1982, 1985). (See chapter 3 for a fuller discussion of this topic.)

An additional deterrent for many women and people of color is that biological research has been and continues to be used to justify social and political inequalities. If any inequity can be scientifically "proven" to have a biological biasis, then the rationale for social pressures to erase that inequity is diminished. In both the nineteenth and twentieth centuries some scientific research has centered on discovering the biological bases for gender differences in abilities to justify women's socially inferior position. Craniometry research and the social Darwinism quickly derived from Darwin's theory of natural selection serve as examples of the flawed science used to "prove" the inferiority of women and nonwhites (Sayers, 1982). Feminist critics have stated that some of the work in sociobiology (Bleier, 1984; Hubbard, 1979) and brain lateralization (Bleier, 1988; Star, 1979) constitutes a twentieth-century equivalent to social Darwinism and craniometry, providing scientific justification for maintaining the social status quo of women and minorities.

Phase IV—Search for Women Scientists and their Unique Contributions   The recovery of the names and contributions of the lost women of science has been invaluable research provided by historians of science who were spurred on by the work of feminists in history. Much of the work has followed the male model, focusing on the great or successful women in science. (See chapter 2 for a fuller treatment of this topic.) Demonstrating that women have been successful in traditional science is important in that it documents the fact that despite the extreme barriers and obstacles, women can do science.

Some historians have rejected this male model and sought to examine the lives and situations of women in science who were not famous. Margaret Rossiter's (1982) *Women Scientists in America: Struggles and Strategies to 1940* is the groundbreaking work that examines how the work of the usual woman scientists suffers from underrecognition due to application of double standards and other social barriers inherent in the structure of the scientific community. Recovering the history of women in science often reveals the history of the use of flawed scientific research against women and people of color. Frequently, biologically deterministic theories, such as sociobiology and those regarding hormonal effects on the brain, have been used to justify women's position in society. Today, the biological determinism question is particularly related to two areas of current research: hormone research and animal behavior. (See chapters three and four for a fuller discussion)

Today's feminist scientists refute the biologically deterministic theories by pointing out their scientific flaws (Birke, 1986; Bleier, 1979; Fausto-Sterling, 1985; Hubbard, 1979, Lowe, 1978; Rosser, 1982). These refutations and warnings about the problems of biologically deterministic assumptions are necessary. Even a century of women scientists pointing out the unscientific bases of the assumptions has not led to their eradication from current scientific theories.

Phase V—Scientific Discoveries by Feminists/Women   Uncovering women scientists and their contributions provides an opportunity to examine differences between their work and that of male scientists. Similarly, awareness of possible biases and flaws introduced into research from the dominance of males and a masculine perspective in science made faculty begin to explore unique aspects of scientific exploration done by women. Three examples of recent work suggest differences in distance between scientist and subject of study, use of experimental subjects, and language between male and female biologists.

1. In her approach towards studying maize, Barbara McClintock indicates a shortening of the distance between the observer and the object being studied and a consideration of the complex interaction between the organism and its environment. Her statements about her work suggest a closer, more intimate relationship with the subject of her research than typically is expressed by the male "objective" scientist. One does not normally associate words such as "a feeling for the organism" (Keller, 1983) with the rational, masculine approach to science. McClintock also rejects the predominant hierarchical theory of genetic DNA as the master molecule that controls gene action to focus on control based on the interaction between the organism and its environment.

2. Models that more accurately simulate functioning, complex biological systems may be derived from using female rats as subjects in experiments. Women scientists such as Hoffman (1982) have questioned the tradition of using male rats or primates as subjects. As Hoffman (1982) points out, the

rhythmic cycle of hormone secretion, as also portrayed in the cycling female rat, appears to be a more accurate model for the secretion of most hormones.

3. As more women have entered primate research, they have begun to challenge the language used to describe primate behavior and the patriarchal assumptions inherent in searches for dominance hierarchies in primates. Lancaster (1975, p. 34) describes a single-male troop of animals as follows: "For a female, males are a resource in her environment which she may use to further the survival of herself and her offspring. If environmental conditions are such that the male role can be minimal, a one-male group is likely. Only one male is necessary for a group of females if his only role is to impregnate them."

Her work points out the androcentric bias of primate behavior theories, which would describe this group as a "harem" and consider dominance and subordination in the description of behavior. Describing the same situation using a gynocentric term such as "stud" reveals the importance of more gender-neutral language in removing bias.

Phase VI—Science Redefined and Reconstructed to Include Us All   The ultimate goal of the methods and curricular changes suggested in phases I–V is the production of curriculum information and pedagogy that includes women and people of color and therefore attracts individuals from those groups to become scientists. Obviously, this curriculum and these methods have not been fully developed yet. Achievement of phase VI should accomplish more than increasing the diversity of individuals who choose to become scientists. Phase VI should also result in a better science that suffers from fewer flaws and biases. As more people from varying backgrounds and perspectives become scientists, they increase the likelihood that the scientific method will be able to function as it should. As long as most scientists come from a relatively homogeneous perspective—that of the white, middle/upper-class Western male—their view of the world and science will be limited by that perspective. When scientific hypotheses are held up for critique to the scientific community, biases and flaws in the hypotheses are likely to go unseen to the extent that the scientific community holds a relatively homogeneous perspective. This homogeneity in gender, race, and class is what caused the scientific community to fail to include women and men of color when defining problems for study, as experimental subjects in drug tests, and in applications of research findings.

THE INTRODUCTORY COURSE

This scheme is a useful tool to assess the progress of the discipline of biology towards curriculum integration. It may be less obvious how an introductory course may be transformed. Including new information about women and the perspective of feminism is crucial in all courses in science and health, but it is particularly crucial in introductory courses. For most students such courses generally serve as the introduction to college science and to all courses in health and biology they will subsequently take. Thus, they set the stage for further study.

Traditionally female students have not gone on in the sciences in large numbers. Women tend to exclude themselves from laboratory science because of cultural influences that dictate gender roles. Women also tend to be excluded from laboratory science by active discrimination. Even when women do choose careers in laboratory science and health care, seldom do they reach the theoretical and decision-making levels (Keller, 1982).

As Fee (1982) points out, there is no feminist science yet. Feminists have only proposed methodological and theoretical changes in small areas of the biological sciences. Currently we are at the stage of a critique of science.

This critique assumes, first, that all investigations are carried out from some perspective. Decisions, either conscious or unconscious, regarding what questions are asked, who is allowed to do the asking, what information is collected, and who interprets that information create a particular vantage point from which knowledge or truth is perceived. The traditional belief in objectivity makes it difficult for scientists to admit the relevance of perspective and therefore even the more obvious perspectives by which their data and theories are influenced. Recognizing the influence of androcentrism (a recognition that has been difficult in the disciplines of the humanities and social sciences in which the concept of perspective in approaching knowledge is more acceptable) is doubly difficult for the scientist. Feminist perspectives insist that women become central to the questions and theories of science and health and that women be studied for their own sake, not as compared to the male; only then does one develop an accurate understanding that permits valid comparisons. With a focus on women, entirely different questions can be asked. Experiments can be set up using the female body as a model, with female rats or monkeys as the experimental subjects. Alternative and multiple interpretations of the data might be encouraged. Thus, females, the other half of humanity, would be included in the scientific descriptions of reality (Minnich, 1982).

Teaching science from a feminist perspectives and setting before all students the examples of great women in science and medicine should make young women realize that science is a field that is open to them. So doing will help dispel the stereotype of scientists as male. Unveiling the stories of women scientists, such as Rosalind Franklin and Barbara McClintock, may stimulate people to do the necessary work on the history of women in science and to begin to shape a feminist science. In short, a feminist critique of science aims at making young women and men aware of the deficiencies, lack of objectivity, and androcentric bias of traditional science.

The question for the introductory biology teacher then becomes how, at present, can one incorporate the recent scholarship on women and science into the biology curriculum in a manner that will inspire further critiques and theoretical changes. How can one integrate into the standard biology curriculum the considerable but diffuse information constituting contemporary feminist perspectives: the critique of biological determinism and androcentric "objectivity," the substantial information about famous and lesser-known women scientists and their discoveries, some remarks about the obvious influence of masculine thinking on the descriptive language of biology, the feminist theoretical changes that have already taken place, and those areas in which the theoretical changes are still needed?

After an introduction to the scientific method, most introductory syllabi and textbooks attempt to cover the following five broad fields within biology: the cell, genetics, development, evolution and animal behavior, and ecology. I will indicate some issues that might be raised, and some methods and activities that might aid students might aid students in understanding these issues.

1. *Scientific Method*: Most beginning biology courses include a presentation of the modern conception of the scientific method. This provides an ideal opportunity for presenting feminist critiques of the methodology of science that can then be applied when assessing the research and data presented in individual areas. In the feminist critiques of the scientific method, the following issues need to be raised: To what extent are the scientific method and the theories derived from it biased by the particular social and historical context of the scientist? To what extent is the language of scientific theories reflective of a particular social and historical context? Is the scientific method really an objective approach to the world or is it androcentric? Is this androcentric bias reflected in experimental design, male subjects and models used for experimentation, and the language and conceptualization of scientific theories?

2. *The Cell*: The area of cell biology is one in which virtually no theoretical changes due to feminist critique have occurred. The integration of a feminist perspective in this area will probably have to be raised in terms of the language and terminology in which the theories are expressed and the very few role models of female scientists who have worked in this area.

3. *Genetics*: The study of genetics and DNA provides an excellent locus to raise the issues of the position of women in science and why women are not accepted as "good" scientists. Questions such as why most of the data collection and technical work are done by women, whereas most of the theorizing and decision making are done by men in science must be addressed. Why are hypotheses suggested by women not accepted? One might

also ask if the unicausal approach to teaching in genetics, which reflects a reductionist view that understanding the genes explains everything about the organism without taking into account its complex interaction with the environment (Hubbard, 1990), is not a male approach to the world.

4. *Development*: The area of developmental biology, including for purposes of an introductory course, endocrinology, provides opportunities to begin to raise the issues of how the male models, experimental subjects, and language used to describe those models are beginning to be transformed by a feminist critique. The evidence from developmental biology that the initial ground plan for development in most species is female (Fausto-Sterling, 1985) will come as a shock to most students who are used to the androcentric Western view that the male is primary in all realms and that female is the ''other'' or secondary (Sherfey, 1973). Learning about parthenogenesis and that in development it is the so-called reacting (an androcentric turn of phrase?) biological system that is important in egg development rather than what is applied to it (the sperm) reemphasizes the importance of the female (Biology and Gender Study Group, 1989; Manning, 1983; Martin, 1991).

The increasing evidence that most hormones operate on a cyclic rather than steady-state basis (Hoffman, 1982) raises the question of why male rats and monkeys are used as experimental subjects when females would obviously provide a more accurate model. Students can begin to see that the ''cleaner'' data derived from male models due to their noncyclicity may lead scientists to oversimplified conclusions. Perhaps the ''messier'' data derived from female models is in fact more reflective of biological complexity. An explanation of the subtle problems that occur with biochemical conversions of hormones within the body (Bleier, 1979) may lead students to ask questions about proper controls and extrapolating from biochemical to behavioral traits. The issue, first raised by E. E. Just in the 1930s and now brought forth by feminist scientists, of the nature of the interaction of the cell surface with the surrounding environment demonstrates a beginning theoretical change caused by feminist critique. Standard theory holds that the cell is in a struggle with the environment; the newer theory, influenced partially by feminist critique, suggests that cooperative processes at the cell surface may be more important (Biology and Gender Study Group, 1989; Manning, 1983).

5. *Evolution*: The field of evolution with its subdiscipline, animal behavior, provides ample opportunity for feminist critiques of the language, experimental subjects, data collection, and theoretical conclusions drawn. One may begin by questioning the extent to which Darwin's theory of natural selection was biased by the Victorian social and historical context of its time. It probably needs to be pointed out to students that his theoretical language (competition, struggle for existence, survival of the fittest) led to theories of biological determinism as a basis for origins of behavioral differences and abilities. These were then used to explain differences of social and economic class and as the basis for the policy of social Darwinism during his time (Rose, 1982). Then many students will be able to understand

the problems of some animal behavior research, in which behavior in lower animals is observed in the framework of a search for "universal" behavior patterns in males of all species or in all males of a particular order or class, such as primates or mammals. The problems raised by then extrapolating these patterns to humans must be addressed. The claims of some sociobiologists that behavior is genetically determined and that differences between males in role, status, and performance are biologically based (Wilson, 1975) can then be refuted by explaining the alternative theories now provided by feminist scientists (Lancaster, 1975) to the classical androcentric and ethnocentric descriptions of animal behavior.

6. *Ecology*: Ecology is one field within biology in which the traditional scientific theory and approach are most in harmony with a feminist approach to the subject. Ecology emphasizes the interrelationships among organisms, including human beings and the earth. Feminists have also focused on the position of human beings as a part of the environmental network. Both ecology and feminism deplore the position that industrialized Western man has taken, that of a superior being who has dominion over and the right to exploit the earth and its other living beings, including women. The fusion of feminist and scientific theory in the field of ecology brings together the ultimate goal of the course: the integration of a feminist perspective into science. It is thus the ideal subject matter on which to end the course.

Taken together, it becomes evident that the inclusion of feminist perspectives and methods leads to changes in models, experimental subjects, and interpretations of the data. These changes entail more inclusive, enriched theories compared to the traditional, restrictive unicausal theories. These alternative, multidimensional theories generally provide a more accurate description for the introductory student to the realities of our complex biological world.

PEDAGOGY IN WOMEN'S STUDIES COURSES FOCUSED ON HEALTH OR BIOLOGY

Just as feminism has had an impact on curricular content in biology, feminist pedagogy has also begun to have an impact on classroom techniques used to teach biology. Most faculty using these techniques first developed them in their women's studies courses. The initial need for the techniques was fueled by the desire to break down hierarchical barriers between faculty and students in the women's studies classroom. Soon the driving force became the recognition that changed curricular content, which includes multiple perspectives, requires a changed pedagogy that reflects those perspectives.

Including perspectives other than those of the white, middle-class, heterosexual female involves rethinking all of the issues of the course, not just adding on material at the end. For instance, widening the focus of a section on birth control means more than including a discussion of the possible complications of various birth-control methods for different ethnic or religious groups such as the particular risks in taking birth control pills to black women who have sickle cell anemia (Ammer, 1983) or the newer methods of using the cervical mucus to determine the exact time of ovulation to aid in rhythm or natural birth control. The issue of birth control itself must be the central focus because it presents itself differently to different groups of women. To many women of color, the testing and forced use of birth control may represent another genocidal threat directed by whites towards other ethnic groups. Puerto Rican women may recall that over one-third of the women on their island have been sterilized during the last 30 years without their consent (Vazquez-Calzadar, 1973) and that the pill was tested on the island's population before it was considered safe to market on the United States mainland (Zimmerman, 1980). African-American women, American Indian women, and Chicanas may feel torn between the group-preservation strategy of ethnic liberation movements and the women's movement advocacy of individual choice. To some lower-income women, birth control and forced sterilizations may represent another humiliation in the guise of reducing reliance on government support (Rodgers, 1973). To many women who are Roman Catholic or of fundamentalist religions, birth control may raise a conflict with religious practice. To most lesbians, birth control may be a nonissue except when gynecologists assume the heterosexual norm (Darty & Potter, 1984) and insist on prescribing a method. Thus, the central focus of the birth-control presentation must be a thorough discussion of the use and misuse of birth control for women in different situations. After that, the issues of particular methods may be addressed.

Sexuality is another area that presents itself very differently for each woman, depending on her race, class, sexual orientation, religion, body, and life experiences. I was made acutely aware of this when discussing some of Shere Hite's (1976) work in which she considers the relative infrequency and longer period of time taken to achieve orgasm when stimulated by vaginal penetration as compared to clitoral stimulation. An African-American student asked what I was talking about. She and the other African-American students made it clear to me that the information I was giving did not correspond to their experience at all. Without recognizing it, I had assumed as the norm the experience of the publicized white female who has less success at achieving orgasm through vaginal penetration than by clitoral stimulation. Other assumptions expressing racial, social, religious, age, and sexual orientation underlie most discussions of sexuality. Some of these assumptions are evident when examining the content of the information that is presented or omitted; more may be inferred from the order in which the topics are considered, who presents the topics, and how questions are handled.

Because our culture is permeated with what Adrienne Rich (1980) refers to as "compulsory heterosexuality," most sexuality is taught from this perspective, even when homosexuality and lesbianism are being discussed. The timing and method by which material is presented may convey subtle negative messages to the students about lesbianism. If material on heterosexuality is presented first, then heterosexuality becomes the norm; lesbianism and bisexuality are automatically seen as deviations, even though the terminology used does not state that directly.

It may be wise to place sexuality on the syllabus before a lengthy section on contraception, pregnancy, and childbirth. This is more in keeping with the sequence of biological development. Presenting the material on lesbianism early in the course should create an atmosphere of respect for women of different sexual orientations who may or may not choose to deal with contraception, pregnancy, and childbirth during their lives. It should be noted, however, that some lesbians do choose to conceive and bear children. One must not automatically assume the contrary.

In handling the inevitable question, "What do lesbians do?" it is important to broaden the answer beyond clitoral stimulation to a discussion of the means of expressing sexuality. It may be helpful to consider the extent to which sexuality is a part of the total person that permeates speech, body language, clothing, posture, and other less erotic aspects of expression. This consideration may then be extended to erotic means of sexual expression such as touching. This expansion does more than encourage students to change their focus from heterosexual intercourse to consider sexual activity in lesbians. It also opens the way for a discussion of sexuality in aging and physically challenged people, as well as among lesbians.

Birth control and sexuality provide examples of the complexity of issues when addressed from multiple perspectives. One must not underestimate the difficulties of trying to include multiple points of view. Although each person has a unique set of experiences that determines her individual perspective, the lives and experiences of women as a group are shaped by belonging to that particular group. Although there is not a single, totally identical racial, ethnic, or religious perspective, there are some commonalities that arise out of such roots. The methods suggested here increase the visibility of the groups while allowing the women to speak of their own experiences.

Team teaching with women who represent different perspectives is probably the best way to include varying points of view on all issues. However, limits of budget, excessive demands placed on ethnic and women's studies faculty time, and demands for increased student–faculty ratios in many institutions make this approach less than feasible. When team teaching is not possible, guest lectures by women from the faculty and the community may provide perspectives on particular issues. Students in the class are also a valuable resource. However, it is important to avoid "spot lighting" the one Chicana in the class by expecting her to represent the "Chicana viewpoint" on every issue. Primary sources such as diaries or accounts of sexuality and reproduction in literature by women provide primary accounts of individual experience, whereas statistics gathered and interpreted by sociologists may distort that experience. Films and tapes provide another way for women to express their own experience.

As another means of broadening the students' views beyond the textbook and classroom discussion, I ask them to interview another woman about a biologic event concerning reproduction or sexuality in her life. The woman is to differ as much as possible from the student with regard to class, ethnicity, religion, age, or sexual orientation, so that the student can see the effect that the difference may have on the biological event and its interpretation. Eighteen- to twenty-one-year-old students report that this provides the best opportunity to learn about reproduction and/or sexual events from another perspective and to see how they affected another woman's life.

CHANGED PEDAGOGY FOR BIOLOGY COURSES

Feminist biologists included multiple perspectives and other feminist pedagogical techniques as they began to transform the biology curriculum. Because the topics and focus of a biology course differ substantially from a women's studies course, the techniques must be modified to suit the curricular content.

A variety of methods not usually employed in introductory biology laboratories may sensitize the students to feminist issues. Repeating Thomas Kuhn's (1970) experiment in which he changes the ace of spades from black to red raises the questions about scientific objectivity. Most students will still see the ace as black, demonstrating that expectation can bias observation. Asking students to decide which electron microscope slides (Gazzam-Johnson, fall 1985 personal communication) were taken by men and which by women, and why, or asking students to determine which articles in a bibliography in which initials replace first names are written by men and which by women, raises the question of androcentrism. Asking the students to draw parallels between scientific language used to describe a particular theory, and language that is classically considered masculine or feminine in our culture, draws their attention to the issue of language as it shapes concepts. Parallel reading of books on the same topic such as *Rosalind Franklin and DNA* by Anne Sayre (1975) and *The Double Helix* by James Watson (1969) demonstrate the positions of men and women in science.

More recently some of us (Rosser, 1990) have sought to apply the schema suggested in *Women's Ways of Knowing* (Belenky, Clinchy, Goldberger, & Tarule, 1986) to analyze why some students, particularly women, are not attracted to the science curriculum as it is currently taught. Based on their research, Belenky et al. examine *Women's Ways of Knowing* and described "five different perspectives from which women view reality and draw conclusions about truth, knowledge, and authority" (1986, p. 3):

> . . . *silence*, a position in which women experience themselves as mindless and voiceless and subject to the whims of external authority; *received knowledge*, a perspective from which women conceive of themselves as capable of receiving, even reproducing, knowledge from the all-knowing external authorities but not capable of creating knowledge on their own; *subjective knowledge*, a perspective from which truth and knowledge are conceived of as personal, private, and subjectively known or intuited; *procedural knowledge*, a position in which women are invested in learning and applying objective procedures for obtaining and communicating knowledge; and *constructed knowledge*, a position in which women view all knowledge as contextual, experience themselves as creators of knowledge, and value both subjective and objective strategies for knowing. (p. 15)

They also distinguish two types of procedural knowing—separate and connected: "When we speak of separate and connected-knowing, we refer not to any sort of relationship between the self and another person but with relationship between knowers and the objects (or subjects) of knowing (which may or may not be persons)" (Belenky et al., 1986, p. 102).

In terms of knowing science, the majority of Americans, both male and female, fall into the first three perspectives on knowledge described by Belenky et al.—silent, received, and subjective knowers. Between 45% and 50% of people (Pion & Lipsey, 1981) think that science and technology have caused some of our problems. A substantial fraction of the population is overwhelmed by science and its methods and feels deaf and dumb in the face of scientific knowledge. For example, an Office of Technology Assessment survey (1987) revealed that only 16% of the U.S. population rates their "own basic understanding of science and technology" as very good; 28% of the U.S. population rates their own understanding of science and technology as poor (OTA, 1987). The jargon of science may have been used to keep people in their places and make them fear questioning anything they hear that is scientific. The extent to which most students, regardless of grades, attempt to avoid science courses represents their fear of science. They seem to feel silenced by the authority of science.

Another considerable fraction of individuals, both male and female, appears to be received knowers. They accept without question and may repeat the information provided by the latest scientific and medical-research findings presented by the scientist or surrogate authority for the scientist. Received knowers may change their life habits (what they eat, medications they give their children, the level of exercise they strive to achieve) without question depending on the latest research findings reported on the evening news. The received knowers constitute the group of health-care consumers who may be overly compliant with physician's instructions. They will continue with medication long after allergic reactions or other adverse side effects become evident. They may request new medications or change their habits based on the latest research findings popularized by the media even if the findings are not relevant to them. They do not have confidence in their own common sense or possess the scientific knowledge to resolve conflicting information and data.

Subjective knowers distrust and may even reject science, its methods and findings. No one really knows what percentage of the American population, both male and female, might fall in this camp. However, 29% of the population rates itself as rather uninterested (11%) or not interested at all (18%) in scientific and technological matters (OTA, 1987).

According to Belenky et al. (1986), the scientific method, with its emphasis on objectivity and distance between observer and object of study, is an example of separate, procedural knowing. As the data collected for *Women's Ways of Knowing* suggest, most college curricula and professors strive for their students to obtain the critical-thinking skills, logical reasoning, and abstract analysis that characterize separate, procedural knowing.

Science as it is taught and practiced in the United States exemplifies this type of knowing. The discomfort of larger numbers of women than men with separate, procedural knowledge may signify one of the reason why fewer women than men are scientists. Considerable research (Keller, 1985) applying feminist theories from psychology such as the work of Chodorow (1978) and Gilligan (1982) explains the selection of individuals who value autonomy, distance, and masculinity as those who feel comfortable in science and succeed in science courses. Feminist philosophers, historians, and scientists have considered the extent to which the mechanistic, objective approach to science that supplanted the hermetic, organic approach of the seventeenth century might be synonymous with a masculine world view (Keller, 1985; Merchant, 1979). Pedagogies that emphasize "connection" rather than separation may be more attractive to women.

Feminist scientists (Fausto-Sterling, 1985; Halpin, 1989; Rosser, 1990) are acutely aware of the predicted shortage of scientists in the United States and that women and people of color are seen as the most likely groups from which the shortage might be filled (OTA, 1987). These facts have pushed us to adopt applications of feminist pedagogies for the purposes of attracting and retaining women in science classrooms. Table 6.1 lists 20 such techniques I have developed and found useful (Rosser, 1990) to attract women to science. Most of these simply represent good teaching techniques; because of this, they often result in more white males, as well as women and men of color, being attracted to science (Kahle, 1985).

TABLE 6.1:   Techniques to Attract Women to Science

1. Expand the kinds of observations beyond those traditionally carried out in scientific research. Women students may see new data that could make a valuable contribution to scientific experiments.

2. Increase the numbers of observations and remain longer in the observational stage of the scientific method. This would provide more hands-on experience with various types of equipment in the laboratory.

3. Incorporate and validate personal experiences women are likely to have had as part of the class discussion or the laboratory exercise.

4. Undertake fewer experiments likely to have applications of direct benefit to the military and propose more experiments to explore problems of social concern.

5. Consider problems that have not been considered worthy of scientific investigation because of the field with which the problem has been traditionally associated.

6. Formulate hypotheses focusing on gender as a crucial part of the question asked.

7. Undertake the investigation of problems of more holistic, global scope rather than the more reduced and limited scale problems traditionally considered.

8. Use a combination of qualitative and quantitative methods in data gathering.

9. Use methods from a variety of fields or interdisciplinary approaches to problem solving.

10. Include females as experimental subjects in experimental designs.

11. Use more interactive methods, thereby shortening the distance between observer and the object being studied.

12. Decrease laboratory exercises in introductory courses in which students must kill animals or render treatment that may be perceived as particularly harsh.

13. Use precise, gender-neutral language in describing data and presenting theories.

14. Be open to critiques of conclusions and theories drawn from observations differing from those drawn by the traditional male scientist from the same observations.

15. Encourage uncovering of other biases such as those of race, class, sexual preference, and religious affiliation that may permeate theories and conclusions drawn from experimental observation.

16. Encourage development of theories and hypotheses that are relational, interdependent, and multicausal rather than hierarchical, reductionistic, and dualistic.

17. Use less competitive models to practice science.

18. Discuss the role of scientist as only one facet that must be smoothly integrated with other aspects of students' lives.

19. Put increased effort into strategies such as teaching and communicating with nonscientists to break down barriers between science and the lay person.

20. Discuss the practical uses to which scientific discoveries are put to help students see science in its social context.

From Rosser, S. V. (1990), *Female Friendly Science*. The Athene Series. New York: Pergamon Press.

The dearth of scientists has also provided feminist biologists with a unique opportunity to communicate feminism to mainstream biologists. Like all scientists, biologists are forced to examine their curricula and pedagogies to make them more attractive and inclusive. Fueled by the fear and necessity engendered by the shortage they are more willing to listen to critiques and new possibilities— including feminism—that fall outside the mainstream. The shortage opens the possibility not only for attracting more women and people of color to science, but it also opens the possibility for changing biology. As more women and people from differing races, classes, and ethnic backgrounds become scientists, the science they evolve is likely to reflect their rich diversity of perspectives.

REFERENCES

American Chemical Society. (1983, November 14). Medalists study charts women chemists' role. *Chemistry and Engineering*, 53.

Ammer, C. (1983). *The A to Z of women's health*. New York: Everest House.

Baker, D. (1983, November). Can the difference between male and female science majors account for the low number of women at the doctoral level in science? *Journal of College Science Teaching*, 102–107.

Belenky, M. F., Clinchy, B. M., Goldberger, N. R., & Tarule, J. M. (1986). *Women's ways of knowing*. New York: Basic Books.

Berryman, S. (1983, November). Who will do science? Minority and female attainment of science and mathematics degrees: Trends and causes. *Rockefeller Foundation Special Report.*

Biology and Gender Study Group. (1989). The importance of feminist critique for contemporary cell biology. In N. Tuana (Ed.), *Feminism and science.* Bloomington and Indianapolis: Indiana University Press.

Birke, L. (1986). *Women, feminism, and biology: The feminist challenge.* New York: Methuen.

Blackwell, A. B. (1976). *The sexes throughout nature.* Westport, CT: Hyperion Press. (Original work published 1875).

Bleier, R. (1979). Social and political bias in science: An examination of animal studies and their generalizations to human behavior and evolution. In R. Hubbard, & M. Lowe (Eds.), *Genes and gender II* (pp. 49-70). Staten Island, NY: Gordian Press.

Bleier, R. (1984). *Science and gender: A critique of biology and its theories on women.* New York: Pergamon Press.

Bleier, R. (1988). *Science* and the construction of meanings in the neurosciences. In S. Rosser (Ed.), *Feminism within the science and health care professions: Overcoming resistance.* Elmsford, NY: Pergamon Press.

Calkins, M. W. (1896). Community of ideas of men and women. *Psychological Review 3*(4), 426–430.

Chodorow, N. (1978). *The reproduction of mothering: Psychoanalysis and the sociology of gender.* Berkeley and Los Angeles: The University of California Press.

Darty, T., & Potter, S. (1984). Lesbians and contemporary health care systems: Oppression and opportunity. In T. Darty & S. Potter (Eds.), *Women identified women.* Palo Alto, CA: Mayfield Publishing Company.

Fausto-Sterling, A. (1985). *Myths of gender.* New York: Basic Books.

Fee, E. (1981). Is feminism a threat to scientific objectivity? *International Journal of Women's Studies, 4*(4), 213–233.

Fee, E. (1982). A feminist critique of scientific objectivity. *Science for the People, 14*(4), 8.

Gilligan, C. (1982). *In a different voice.* Cambridge: Harvard University Press.

Hall, R., & Sandler, B. (1982). *The classroom climate: A chilly one for women?* Washington, DC: Association of American College Project on the Status and Education of Women.

Halpin, Z. T. (1989). Scientific objectivity and the concept of "the other." *Women's Studies International Forum, 12*(13), 285–294.

Hite, S. (1976). *The Hite report: A nationwide study of female sexuality.* New York: Dell.

Hoffman, J. C. (1982). Biorhythms in human reproduction: The not-so-steady states. *Signs: Journal of Women in Culture and Society, 7*(4), 829–844.

Howe, F. (1984). *Myths of coeducation.* Bloomington: Indiana University Press.

Hrdy, S. (1981). *The woman that never evolved.* Cambridge, MA: Harvard University Press.

Hubbard, R. (1979). Have only men evolved? In R. Hubbard, M. S. Henifin, & B. Fried (Eds.), *Women look at biology looking at women.* Cambridge, MA: Schenkman Publishing Co.

Hubbard, R. (1990). *Politics of women's biology.* New Brunswick, NJ: Rutgers University Press.

Kahle, J. (1983). *The disadvantaged majority: Science education for women.* Burlington, NC: Carolina Biological Supply Co.

Kahle, J. (1985). *Women in science.* Philadelphia: Falmer Press.

Keller, E. (1977). The anomaly of a woman in physics. In S. Ruddick & P. Daniels (Eds.), *Working it out.* New York: Pantheon.

Keller, E. (1982). Feminism and science. *Signs: Journal of Women in Culture and Society*, *7*(3), 589–602.

Keller, E. (1983). *A feeling for the organism: The life and work of Barbara McClintock*. New York: W. H. Freeman Co.

Keller, E. F. (1985). *Reflections on gender and science*. New Haven, CT: Yale University Press.

Kuhn, T. S. (1970). *The structure of scientific revolutions*, 2nd ed. Chicago: University of Chicago Press.

Lancaster, J. (1975). *Primate behavior and the emergence of human culture*. New York: Holt, Rinehart, Winston.

Lerner, G. (1975). Placing women in history: A 1975 perspective. *Feminist Studies*, *3*(102), 5–15.

Lowe, M. (1978). Sociobiology and sex differences. *Signs: Journal of Women in Culture and Society*, *4*(1), 118–125.

McIntosh, P. (1984). The study of women: Processes of personal and curricular re-vision. *The Forum for Liberal Education*, *6*(5), 2–4.

Manning, K. (1983). *Black Apollo of science*. Oxford: Oxford University Press.

Martin, E. (1991). The egg and the sperm: How science has constructed a romance based on stereotypical male-female roles. *Signs: Journal of Women in Culture and Society*, *16*(3), 485–501.

Matyas, M. L. (1985). Obstacles and constraints on women in science. In J. B. Kahle (Ed.), *Women in science*. Philadelphia: Falmer Press.

Merchant, C. (1979). *The death of nature: Women, ecology and the scientific revolution*. New York: Harper & Row.

Minnich, E. K. (1982). A feminist critique of the liberal arts. In *Liberal education and the new scholarship on women: Issues and constraints in institutional change* (pp. 22–38). Washington, DC: Association of American Colleges.

National Science Foundation. (1990). *Women and minorities in science and engineering* (NSF 90–301). Washington, DC: Author.

Office of Technology Assessment. (1987). *New developments in biotechnology background paper: Public perceptions of biotechnology* (OTA-BP-BA-45). Washington, DC: Author.

Pion, G. M., & Lipsey, M. W. (1981). Public attitudes toward science and technology: What have the surveys told us? *Public Opinion Quarterly 45*.

Rawls, M., & Fox, J. S. (1978 September 11). Women in academic chemistry find rise to full status difficult. *Chemical and Engineering News. 56*: 26–32; 36.

Rich, A. (1980). Compulsory heterosexuality and lesbian existence. *Signs: Journal of Women in Culture and Society* (Summer).

Rodgers, J. (1973). Rush to surgery. *New York Times Magazine*, 34.

Rose, S. ed. (1982). *Towards a liberatory biology*, New York: Allison and Busby.

Rosser, S. V. (1982). Androgyny and sociobiology. *International Journal of Women's Studies 5*(5), 435–444.

Rosser, S. V. (1985). Feminist perspectives on science: Is reconceptualization possible? *Journal of the National Association for Women Deans, Administrators, and Counselors*, *49*, 29–36.

Rosser, S. V. (1990). *Female friendly science*. New York: Pergamon Press.

Rossiter, M. W. (1982). *Women scientists in America: Struggles and strategies to 1940*. Baltimore: Johns Hopkins University Press.

Sayers, J. (1982). *Biological politics: Feminist and anti-feminist perspectives*. London and New York: Tavistock Publications.

Sayre, A. (1975). *Rosalind Franklin and DNA: A vivid view of what it is like to be a gifted woman in an especially male profession*. New York: W. W. Norton & Co.

Schuster, M., & Van Dyne, S. (1984). Placing women in the liberal arts: Stages of curriculum transformation. *Harvard Educational Review*, *54*(4), 413–428.

Sherfey, M. J. (1973). *The nature and evolution of female sexuality*. New York: Random House.

Star, S. L. (1979). The politics of right and left: Sex differences in hemispheric brain asymmetry. In R. Hubbard, M. S. Henifin, & B. Fried (Eds.), *Women look at biology looking at women*. Boston: Schenkman Publishing Co.

Tetreault, Mary K. (1985). Stages of thinking about women: An experience-derived evaluation model. *Journal of Higher Education, 5*. 368–384.

Thompson (Woolley), H. B. (1903). *The mental traits of sex*. Chicago: The University of Chicago Press.

Vazquez-Calzadar, J. (1973, September). La esterilizacion feminina en Puerto Rico. *Revista de Ciencias Sociales, 17*(3), 281–308.

Vetter, B. (1988). Where are the women in the physical sciences? In S. V. Rosser (Ed.), *Feminism within the science and health care professions: Overcoming resistance*. Elmsford, NY: Pergamon Press.

Vetter, B. (1980, March). Sex discrimination in the halls of science. *Chemical and Engineering News, 58* 37–38.

Watson, J. D. (1969). *The double helix*. New York: Atheneum.

Weisstein, N. (1979). Adventures of a woman in science. In R. Hubbard, M. S. Henifin, & B. Fried (Eds.), *Women look at biology looking at women*. Boston: Schenkman Publishing Co.

Zimmerman, B., et al. (1980). People's science. In R. Arditti, P. Brennan, and S. Cavrak (Eds.), *Science and Liberation* (pp. 299–319). Boston: South End Press.

7.

PRACTICAL APPLICATIONS
OF FEMINISM TO BIOLOGY

As the significance of feminist critiques becomes more widely recognized and dispersed, their influences are felt beyond the curriculum and research of the academy. Providing theoretical frameworks and methods for the examples of hazards noted by activists, feminist critiques and perspectives are beginning to affect public policy and research controls in some areas of biology. Feminism has begun to play a substantial role in policies, funding, and technological development and application in the areas of women's health, reproductive technologies, and the environment. A factor uniting activism in these three areas of biological application is the recognition by feminists of men's domination and control of women's bodies and the earth. Many feminists have felt solidarity with other women and with other species on the earth because of the harmful ways that men have used biology and its technologies to exploit and dominate women's bodies and the ecosystem.

WOMEN'S HEALTH

With the expense of sophisticated equipment, maintenance of laboratory animals and facilities, and salaries for qualified technicians and researchers, virtually no medical research is undertaken today without Federal or foundation support. Gone are the days when individuals had laboratories in their homes or made significant discoveries working in isolation using homemade equipment. In fiscal 1987, the National Institutes of Health (NIH) funded approximately $6.1 billion of research (*Science and Government Report,* 1988). Private foundations and state governments funded a smaller portion of the research (*NSF Science and Engineering Indicators*, 1987).

The choice of problems for study in medical research is substantially determined by a national agenda that defines what is worthy of study through the allocations of funds. As Marxist (Zimmerman, 1980), African-American (McLeod, 1987), and feminist critics (Hubbard, 1983, 1990) of scientific research have pointed out, the scientific research that is undertaken reflects the societal bias towards the powerful who are overwhelmingly white, middle/upper class, and male in the United States. Obviously, the members of Congress who appropriate the funds for NIH and other Federal agencies are overwhelmingly white, middle/upper class, and male, an image reinforced in many women's minds after they viewed the confirmation hearings of Clarence Thomas on TV. They are more likely to vote funds for research that they view as beneficial to health needs, as defined from their perspective.

It may be argued that actual priorities for medical research and allocations of funds are not set by members of Congress but by leaders in medical research who are employees of the NIH or other Federal agencies or who are brought in as consultants. Unfortunately the same descriptors—white, middle/upper class, and male—must be used to characterize the individuals in the theoretical and decision-making positions within the medical hierarchy and scientific establishment.

Women are lacking even at the level of the peer-review committee, which is how NIH determines which of the competitive proposals submitted by researchers in a given area are funded. In the 10 year interval 1975–84, women went from 16.9% of NIH peer-review committee members to only 17.9%; during this time, the total number of members nearly doubled from 733 to 1,264 (Filner, 1982). Because the percentage of female postdoctoral fellows increased by 32% during the same time period, it seems likely that qualified women were available, but not used.

I believe that the results of having a huge preponderance of male leaders setting the priorities for medical research have definite effects on the choice and definition of problems for research.

1.   Hypotheses are not formulated to focus on gender as a crucial part of the question being asked. Because it is clear that many diseases have different frequencies (heart disease, lupus), symptoms (gonorrhea), or complications

(most sexually transmitted diseases) in the two sexes, scientists should routinely consider and test for differences or lack of differences based on gender in any hypothesis being tested. For example, when exploring the metabolism of a particular drug, one should routinely run tests in both males and females. Two dramatic, widely publicized recent examples demonstrate that gender differences are *not* routinely considered as part of the question asked. In a longitudinal study of the effects of cholesterol-lowering drugs, gender differences were not tested as the drug was tested on 3,806 men and no women (Hamilton, 1985). In a similar test of the effects of aspirin on cardiovascular disease, which is now used widely by the pharmaceutical industry to support "taking one aspirin each day to prevent heart attacks," no females were included (Steering Committee of the Physicians Health Study Research Group, 1988). Since estrogen influences cholesterol levels, it is not unreasonable to assume that the studies cannot be directly extrapolated from males to females.

2. Some diseases that affect both sexes are defined as male diseases. Heart disease is the best example of a disease that has been so designated because of the fact that heart disease occurs more frequently in men at younger ages than it does women. Therefore, most of the funding for heart disease has been appropriated for research on predisposing factors for the disease (such as cholesterol level, lack of exercise, stress, smoking, and weight) using white, middle-aged, middle-class males.

    This "male-disease" designation has resulted in very little research being directed toward high-risk groups of women. Heart disease is a leading cause of death in older women (Kirschstein, 1985) who live an average of eight years longer than men (Boston Women's Health Book Collective, 1984). It is also frequent in poor black women who have had several children (Manley, Lin-Fu, Miranda, Noonan, & Parker, 1985). Virtually no research has explored predisposing factors for these groups who fall outside the disease definition established from an androcentric perspective. The male disease descriptor may influence clinical diagnosis, leading to underdiagnosis in women. Studies indicate that (Steingart, Packes, Hamm, Coglianese, Gersh, Geltman, 1991) women had angina before myocardial infarction as frequently and with more debilitating effects than men, yet women are referred for cardiac catheterization only half as often. Recent data indicate that the designation of AIDS as a disease of male homosexuals and drug users has led researchers and health-care practitioners to fail to understand the etiology and diagnosis of AIDS in women (Norwood, 1988).

3. Research on conditions specific to females receives low priority, funding, and prestige. Some examples include dysmenorrhea, incontinency in older women, and nutrition in postmenopausal women. Effects of exercise level and duration on alleviation of menstrual discomfort and length and amount of exposure to VDTs that have resulted in the "cluster pregnancies" of women giving birth to deformed babies in certain industries have also received low priority. In contrast, significant amounts of time and money are expended on clinical research on women's bodies in connection with other

aspects of reproduction. In this century up until the 1970s, considerable attention was devoted to the development of contraceptive devices for females
rather than for males (Cowan, 1980; Dreifus, 1978). Furthermore, substantial clinical research has resulted in increasing medicalization and control of
pregnancy, labor, and childbirth. Feminists have critiqued (Ehrenreich &
English, 1978; Holmes, 1981) the conversion of a normal, natural process
controlled by women into a clinical, and often surgical, procedure controlled
by men. More recently, the new reproductive technologies such as amniocentesis, in-vitro fertilization, and artificial insemination have become a major
focus as means are sought to overcome infertility. Feminists (Arditti, Klein,
& Minden, 1984; Corea & Ince, 1987; Corea, Hamner, Hoskins, Raymond,
Duelli-Klein, and Holmes, 1987) have warned of the extent to which these
technologies place pressure on women to produce the "perfect" child while
placing control in the hands of the male medical establishment.

4. Suggestions of fruitful questions for research based on the personal experi-
    ence of women have also been ignored. In the health-care area, women have
    often reported (and accepted among themselves) experiences that could not
    be documented by scientific experiments or were not accepted as valid by
    the researchers of the day. For decades, dysmenorrhea was attributed by
    most health-care researchers and practitioners to psychological or social
    factors despite the reports from an overwhelming number of women that
    these were monthly experiences in their lives. Only after prostaglandins were
    "discovered" was there widespread acceptance among the male medical
    establishment that this experience reported by women had a biological com-
    ponent (Kirschstein, 1985).

These four types of bias raise ethical issues. Health-care practitioners must
treat the majority of the population, which is female, based on information
gathered from clinical research in which drugs may not have been tested on
females, in which the etiology of the disease in women has not been studied,
and in which women's experience has been ignored.

APPROACHES AND METHODS

1. The scientific community has often failed to include females in animal
    studies in basic research as well as in clinical research unless the research
    centered on controlling the production of children. The reasons for the
    exclusion (cleaner data from males due to lack of interference from estrus
    or menstrual cycles, fear of inducing fetal deformities in pregnant subjects,
    and higher incidence of some diseases in males) are practical when viewed
    from a financial standpoint. However, the exclusion results in drugs that
    have not been adequately tested in women subjects before being marketed
    and lack of information about the etiology of some diseases in women
    (Rosser, 1989). Using the male as the experimental subject not only ignores

the fact that females may respond differently to the variable tested, it may also lead to less accurate models even in the male. Models that *more accurately* simulate functioning complex biological systems may be derived from using female rats as subjects in experiments (Hoffman, 1982).

2. When females have been used as experimental subjects, often they are treated as not fully human. In his attempts to investigate the side effects (Goldzieher, Moses, Averkin, Schell, & Taber, 1971a) nervousness and depression (Goldzieher, Moses, Averkin, Schell, & Taber, 1971b) attributable to oral contraceptives, Goldzieher gave dummy pills to 76 women who sought treatment at a San Antonio clinic to prevent further pregnancies. None of the women was told that she was participating in research or receiving placebos (Cowan, 1980; Veatch, 1971). The women in Goldzieher's study were primarily poor, multiparous, Mexican Americans. Research that raises similar issues about the ethics of informed consent was carried out on poor Puerto Rican women during the initial phases of testing the effectiveness of the pill as a contraceptive (Zimmerman, et. al., 1980).

    Frequently it is difficult to determine whether these women are treated as less than human because of their gender or whether race and class are more significant variables. From the Tuskegee Syphilis Experiment in which the effects of untreated syphilis were studied in 399 men over a period of 40 years (Jones, 1981), it is clear that men who are black and poor may not receive appropriate treatment or information about the experiment in which they are participating. Feminist scholars (Dill, 1983; Ruzek, 1988) have begun to explore the extent to which gender, race, and class become complex, interlocking political variables that may affect access to and quality of health care.

3. Current clinical research sets up a distance between the observer and the human subject being studied. Several feminist philosophers (Haraway, 1978; Harding, 1986; Hein, 1981; Keller, 1985) have characterized this distancing as an androcentric approach. Distance between the observer and experimental subject may be more comfortable for men who are reared to feel more comfortable with autonomy and distance (Keller, 1985) than for women who tend to value relationship and interdependency (Gilligan, 1982).

4. Using only the methods traditional to a particular discipline may result in limited approaches that fail to reveal sufficient information about the problem being explored. This may be a particular difficulty for research surrounding medical problems of pregnancy, childbirth, menstruation, and menopause for which the methods of one discipline are clearly inadequate.

    Methods that cross disciplinary boundaries or include combinations of methods traditionally used in separate fields may provide more appropriate approaches. For example, if the topic of research is occupational exposure that presents a risk to the pregnant woman working in a plant in which toxic chemicals are manufactured, a combination of methods traditionally used in social-science research with methods frequently used in biology and chemistry may be the best approach. Checking the chromosomes of any miscarried fetuses, chemical analysis of placentae after birth, Apgar Scores of the babies at birth, and blood samples of the newborns to determine trace amounts of the toxic chemicals would be appropriate biological and chemical methods used to gather data about the problem. In-depth interviews with women to discuss how they are feeling and any irregularities they detect during each month of the pregnancy, or evaluation using weekly written questionnaires regarding the pregnancy progress are methods more traditionally used in the social sciences for problems of this sort.

Jean Hamilton has called for interactive models that draw on both the social and natural sciences to explain complex problems.

> Particularly for understanding human, gender-related health, we need more interactive and contextual models that address the actual complexity of the phenomenon that is the subject of explanation. One example is the need for more phenomenological definitions of symptoms, along with increased recognition that psychology, behavioral studies, and sociology are among the "basic sciences" for health research. Research on heart disease is one example of a field where it is recognized that both psychological stress and behaviors such as eating and cigarette smoking influence the onset and natural course of a disease process. (1985, vi–62)

Perhaps more women holding decision-making positions in designing and funding clinical research would result in more interdisciplinary research to study issues of women's health care such as menstruation, pregnancy, childbirth, lactation, and menopause. Those complex phenomena fall outside the range of methods of study provided by a sole discipline. The interdisciplinary approaches developed to solve these problems might then be applied to other complex problems to benefit all health-care consumers, both male and female.

THEORIES AND CONCLUSIONS DRAWN FROM THE RESEARCH

The rationale that is traditionally presented in support of the "objective" methods is that they prevent bias. Emphasis on traditional disciplinary approaches that are quantitative and maintain the distance between observer and experimental subject supposedly remove the bias of the researcher. Ironically, to the extent that these "objective" approaches are in fact synonymous with a masculine approach to the world, they may introduce bias. Specifically, androcentric bias may permeate the theories and conclusions drawn from the research in several ways as discussed below:

1. First, theories may be presented in androcentric language. Much feminist scholarship has focused on problems of sexism in language and the extent

to which patriarchal language has excluded and limited women (Kramarae & Treichler, 1986; Lakoff, 1975; Thorne, 1979). Sexist language is a symptom of underlying sexism, but language also shapes our concepts and provides the framework through which we express our ideas. The awareness of sexism and the limitations of a patriarchal language that feminist researchers have might allow them to describe their observations in less gender-biased terms.

An awareness of language should aid experimenters in avoiding the use of terms such as "tomboyism" (Money & Erhardt, 1972), "aggression," and "hysteria" that reflect assumptions about gender-appropriate behavior (Hamilton, 1985) that permeate behavioral descriptions in clinical research. The limited research on AIDS in women focuses on women as prostitutes or mothers. Describing the woman as a vector for transmission to men (prostitute) or the fetus (mother) has produced little information on the progress of the AIDS disease in women themselves (Rosser, 1991). Once the bias in the terminology is exposed, the next step is to ask whether that terminology leads to a constraint or bias in the theory itself.

2. An androcentric perspective may lead to formulating theories and conclusions drawn from medical research to support the status quo of inequality for women and other oppressed groups. Building on their awareness of these biases, women scientists have critiqued the studies of brain–hormone interaction (Bleier 1984) for their biological determinism used to justify women's socially inferior position. Perhaps male researchers are less likely to see flaws in and question biologically deterministic theories that provide scientific justification for men's superior status in society because they as men gain social power and status from such theories. Researchers from outside the mainstream (women, for example) are much more likely to be critical of such theories because they lose power from those theories. In order to eliminate bias, the community of scientists undertaking clinical research needs to include individuals from backgrounds of as much variety and diversity as possible with regard to race, class, gender, and sexual orientation (Rosser, 1988). Only then is it likely that the perspective of one group will bias research design, approaches, subjects, and interpretations.

HINTS OF REVISIONING

Some changes in clinical research have come about because of the recognition of flaws and ethical problems for women. Some of the changes are the result of critiques made by feminists and women scientists; some of the changes have been initiated by men.

1. The rise of the women's health movement in the 1970s encouraged women to question established medical authority, take responsibility for their own bodies (Boston Women's Health Book Collective, 1984; Cowan, 1980), and

express new demands for clinical research and for access to health care. Feminist demands have led to increased availability of health-related information to women consumers. Litigation and Federal affirmative-action programs have resulted in an increase from about 6% to about 40% of women medical students from 1960 to present (Altekruse & Rosser, 1992). Consumer complaints and suggestions have fostered minor reforms in obstetrical care. The decor, ambiance, and regimens of birthing facilities have improved to provide personal and psychological support for the mother and to promote infant–parent bonding. However, concurrent with modest obstetrical modifications in hospitals, nurse midwives in most states have felt the backlash of professional efforts to control their practice and licensure status (Altekruse & Rosser, 1992). Efforts to increase the understanding of the biology of birth and translate that knowledge into clinical care expressed as acceptable infant mortality rates remain inadequate.

2. Guidelines have been developed that require any research project that is Federally funded to ensure humane treatment of human subjects and fully informed consent. The impetus for the formation of the National Commission for the Protection of Human Subjects of Biomedical and Behavioral Research was the revelation of the abuses of human subjects during the Nuremberg War Crimes Trials and the Tuskegee Syphilis Experiments (*Belmont Report*, 1978). However, the attention drawn by men such as Veatch (1971) to unethical issues surrounding the testing of oral contraceptives in women helped to ensure that women, especially pregnant women, were given particular consideration in the papers forming the basis of the Belmont Report (Levine, 1978).

3. In recent years U.S. government agencies have shown increased sensitivity to clinical research surrounding women's health issues and the difficult ethical issues of including women in pharamacological research. The Public Health Service (PHS) Task Force on Women's Health Issues was commissioned to aid the PHS "as the agency works within its areas of jurisdiction and expertise to improve the health and well-being of women in the United States" (U.S. Department of Health and Human Services, 1985). In her insightful commissioned paper "Avoiding Methodological and Policy-Making Biases in Gender-Related Health Research" for the Report to the Task Force, Jean Hamilton makes strong recommendations:

PHS consensus-development conference on "Gender-related Methods for Health Research" (for the development of guidelines) should be held. . . . The feasibility of including women in certain types of research needs to be reexamined. . . . A number of working-groups should be formed: A working-group to reconsider the difficult ethical issues of including women in pharmacological research (e.g., extra-protection for women as research subjects, versus other means for informed consent). . . . A working-group to identify and to consider mechanisms to enhance the kind of multi-center, *collaborative or clinical research center* studies that would be most efficient in advancing our understanding of women and their health. . . . A working-group or committee to consider ways to foster subject-selection in a way that allows for an examination of possible age, sex, and hormonal status effects. (Hamilton, 1985, iv–63–64)

Bernadine Healy, the recently appointed Director of the National Institutes of Health, has made a major commitment to research on women's health and illness, including the establishment of The Women's Health Initiative and the Office of Research on Women's Health (Healy, 1991a, 1991b).

4.   Some attempts at patient involvement in research design and implementation have provided a mechanism to shorten the distance between the observer and subjects observed. Elizabeth Fee describes an account of occupational health research in an Italian factory.

Prior to 1969, occupational health research was done by specialists who would be asked by management to investigate a potential problem in the factory. . . . The procedure was rigorously objective, the results were submitted to management. The workers were the individualized and passive objects of this kind of research. In 1969, however, when workers' committees were established in the factories, they refused to allow this type of investigation. . . . Occupational health specialists had to discuss the ideas and procedures of research with workers' assemblies and see their "objective" expertise measured against the "subjective" experience of the workers. The mutual validation of data took place by testing in terms of the workers' experience of reality and not simply by statistical methods; the subjectivity of the workers' experience was involved at each level in the definition of the problem, the method of research, and the evaluation of solutions. Their collective experience was understood to be much more than the statistical combination of individual data; the workers had become the active subjects of research, involved in the production, evaluation, and uses of the knowledge relating to their own experience. (1983, p. 24)

Replacing the androcentrism in the practice of medical research and the androcentric bias in the questions asked, methods used, theories and conclusions drawn from data gathered with a feminist approach represents a major change with profound ethical implications. Lynda Birke, a feminist scientist, suggests that feminism will change science and medicine from research that is oppressive to women and potentially destructive to a liberating system with improvement for everyone.

Perhaps this discussion of creating a feminist science seems hopelessly utopian. Perhaps. But feminism is, above all else, about wanting and working for change, change towards a better society in which women of all kinds are not devalued, or oppressed in any way. Working for change has to include changing science, which not only perpetuates our oppression at present, but threatens also to destroy humanity and all the other species with whom we share this earth. (Birke, 1986, p. 171)

REPRODUCTION AND REPRODUCTIVE TECHNOLOGIES

Reproduction is an aspect of women's health of particular concern to feminists. As previously suggested, considerable resources and attention are devoted to women's health issues which permit men to have more control over the production of children. The new reproductive technologies have been critiqued by feminists because of their potential physical and psychological health risks for women and because they provide men with more control over reproduction. The pervasiveness, risk to health, and escalating costs of these new technologies have led feminists to develop entire journals such as *Reproductive and Genetic Engineering: Journal of International Feminist Analysis* and write numerous books, for example, *The Mother Machine* (Corea, 1985), and *Test-tube Women* (Arditti, & Minden, Klein, 1984), which examine the pitfalls of these technologies for women's health and their implications for exacerbating racism, classism, homophobia, and difficulties for the physically challenged in our society.

> What we have is patriarchal rear-hegemony of technology, information, medicine and facilities affecting female reproduction. And who exactly are these men who dominate female reproductive lives? They are males raised, as we all have been, in a society steeped deep in woman-hatred. Only these men have unique on-the-job opportunities to act out their misogyny. (Dreifus, 1977, xix)

This quotation comes from the Introduction to *Seizing Our Bodies*, which was written in 1977. Since that time, even more technologies have been invented, which are imposed more frequently, even routinely, on women's reproductive lives.

In our society, the technologies are not only based in androcentric scientific theories, but the control of those technologies is also primarily in the hands of men (Albury, 1984). An evaluation of these technologies from a feminist perspective is essential, because they represent very powerful tools in the continued struggle for domination and control over women's bodies.

The source of men's desire for this control is unclear. Some sociologists (Levi-Strauss, 1969) have suggested that the desire comes from men's jealousy over women's ability to bear children and their view that marriage is a contract between *men*, in which there is a formalized exchange of women as commodities. Sociobiologists, arguing from the perspective of men's insecurity about paternity, would agree that once men's minor role in reproduction (contribution of the sperm) was understood, men set up all sorts of legal and social conditions to ensure that the child whom they might be protecting or supporting in some way was genetically theirs (Daly & Wilson, 1978). Brownmiller (1975) suggests that women accepted some of these sociolegal arrangements, such as monogamy and marriage, as a trade-off for protection against being raped by more than one man. Whatever its sources, in patriarchal societies women (and their offspring) are viewed as the property of the men.

In the past and at present in other countries, men often controlled the sexuality and reproduction of their "property" through physical as well as social and legal means: chastity belts (Davis, 1971), foot-binding (Daly, 1978), and clitoridectomy (still common today in many Moslem countries) (Hosken, 1976). In the United States today, forced sterilizations (CARASA, 1979), hysterectomies performed too frequently (Centers for Disease Control, 1980), lack of Medicaid funding for abortion, threatened loss of legal abortion, and denial of access to lesbians for artificial insemination (Hornstein, 1984) are simply examples of the ways women's sexuality and reproduction are regulated by the medical establishment. Not coincidentally, the medical establishment, particularly the decision-making portion dealing with women's reproduction, is strongly dominated by men.

The history of gynecology in the United States has shown a distinct pattern of takeover and control of the childbirth and reproductive procedures by male doctors from female midwives, from the mid-nineteenth century (Ehrenreich & English, 1978; Wertz & Wertz, 1979) to the present time. Considering this history and the current abuses, can we expect that the new reproductive technologies, developed and controlled by a scientific and medical establishment dominated by men, will be completely positive for women? Technologies such as amniocentesis, chorionic villi biopsy, artificial insemination, and in-vitro fertilization are heralded by the media as "liberating" women. They permit women who are older, who do not wish to have intercourse, or who have blocked oviducts to bear children. However, on closer examination, each of these new technologies also has an oppressive side; each may also be used in a way to control or limit women's sexuality or reproductive access. Amniocentesis and chorionic villi biopsy may be used to abort a child of an unwanted sex, usually female (Hoskins & Holmes, 1984; Hubbard, 1990; Roggencamp, 1984). In most localities, artificial insemination is denied women who are unmarried or open about their lesbianism (Hornstein, 1984; Hubbard, 1990). In-vitro fertilization is very expensive, $5000 per insemination with a 23% chance of success, and available only to married couples (Gold, 1991).

As with most technologies, intrinsically the new reproductive technologies are neither good nor bad; it is the way they are used that determines their potential for benefit or harm. The androcentric scientific and medical establishment creates and controls these technologies. Using our biological and medical knowledge, we must evaluate them from a feminist perspective to begin to appreciate the full implications of these technologies for women before we can assess their benefits or hazards.

The example of amniocentesis provides an opportunity to examine positive and negative aspects of the technique for women. The technology's benefits include the ability to detect some 70 abnormalities including Trisomy 21, Edwards' Syndrome, and spina bifida (Ritchie, 1984), and to provide peace of mind during the latter half of the pregnancy based on the assumption that no genetic defects are present in the fetus, providing the test has been accurately administered, cultured, and read. Some of its risks include 1.0%–1.5% increased chance of miscarriage or fetal abnormalities, like clubfoot or dislocated hip, breathing difficulties at birth, and Rh sensitization (Ritchie, 1984); necessity of a second trimester abortion if the woman wishes to terminate the pregnancy after learning the results; the physical discomfort of the procedure; psychological discomfort of waiting three to four weeks for the results; and a false sense of security fostered by the assumption that most "defects" may be detected by the procedure when developmental and other nongenetic defects cannot. When the amniocentesis is considered from the perspectives of class and religion, it is restricted mostly to middle-class women whose religious background has limited sanctions against abortion. The issue of amniocentesis raises questions about what it means to be labelled *abnormal* or defective in our society and about who decides who is "normal," therefore worthy of life, and who is "abnormal," and should be aborted. Women of color have pointed out that other tests of normality (IQ) have often been used to screen out nonwhites and represent people of color as inferior (Chase, 1980). This point becomes even clearer when looking at international data. In India (Chacko, 1982; Roggencamp, 1984), China (Campbell, 1976), and probably in some clinics in the United States (Hubbard, 1990; Roggencamp, 1984), amniocentesis is used to abort fetuses who are female. All women react strongly to the fact that this reproductive technology may be used to define who is worthy of living, and that in many cases, this decision would exclude women. Thus, the technology that has been represented by the media and medical profession as a benefit to women, that allows women to delay childbearing and still guarantee a healthy baby, may also be used to enforce societal restrictions on physical and mental norms and even limit women in subsequent generations.

Men in patriarchal societies have used a variety of means to control the sexuality of women and their offspring, who the men view as their property. An examination of access to contraception and abortion and the statistics regarding sterilization reveal the medical means by which the sexuality of heterosexual women is manipulated. Women have fought hard for their reproductive rights: choice of contraception, abortion, and sterilization. However, access to and control of these procedures is in the hands of men, which means that the procedures may also be used to manipulate women's sexuality. The recent Supreme Court decision (*Rust v. Sullivan*, 1991) preventing health-care personnel (recently modified to exempt physicians) from providing information on abortion to women receiving care in Federally funded clinics serves as a dramatic example of such manipulation.

Most of the new reproductive technologies have been developed to control conception and infertility in a woman's reproductive life. For some individual women these technologies may be liberating; they permit women to have children who cannot conceive due to blocked oviducts or who do not wish to have intercourse. However, these technologies are often limited only to married women in order to produce "perfect" offspring, indicating that their usage may be oppressive. The scientists who developed the technologies describe the women contributing the eggs for in-vitro fertilization as *egg farms* and *egg factories* (Murphy, 1984). They envision a day when, through a combination of supraovulation, in-vitro fertilization, sex selection, and artificial wombs, women need only be a small percentage of the population (Klein, 1989; Postgate, 1973), which makes evident some scientists' plans for use of these technologies.

The future development of artificial wombs may free women from pregnancy and permit the development of healthy offspring. As envisioned by Shulamith Firestone in her utopian feminist fantasy (1970), this would only bring about a better world if men were not using the technology to eliminate women and other "defectives."

The current use of surrogate mothers has become a clear way in which women's bodies are used to produce the property of men (Ince, 1984). The new technologies that currently permit women to increase the chances of having healthy babies place extreme pressure on the individual woman to produce a "perfect piece of property" (Hubbard, 1990). The information now available about the effects of alcohol, drugs, smoking, disease, and nutrition during pregnancy and the availability of amniocentesis and chorionic villi biopsy place on individual women the guilt of bearing a child with a "defect." By placing the burden of guilt on individual women, men and society lose sight of their responsibility to care for these children. Although the vast majority of physical and mental disabilities are not due to diseases or abnormalities detectable by amniocentesis or to the maternal environment during pregnancy, the current trend leaves people with the impression that they are. Therefore, society as a whole feels that the woman is responsible for "producing" (or failing to abort) this "defective" child, and so must care for it (Hubbard, 1990). At the same time funding is reduced for nutritional needs and prenatal care for poor women, despite evidence demonstrating the role of poor nutrition and lack of care in producing defective children.

Childbirth is an area in which the male scientific and medical establishments have developed and used technologies for over a century. Some of these technologies have greatly benefitted women in their potential to save the lives of both mothers and babies. Once again, the difficulty is in the control and overuse of these technologies by the medical profession to speed normal deliveries, make money, and enhance hospital procedure at the cost of a normal delivery by women who might not have needed medical intervention.

The medical profession's use of technology in menopausal and aging women further demonstrates the desire of men to control women's sexuality and reproduction. Many doctors advise women past childbearing age to agree to removal of the uterus, as it has the potential to become cancerous (Taylor, 1979). Do doctors ever suggest removing the prostate in men because it too has the potential—much higher than the uterus—to become cancerous?

Although the advantages and disadvantages of hormone-replacement therapy to a woman's health are still being explored, the pharmaceutical ads in medical journals appeal to physicians to put their patients on hormone-replacement therapy to keep the woman looking young. Little study has been undertaken to evaluate alternatives to estrogen that would reduce osteoporosis. The implication is that, with aging as with other aspects of women's health, women's bodies are manipulated to conform to the standards of society regarding sexuality and reproduction.

ECOFEMINISM

Recently, feminists have begun to decry the commercial interests and the scientific enterprise that sell biotechnologies as cures for world hunger and infertility while masking the environmental ravages that result in crop failures in third-world countries and reduced fertility in developed countries. Feminists trained in environmental protection such as Patricia Hynes (1989) reveal biotechnologies to be the latest technical turnkeys that exploit nature and women for the benefit of men.

Hynes points out the shocking fact that because of the work of Rachel Carson (1962) nature now holds superior standing legislatively compared to women's bodies. On the groundwork laid by Carson for nature-centered environmental protection, Hynes builds a health-centered system for protection of women for the new reproductive technologies. ''The ethical questions raised about the new reproductive technologies have been centered on the embryo and 'respect for human life,' not the life of the woman. I will draw from the principles of environmental protection inspired by *Silent Spring* to make recommendations for policy on the new reproductive technologies and the protection of women in the work place which is centered on women's right to self-defined, not fetal-defined, fertility-defined, nor male-defined, existence'' (1989, p. 26).

The ecofeminist movement provides an explicit outlet for women to recognize their unity with other species and to seek to prevent their joint exploitation and control by men. Feminists suggest critiques of science (Birke, 1986; Bleier, 1984; Keller, 1985, 1987) and use of feminist interdisciplinary (Rosser, 1989), holistic (Hubbard, 1983), and qualitative methods (Harding, 1986) as more humane approaches to science and the environment. Keller (1983) and Goodfield (1981) discuss the ways in which women scientists shorten the distance between themselves as the observer and their object of study, suggesting that their relationship with their experimental subject makes them less likely to exploit or harm that subject.

Other feminists in science (Hamilton, 1985; Lancaster, 1975) have revealed the hidden ''male-as-norm'' research protocol that has led to women's routine exclusion as experimental subjects in drug trials and in testing of effects of hazardous materials such as pesticides and radioactive nuclear waste. Based on the recognition of the biological reality that pregnant women and their offspring may be particularly sensitive to teratogenic effects of such drugs and materials and not wishing to run the risk of a pregnant woman inadvertently being tested, the initial impetus for such exclusionary protocols was protective. However, the reality is that these drugs and materials are then used without ever having been tested on women.

Feminists have delineated the extent to which interdisciplinary approaches and combinations of qualitative and quantitative methods are more appropriate to study important questions in women's health in areas such as childbirth, pregnancy, and menopause (Hamilton, 1985; Rosser, 1989). These interdisciplinary and combinations of qualitative and quantitative methods typically also provide the most fruitful information for solutions to environmental problems. As Hynes (1984, 1989) points out, (see chapter 3) many of the classic tests used in ecology were developed by women.

All of the feminists who critique science call for a consideration of the potential use of the research and its possible social and environmental effects as part of the determination of whether or not the research should be undertaken (Birke, 1986; Bleier, 1984; Fausto-Sterling, 1985; Hubbard, 1983; Rosser, 1988). These writers claim that the division between basic and applied should be blurred and research that is militaristic, destructive, and exploitative of the environment and certain groups of people, should not be permitted. As Bleier states, ''it would aim to eliminate research that leads to the exploitation and destruction of nature, the destruction of the human race and other species, and that justifies the oppression of people because of race, gender, class, sexuality, or nationality'' (1986, p. 16). In this sense both ecologists and feminists share the same commitment to political and social action based on their principles.

The science of ecology and the ecological movement stress the necessity for human beings to see themselves as part of the holistic environment. Ecology sees all life and all species (including human beings) as part of an interconnected web. Relationship and mutual interdependence with other species rather than separation, hierarchy, and domination are emphasized in ecological theory and particularly in ecofeminism (Davis, 1988).

REFERENCES

Albury, R. (1984). Who owns the embryo? In R. Arditti, R. Duelli Klein, & S. Minden (Eds.), *Test-tube women* (pp. 54–67). London: Pandora Press.

Altekruse, J., & Rosser, S. V. (1992). "Feminism and Medicine." In D. Kramerae & C. Spender (Eds.), *Knowledge explosion: Generations of Feminist Scholarship*. New York: Teachers College Press.

Arditti, R., Duelli Klein, R., & Minden, S. (1984). *Test-tube women: What future for motherhood*? London: Pandora Press.

Belmont Report. (1978). Washington, DC: Department of Health Education and Welfare. (Publication No. OS 78–0012).

Birke, L. (1986). *Women, feminism, and biology*. New York: Methuen.

Bleier, R. (1984). *Science and gender: A critique of biology and its theories on women*. New York: Pergamon Press.

Bleier, R. (1986). Sex differences research: Science or belief? In R. Bleier (Ed.), *Feminist approaches to science*. New York: Pergamon Press.

Boston Women's Health Book Collective. (1984). *The new our bodies, ourselves*. New York: Simon & Schuster.

Brownmiller, S. (1975). *Against our will: Men, women & rape*. New York: Simon & Schuster.

Campbell, C. (1976). "The manchild pill." *Psychology Today* (August): 86–91.

CARASA (Committee for Abortion Rights and Against Sterilization Abuse). (1979). *Women under attack: Abortion, sterilization and reproductive freedom*. New York: Author.

Carson, R. (1962). *Silent spring*. New York: Fawcett Press.

Centers for Disease Control. (1980). *Surgical sterilization surveillance: Hysterectomy in women aged 15–44, from 1970–1975*. Atlanta, GA: CDC.

Chacko, A. (1982, November). Too many daughters? India's drastic cure. *World Paper*, 8–9.

Chase, A. (1980). *The legacy of Malthus*. Urbana: University of Illinois Press.

Chodorow, N. (1978). *The reproduction of mothering*. Berkeley: University of California Press.

Corea, G. (1985). *The mother machine: Reproductive technologies from artificial insemination to artificial wombs*. New York: Harper & Row.

Corea, G., Hamner J., Hoskins, B., Raymond, J., Duelli Klein, R., Holmes, H. B., Keshwar, M., Rowland, R., Steinbacker, R., (Eds.). (1987). *Man-made women: How new reproductive technologies affect women*. Bloomington: Indiana University Press.

Corea, G., & Ince, S. (1987). Report of a survey of IVG clinics in the USC. In P. Spallone & D. L. Steinberg (Eds.), *Made to order: The myth of reproductive and genetic progress*. Oxford: Pergamon Press.

Cowan, B. (1980). Ethical problems in government-funded contraceptive research. In H. Holmes, B. Hoskins, & M. Gross (Eds.), *Birth control and controlling birth: Women-centered perspectives* (pp. 37–46). Clifton, NJ: Humana Press.

Daly, M. (1978). *GynEcology: The metaethics of radical feminism*. Boston: Beacon Press.

Daly, M., & Wilson, M. (1978). *Sex, evolution and behavior*. North Scituate, MA: Duxbury Press.

Davies, K. (1988, Spring). What is ecofeminism? *Women and Environments, 10*, 4–6.

Davis, E. G. (1971). *The first sex*. New York: G. P. Putnam.

Dill, B. T. (1983). Race, class and gender: Prospects for an all-inclusive sisterhood. *Feminist Studies, 9*: 1.

Dreifus, C. (1977). *Seizing our bodies*. New York: Vintage Books.

Ehrenreich, B., & English, D. (1978). *For her own good*. New York: Anchor Press.

Fausto-Sterling, A. (1985). *Myths of gender*. New York: Basic Books.

Fee, E. (1983). Women's nature and scientific objectivity. In M. Lowe & R. Hubbard (Eds.), *Woman's nature, rationalizations of inequality*. New York: Pergamon Press.

Filner, B. (1982, July/August). President's remarks. *AWIS; XV*(4).

Firestone, S. (1970). *The dialectic of sex*. New York: Morrow.

Gilligan, C. (1982). *In a different voice: Psychological theory and women's development*. Cambridge, MA: Harvard University Press.

Gold, M. (1985). The baby makers. *Science, 85 6* (3): 26–38.

Goldzieher, J. W., Moses, L., Averkin, E., Scheel, C., & Taber B., (1971a). A placebo-controlled double-blind crossover investigation of the side effects attributed to oral contraceptives. *Fertility and Sterility, 22* (9), 609–623.

Goldzieher, J. W., Moses, L., Averkin, E., Scheel, C., & Taber, B. (1971b). Nervousness and depression attributed to oral contraceptives: A double-blind, placebo-controlled study. *American Journal of Obstetrics and Gynecology, 22*, 1013–1020.

Goodfield, J. (1981). *An imagined world*. New York: Penguin Books.

Hamilton, J. (1985). Avoiding methodological biases in gender-related research. In *Women's health report of the public health service task force on women's health issues*. Washington, DC: U.S. Dept. of Health and Human Service Public Service.

Haraway, D. (1978). Animal sociology and a natural economy of the body politic, Part I: A political physiology of dominance; and animal sociology and a natural economy of the body politic, Part II: The past is the contested zone: Human nature and theories of production and reproduction in primate behavior studies. *Signs: Journal of Women in Culture and Society, 4* (1); 21–60.

Harding, S. (1986). *The science question in feminism*. Ithaca, NY: Cornell University Press.

Healy, B. (1991a). Women's health, public welfare. *Journal of the American Medical Association, 264* (4); 566–568.

Healy, B. (1991a). The Yentl Syndrome. *New England Journal of Medicine, 325* (4); 274–276.

Hein, H. (1981). Women and science: Fitting men to think about nature. *International Journal of Women's Studies, 4*l; 369–377.

Hoffman. J. C. (1982). Biorhythms in human reproduction: The not-so-steady states. *Signs: Journal of Women in Culture and Society, 7* (4); 829–844.

Holmes, H. B. (1981). Reproductive technologies: The birth of a women-centered analysis. In H. B. Holmes, *et al*, (Eds.), *The custom-made child?* NJ: Humana Press.

Holmes, H. B., Hoskins, B. B., & Gross, M. (1980). *Birth control and controlling birth: Women-centered perspectives.* Clifton, NJ: Humana Press.

Hornstein, F. (1984). Children by donor insemination: A new choice for lesbians. In R. Arditti, R. Duelli Klein, & S. Minden (Eds.), *Test-tube women* (pp. 373–381). London: Pandora Press.

Hosken, F. P. (1976). *WIN News, II* 3.

Hoskins, B., & H. Holmes. (1984). Technology and prenatal femicide. In R. Arditti, R. Duelli Klein, & S. Minden (Eds.), *Test-tube women* (pp. 237–255). London: Pandora Press.

Hubbard, R. (1983). Social effects of some contemporary myths about women. In M. Lowe & R. Hubbard (Eds.), *Woman's nature: Rationalizations of inequality.* New York: Pergamon Press.

Hubbard, R. (1990). *The politics of women's biology.* New Brunswick, NJ: Rutgers University Press.

Hynes, H. P. (1984, November-December). Women working: A field report. *Technology Review*, 37.

Hynes, H. P. (1989). *The recurring silent spring.* Elmsford, NY: Pergamon Press.

Ince, S. (1984). Inside the surrogate industry. In R. Arditti, R. Duelli Klein, & S. Minden (Eds.), *Test-tube women* (pp. 99–116). London: Pandora Press.

Jones, J. H. (1981). *Bad blood: The Tuskegee syphilis experiment.* New York: Free Press.

Keller, E. F. (1983). *A feeling for the organism: The life and work of Barbara McClintock.* New York: W. H. Freeman.

Keller, E. F. (1985). *Reflections on gender and science.* New Haven, CT: Yale University Press.

Keller, E. F. (1987). Women scientists and feminist critics of science. *Daedalus, 116*, 77–91.

Kirschstein, R. L. (1985). *Women's health: Report of the public health service task force on women's health issues.* Vol. 2. Washington, DC: U.S. Dept. of Health and Human Services Public Health Service.

Klein, R. D. (1989). *Infertility.* London: Pandora Press.

Kramarae, C., & Treichler, P. (1986). *A feminist dictionary.* London: Pandora Press.

Lakoff, R. (1975). *Language and woman's place.* New York: Harper & Row.

Lancaster, J. (1975). *Primate behavior and the emergence of human culture.* New York: Holt, Reinhart and Winston.

Levi-Strauss, C. (1969). *The elementary structures of kinship.* Boston: Beacon Press.

Levine, R. J. (1978). The nature and definition of informed consent. *The Belmont Report: Ethical principles and guidelines for the protection of human subjects of research.* Appendix 1. (DHEW Publication No. OS 78–0013.)

Levine, R. J. (1986). *Ethics and regulation of clinical research.* (2nd ed.). Baltimore: Urban and Schwarzenberg.

McLeod, S. (1987). *Scientific colonialism: A cross-cultural comparison.* Washington, DC: Smithsonian Institution Press.

Manley, A., Lin-Fu, J., Miranda, M., Noonan, A., & Parker, T. (1985). Special health concerns of ethnic minority women in women's health. *Report of the public health service task force on women's health issues.* Washington, DC: U.S. Dept. of Health and Human Services.

Merchant, C. (1979). *The death of nature: Women, ecology and the scientific revolution.* New York: Harper & Row.

Money, J., & Erhardt, A. (1972). *Man and woman, boy and girl.* Baltimore: Johns Hopkins University Press.

Murphy, J. (1984). Egg farming and women's future. In R. Arditti, R. Duelli Klein, & S. Minden (Eds.), *Test-tube women* (pp. 68–75). London: Pandora Press.

National Science Foundation. (1986). *Report on women and minorities in science and engineering*. Washington, DC: Author.

National Science Foundation Science and Engineering Indicators. (1987). Washington, DC: Author (NSB-1, Appendix Table 4–10).

Norwood, C. (1988, July). *Alarming rise in deaths. Ms.*, 65–67.

Postgate, J. (1973). Bat's chance in hell. *New Scientist, 5*: 11–16.

Ritchie, M. (1984). Taking the initiative: Information versus technology in pregnancy. In R. Arditti, R. Duelli Klein, & S. Minden (Eds.), *Test-tube women* (pp. 402–413). London: Pandora Press.

Roggencamp, V. (1984). Abortion of a special kind: Male sex selection in India. In R. Arditti, R. Duelli Klein, & S. Minden (Eds.), *Test-tube women* (266–278). London: Pandora Press.

Rosser, S. V. (1988). Women in science and health care: A gender at risk. In S. V. Rosser (Ed.), *Feminism within the science of health care professions: Overcoming resistance*. Elmsford, NY: Pergamon Press.

Rosser, S. V. (1989). "Revisioning Clinical Research: Gender and the Ethics of Experimental Design" *Hypatia 4* (2): 125–139.

Rosser, S. V. (1989). Teaching techniques to attract women to science. *Women's Studies International Forum, 12*(3), 363–378.

Rosser, S. V. (1991). AIDS and women. *AIDS Education and Prevention, 3*(3); 230–240.

Rust v. Sullivan (1991).

Ruzek, S. (1988). *Women's health: Sisterhood is powerful, but so are race and class.* Keynote address delivered at Southeast Women's Studies Association Annual Conference, February 27 at University of North Carolina-Chapel Hill.

Science and Government Report. (1988). Washington, DC, March 1, 18 (4): 1. Steering Committee of the Physician's Health Study Research Group. 1988. *Special report: Preliminary report of findings from the aspirin component of the ongoing physician's health study. New England Journal of Medicine 318*, 4, 262–264.

Steingart, R. M., Packer, M., Hamm, P., Coglianese, M. E., Gersh, B., Geltman, E. M et al. (1991). Sex differences in the management of coronary artery disease. *New England Journal of Medicine, 325*; 226–230.

Taylor, R. (1979). *Medicine out of control*. Melbourne: Sun Books.

Thorne, B. (1979). *Claiming verbal space: Women, speech and language in college classrooms*. Paper presented at the Research Conference on Educational Environments and the Undergraduate Women, September 13–15, Wellesley, MA: Wellesley College.

US Department of Health and Human Services. (1985). *Women's health: Report of the Public Health Service Task Force on Women's Issues*. Vol. 2. Washington, DC: Public Health Service.

Veatch, R. M. (1971). *Experimental pregnancy*. Hastings Center report. 1: 2–3.

Wertz, R. W., & Wertz, D. (1979). *Lying-in*. New York: Schocken

Zimmerman, B. *et al.* (1980). People's science. In R. Arditti, P. Brennan, & S. Cavrak (Eds.), *Science and Liberation* (pp. 299–319). Boston: South End Press.

8.

A LOOK TOWARDS
THE FUTURE:
THE INFLUENCE OF
BIOLOGY ON FEMINISM

In this volume I have attempted to examine feminism and biology. As a branch of science, biology has been defined as a masculine pursuit (Keller, 1982; 1985; Hein, 1981; Haraway, 1978) in that historically and at the present time, more men than women have been trained as biologists. The male predominance in the profession has resulted in a biology that reflects a masculine world view that has suffered from androcentric biases.

In recent times substantial numbers of women have entered biology. Biology now includes more women than any other physical or natural science, although the overwhelming majority of biologists are still men. A small number of the women in biology were or became feminists. For almost two decades these feminists have used the lens of gender to critique the extent to which androcentric bias has distorted the theory and practice of science. They have developed substantial feminist critiques focused on the organismal level, particularly in the subdisciplines of evolutionary biology, animal behavior, and ecology. For the cellular and molecular levels of biology, in the subdisciplines of developmental biology, endocrinology, cell biology, and the neurosciences the critiques are less well developed but are evolving. Feminist biologists are also evolving new approaches and methods for biological research that are grounded in feminist theory; in turn these methods may result in new theories and conclusions drawn

152

from data. These critiques and methodologies have begun to transform curricular content and pedagogy in the biology classroom. They have also started to have an impact on public policy and research funding and applications, particularly as activists recognize male domination and exploitation of both women and the environment.

Most of the material in this volume has dealt with the effect of feminism on biology. In my opinion, this accurately represents the relationship between feminism and biology at the present time. We are primarily at the stage of feminist critiques and transformations of the discipline. Very little has emerged from biology that is used to critique or transform feminist theories and methodologies. In this respect, biology has had much less influence than many of the disciplines in the humanities and social sciences on feminism.

Recognizing the contributions of other disciplines to feminism and the original importance of women's health and environmental issues to feminism, it seems likely that the discipline of biology eventually will contribute substantially to feminism. I would like to conclude this volume with an exploration of a future direction I envision for the feminism and biology relationship: lessons, critiques, and contributions for feminism from biology. I choose as an example the subdiscipline of ecology to explore how its theories, methods, and practice might add to a critique of feminism. In their fusion as ecofeminism both ecological and feminist theory can intertwine and complement to form a strong framework for praxis.

Unlike most fields both ecology and feminism represent academic areas closely linked with current political activism. This connection permits the evolving theory of each to be informed and transformed by the praxis of ecologists and feminists. Perhaps it was this connection with praxis that allowed the ecofeminist movement, beginning in the mid-1970s (Davies, 1988), to explore similarities and overlaps that exist in the way women and the environment are controlled, exploited, and dominated by white, middle-class men in Western society.

Feminists have successfully used the lens of gender to critique the extent to which androcentric bias has distorted the theory and practice of science. Merchant (1979) and Griffin (1978, 1989) begin their documentation of science's historical roots with the seventeenth-century shift from an organic hermetic approach to science in which men revered and saw themselves as part of the environment and nature (and women as identified with nature), to a mechanistic, objective approach in which the objective distance endorsed men's domination and exploitation of the environment (and women) (Keller, 1985).

In their critique of science, its theories, methods, and uses, feminists have delineated an improved science that would result from less androcentrism (Keller,

1982). Ecofeminists have made explicit the connection between the domination of both women and the environment through the androcentrism of modern science (Harding, 1986; King, 1983, 1989). They propose that science, including our approach to ecology because it has suffered from androcentrism, has much to learn from feminism.

Although considerable work has focused on what science and ecology can learn from feminism, rarely has the question been posed in the opposite direction: What can feminism learn from ecology and science? Indeed, out of enthusiasm for recognizing the importance of feminism for revealing androcentric distortion in theories, methods, applications, and teaching of science, my own work (Rosser, 1986; 1988; 1990) has suffered from this same unidirectional thinking. On rare occasions (Rosser, 1986) I note that feminist theory and ecological theory are parallel, overlapping, and possibly even congruent in some aspects. However, I have not considered that the science of ecology in its theories, methods, and practice might contribute to the critique of feminism. In thinking about important issues and current debates in Women's Studies and feminism, I now recognize that ecology can provide information and insights on some of the topics. In retrospect this does not seem so surprising as even the science of ecology is older than this phase of feminism; theories in ecology have benefited from the maturity and complexity that may evolve in an older field. More fundamentally, though, in dealing with the intricacies of a web of interconnected beings, ecology has developed principles that may well serve as models for a better understanding of the way feminism functions with the worlds that surround it.

The science of ecology and the ecological movement stress the necessity for human beings to see themselves as part of the holistic environment. Ecology sees all life and all species (including human beings) as part of an interconnected web. Relationship and mutual interdependence with other species rather than separation, hierarchy, and domination are emphasized in ecological theory and particularly in ecofeminism (Davies, 1988).

The philosophical origins of feminism emphasize that it is man's conception of woman as "other" that has led to his willingness to dominate and exploit her. Many examples suggest that man's view of woman as other stretches to the point that his interactions and treatment of her are similar to his interactions with another species.

Anne Fausto-Sterling (1985) suggests that male scientists demonstrate more interest in studying males of other species than in studying female human beings. She also refers to the work of sociobiologist David Symons (1979) who "argues that male and female sexuality are so different, so at odds, that it makes sense to think of the two sexes as separate species" (Fausto-Sterling, 1985, p. 4).

Writing in the nineteenth century, but echoed by sociobiologists (Barash, 1977; Wilson, 1978) in this century, Charles Darwin (1867) remarks specifically on the vast differences between males and females. What amazed him was the fact that such different beings belong to the same species (see chapter 3).

As Darwin depicts male–female interaction, it seems that the former constitute something like a separate group, interacting mainly with each other in relation to another quite separate group. In order to make the differentiation between males and females as strong as possible, the theory of sexual selection is needed. It is the agent of differentiation, that which assures an ever-increasing separation between the sexes, their operation in two quite distinct realms that touch only for the purpose of procreation. At one point Darwin even suggests that it is as preposterous to suggest that a human male should be born of a female as it is that "a perfect kangaroo were seen to come out of the womb of a bear" (Darwin, 1967, p. 425).

Darwin's suggestion that human females and males differ as much as separate species has stuck in my mind ever since I first studied the passage some 14 years ago. Early this year while rereading in an introductory biology text the standard definitions of interactions between species, this passage from Darwin again came to mind. It occurred to me that the metaphor of woman as a separate species might provide a useful concept for ecofeminism. Although the metaphor of woman as a class has practical flaws (Barrett, 1988), women as a class has served as a useful construct for evolution of some Marxist-feminist theory.

The metaphor of women as a separate species suggests an angle from which to view the maximalist versus minimalist debate erupting in so many disciplinary and interdisciplinary areas within feminism. As was the case with nineteenth-century feminism and the struggle for the vote, considerable debate in feminist circles currently centers on the issue of whether or not differences between men and women should be maximized or minimized. In biology the question has been posed as a reexamination of the nature–nurture controversy. Much research has focused on whether the source of differences is biological (Barash, 1977; Wilson, 1975; 1978) or environmental (Bleier, 1984; Gould, 1981; Webster & Webster, 1977). The research of most feminist scientists, including my own work, has pointed out the impossibility of distinguishing between the relative contribution of nature and nurture, given that the two may not be separated. As Bleier (1984) states:

> Since we tend to take for granted (or ignore) the normal physiological milieu as an essential part of development, it is easier to recognize the influence of environmental milieu on genetic expression if we consider external environmental factors that affect fetal development in humans through their disruptive

effects on the maternal milieu. The mother's diet, drug ingestion (for example, thalidomide, DES, alcohol), virus infections (such as herpes and German measles), stress, and other known factors may have serious effects on the physical characteristics of the developing fetus. In some way all of these environmental factors have the capacity to induce abnormalities in the environmental milieu of the fetus, and it is the interactions between genetic factors and disturbed internal environmental factors that result in altered fetal development. There is no way to tease apart genetic and environmental factors in human development or to know where genetic effects end and environmental ones begin; in fact, this is a meaningless way to view the problem since from conception the relationships between the gene's protein synthesizing activity and the fetus' maternal environment are interdependent. (p. 43)

Whatever their source, some differences do exist between males and females in our current society. The question remains as to whether feminism should deemphasize or stress these differences. Stimpson (1973) notes that at first feminism sought to minimize the differences; more recently the focus has been on maximizing of difference. Mansbridge (1986) suggests that a reason for failure of the ERA was the perception that it promoted similarity in areas such as the draft and unisex toilets where people wished to retain difference. Perhaps the best strategy for survival, as suggested by ecological examples, varies depending on the surrounding environment. In her introduction to *The Impact of Feminist Research in the Academy* (1987), Farnham describes a similar explanation for feminism:

> Both strategies in the struggle for women's autonomy, i.e., the argument for equality and the argument for differences, have produced gains. The argument for equality is most appealing in the heady days of a movement when all things seem possible, the argument for differences when disillusionment sets in. The egalitarian argument encourages the development of analyses of opportunity structures, and it benefits from the cultural consensus that exists around democratic values. But, as other ethnic and racial groups have discovered, something is lost in the process. Not everything about the dominant culture is worthy of emulation, and not everything developed within the confines assigned by the dominant class is thereby worthless, simply because it developed out of victimization or dependency or limited opportunity or by filling the interstices of the system that the dominant class found of too little value to occupy. There is no equality if the standards of the dominant class are the only ones applied and the positive attributes of the victims are ignored. Yet, the celebration of differences increases women's vulnerability to oppression by providing for its rationalization, even as the insistence upon equality obscures what has been forged in the crucible of adversity. (Farnham, 1987, p. 5)

The current political situation and much of the current feminist research favor the maximalist position of emphasis upon differences between men and women. The woman as a separate species metaphor represents the extreme maximalist position.

The basis for the definition of species rests on the ability of a population to breed under natural conditions and produce fertile offspring. Because men and women clearly can do this, the woman as separate species metaphor has obvious practical flaws. Other dangers or practical problems might also be implied by use of the metaphor. For example, emphasizing separation or differences between males and females often leads to a form of biological determinism implying that differences in social and cultural role, status, and behavior are caused by genetic, hormonal, or anatomical differences between the sexes.

Use of a metaphor that emphasizes separation and differences between the sexes might also be interpreted to deemphasize differences of race, class, ethnic origin, and sexual orientation among women. A bias of much of the early work done by white middle-class feminists was that it assumed that gender is the main difference responsible for social inequalities and oppression in our society. As women of color (Almquist, 1975; Dill, 1983; Hooks, 1989) and women with perspectives on class (Abbott & Sapsford, 1988; Rubin, 1976) quickly pointed out, gender must be seen as one factor along with race, class, and others that create complex political interactions and positions in our society.

In proposing the metaphor of woman as separate species I do not wish to imply biological determinism or fail to recognize the wide diversity among women and the varying sources of that diversity. I also do not wish to ignore the fact that according to the biological definition, human males and females clearly do belong to the same species.

Before exploring the implications of the metaphor, it is useful to understand types of interactions that occur between species. Recurring interactions between species constitute forms of symbiosis or ''living together'' and can range from negative through neutral to positive for one or both species:

Competition is the only interaction that is negative for both species. Because resources are limited, the activity of each individual using a resource depletes or limits it, therefore affecting the ability of others to use the resource. Within ecology, several different types of competition can be distinguished. Competitive exclusion refers to the situation of two species competing intensely for the same limited resource; it leads to the disappearance of one of the species as complete competitors cannot coexist. Exclusion or extinction of one of the competitors can occur either by exploitative competition, in which one species depletes a necessary resource thereby excluding the other species, or by interference competition, in which one species denies another species access to a limited resource, usually by aggressive behavior.

Coexistence of two or more species that compete in the same resource category can occur when each specializes within a narrow range of the resource gradient (part of resource availability); coexistence may also occur through resource partitioning, whereby species share the same resource (although not always equally) in different ways, in different areas, or at different times.

Predation is one kind of interaction that is positive for one species and negative for the other. In short, one species devours the other. Predation typically results in the interacting species coevolving through reciprocal selection pressures. The coevolution is often demonstrated through evolutionary adaptations such as warning coloration and mimicry in which edible prey species try to resemble inedible prey, camouflage that enables prey to blend with its surroundings to escape detection, and various behavioral and chemical defenses that deter a potential attacker.

Parasitism is a second interaction that is positive for one species and negative for the other. True parasites obtain nourishment from living organisms but typically do not kill their hosts outright; frequently the host is weakened and dies from secondary infections. In social parasitism, one species depends on the social behavior rather than the tissues of another to complete its life cycle. For example, the North American brown-headed cowbird lays its eggs in another bird's nest. The other bird hatches and raises the cowbird, which pushes the other nestlings out or eats all their food so that they die. In contrast to true parasites, parasitoids kill their host by consuming its tissues. For example some insect larvae kill their host by completely consuming its soft tissues.

Predation and parasitism are clearly negative for one species and positive for the other. It is not in the best interests of the predator or parasite to eliminate all members of the other species (prey or host) as that would result in loss of the food source for the predator or parasite. This results in predator/prey cycles and coevolutionary mechanisms and links changes in one species to changes in the other species.

Commensalism is positive for one species and neutral for the other. Robins, for example may benefit from human lawn maintenance activities that tend to increase the number of earthworms. However, the worm-gathering activities of robins are not particularly beneficial for humans. *Protocooperation* is beneficial but not obligatory. For example, honeybees concentrate on collecting food from clover when it blooms profusely. But the honeybees may also feed on honeysuckle, apple blossoms, and flowers in the absence of clover. Similarly, clover may be pollinated by moths, butterflies, and bumblebees, as well as honeybees. Although the interaction is not necessary for the survival of either clover or honeybees, both benefit from the positive interaction.

In *mutualism*, the positive benefits that exists are crucial to the survival of both species, making the interaction obligatory. For example, the yucca moth feeds exclusively on the yucca plant, even in its larval form. The yucca plant depends exclusively on the yucca moth for its pollination, and hence its reproductive success.

Applying these descriptions of interspecific interactions to particular human male–female problematic interactions might shed some light on which types of interactions are likely to be least harmful to women living in a cultural and historical environment in which both sameness and differences are alternately emphasized. This application assumes a heterosexual couple, as the metaphor of woman as a separate species would not be appropriate for lesbian or male homosexual interaction.

Application of terms from ecology that describe interspecific interactions to behavioral interactions between human males and females might reveal which types of interactions are likely to be more beneficial.

Two issues have proven particularly thorny as traditional roles for women and men have changed within the last two decades and might be clarified by application of the women as another species metaphor. Male–female interactions over both child custody and economics in intimate relationships seem to suffer from vacillations between maximalist and minimalist perspectives.

Competition, as used to describe interspecies behavior, predicts the negative consequences particularly for females, but also for males, of the current job and wage situation. In the United States, the average woman still earns only 66% for every $1 that men earn (Wallis, 1989). Although a fraction of the discrepancy can be explained by differing amounts of education, on-the-job training, and time out for childbearing, over 55% of the discrepancy can be attributed to discrimination only (Bergmann, 1986). The labor market is stratified by gender. Jobs traditionally held by women are not given comparable worth to jobs requiring the same level of skills that are traditionally held by men. Under this current system, women competing with men will earn considerably less money, as gender differences have historically played a major role in job stratification and pay. The gender-stratified labor market is an example of coexistence through resource partitioning.

This system also has negative consequences for a man involved with a woman in a long-term relationship in which one of the goals is to maximize income overall for the couple. As long as jobs are valued significantly by gender rather than skill, all women and men in relationships with women working in traditional occupations for women will lose money. This leads many male–female couples into the trap of giving the man's career priority because he can be expected to contribute more money to the family coffers. Faced with earning less money for working, while holding similar training and working as hard as a man, many women eventually leave a particular job or the work force entirely when geographic relocation or other conflicts with the man's career arise. This situation demonstrates the exclusion or extinction of a career (and possibly the women's self-esteem) that is predicted by the model of competition.

Marriage or other intimate male–female relationships may lead to economic arrangements that resemble predation and parasitism in that they are negative for one individual and positive for the other. The classic case that would exemplify this type of interaction is the woman who gives up or defers her own education or job promotions to put her husband through graduate or professional school and/or rear children. After he is well established in his career, earning a good salary, he rejects her for a younger woman who is his professional equal. Depending on whether or not she receives financial support until she can get established, who has custody of the children, and other financial and psychological factors, this might be classified as parasitism or predation.

Although women may more frequently be the victims of economic parasitism and predation, men are certainly not immune. Common parlance suggests in fact that women search for "male prey" presumably to live happily ever after in a marriage in which she will be the parasite who receives the economic benefits from his hard work. This language suggests that marriage has economic advantages for females and disadvantages for males. The true economic backdrop that lends some validity to the female as a financial parasite in a male–female relationship is the fact that women earn only 66% for every $1 males earn, that unpaid labor in the home such as housework and child care are not counted in the Gross National Product (GNP), and that in the first year after divorce a man's standard of living increases by 42%, whereas that of the female decreases by 73% (Weitzman, 1985).

Commensal interactions, positive for one species and neutral for the other, may also be applied to male–female interactions when a man and a woman in a relationship have agreed to keep all of their finances separate. If one then receives a substantial raise, windfall, or inheritance, this would presumably be positive for him or her and have no effect on the other partner on the theoretical level. To the extent that standard of living is directly influenced by financial resources in the twentieth-century United States, a substantial change in the financial resources of one partner is likely to have a negative practical effect on the relationship, permitting one partner to live better than the other, if those resources are not shared in some fashion.

Both protocooperation and mutualism represent interactions that are positive for both species. Assume a relationship in which a male and female work at the same type of job for equal pay, have equal opportunity for advancement, and work for a firm or agency that truly does not discriminate in any way on the basis of gender. Both the male and female could survive comfortably and support dependents on his or her own salary, but they save money by living together and sharing expenses. The interaction may be more beneficial for the male if they desire their own biological children, since he needs a female in order to become a biological father. This situation represents commensalism as the interactions are beneficial but not obligatory. If both the male and female must live together and share expenses to survive comfortably and support dependents, the interaction is mutual.

Application of the ecological descriptions of interspecies interactions to human male–female relationships in examining financial interactions suggests that protocooperation and mutualism are positive for both men and women. Both protocooperation and mutualism require that men and women have equal salary, equal access to jobs, advancement, and opportunity, and experience equal discrimination. Protocooperation and mutualism assume the minimalist stance, an absence of difference between men and women.

Unfortunately, the real world includes a gender-stratified labor market, covert or overt discrimination based on gender for opportunities and advancement, the biological reality that women, not men, give birth to children, and sexism in social role expectations. Given these realities, one of the other interspecific models may shed more insight about the realities for women. Competition, which the model predicts to be negative for both species, is particularly negative for women as it too assumes similarity rather than differences as a starting point for the competition. Predation, parasitism, and commensalism result in differences (positive for one species, and negative or neutral for the other). These three models for interaction provide further insight for how changes that assume equality or sameness may work to the detriment of women when the biological, historical, and social reality includes difference and inequality. The example of child custody is another case in point.

As several studies (Weiss, 1984; Weitzman, 1985) of the history of divorce in the United States have illustrated, the parent who is seen as the more appropriate or "fit" individual to have custody of minor children has changed over time. In the nineteenth century, the father automatically received custody of minor children in the rare cases of divorce. Both women and children were viewed as the property of men. Ability to provide economically for the children was deemed the major factor for determination of fitness to be the custodial parent. Because women had few, if any, means of economic support for themselves and their children, most women stayed in unhappy marriages rather than risk losing their children through divorce. Maximum difference was assumed in the ability of the two sexes to compete for economic resources. With economic viability as the sole criterion for custody determination most females were competitively excluded.

In the twentieth century up until the 1970s, the mother usually was considered the appropriate person to receive custody of minor children. Although rarely articulated directly, the rationale was that the mother was more fit either for reasons of biological determinism or socialization to nurture the children. A typical court decision (*Muller v. Muller, 1948*) articulated this maternal or "tender-years presumption": "The mother is the natural custodian of her child in tender years, and . . . if she is a fit and proper person other things being equal, she should be given custody" (*Muller v. Muller*, 1948 as quoted in Sapiro, 1990, p. 334). The father was supposed to provide economic support for the children, and in some cases, the ex-wife. This division into custodial and economic support roles based on gender attempted to ensure some degree of mutualism or protocooperation for the sake of the children based on a recognition of differential economic access and psychological characteristics depending on gender. Although based on differences between the sexes, this model assumed a type of equality or similarity between the sexes. Each sex had something significant that was different from what the parent of the other sex could contribute to the welfare of the child. The mother could better contribute physical and emotional nurturance; the father could better contribute to the financial security of the child.

Beginning in the 1970s, an attitude has begun to emerge that the characteristics and abilities that determine parental fitness and custodial roles are not related to sex. Most divorcing couples still assume the roles of the custodial mother with the father providing child support. However, in a significant number of cases, other interactions occur that are harmful to the child and one or both parents.

1. The father kidnaps the child of whom he has been denied custody. (An example of predation?)

2. The father stops paying child support for the children for which he does not have custody. (Parasitism?) A 1985 study (Rix, 1989) revealed that 26% of the fathers were paying none of the support they owed; only 48% were giving the full court-ordered payment. The social dimensions of the problems caused by these men who are parasites on their ex-wives and children is immense.

3. During a custody battle, a mother loses custody of the children to her ex-husband. A major factor determining his superior fitness is his substantially higher income, which will permit him to have a full-time maid and provide better after-school child care. The facts that the mother stopped her education to put the father through medical school and then stayed at home to rear the child during his/her preschool years were not weighted heavily in determining parental fitness. (Competitive exclusion?)

These three examples illustrate some of the dilemmas that arise when policies based on attitudes about differences and similarities between males and females change. The U.S. divorce laws until the 1970s reflected a maximalist stance on differences between males and females. Most feminists, including me, were eager to see the divorce laws change to reflect more equality between men and women. What we failed to foresee were the negative consequences that can occur from changing one part of the system to reflect similarity while other parts of the system continue to reflect difference. Asking for a minimalist stance in determining parental fitness may prove disadvantageous to some women in a society in which economic resources are critical and the labor market is based on difference in the form of gender stratification that puts women at a disadvantage.

Decisions about the maximalist–minimalist stance become especially crucial over issues such as divorce and child custody. It is at those times that the male and female are particularly estranged. Each is likely to feel separated and emphasize the "otherness" of their former partner. Factors of socialization (Lamke, 1982; Weitzman, 1979), psychological development (Chodorow, 1978; Dinnerstein, 1976), and patriarchal culture (Lerner, 1986; Ruether, 1974; Stichter and Porpart, 1988) further reinforce men's ability to see women as other. Their economic power, social status, and physical strength permit men to dominate and control those they see as "other," thus reinforcing their separation.

The metaphor of woman as separate species may provide some guidelines for setting policies and models of interaction that are less harmful to women. Examination of true interspecific interactions suggests three types of interaction that are negative for neither species: commensalism, protocooperation, and mutualism. These three types of interaction are at least neutral and at best positive for women. They ensure some measure of equality, even when the underlying assumption is difference. The changes in divorce laws in the 1970s with their consequent negative effects on custodial and economic status of women might have been predicted from an understanding of competitive, predatory, and parasitic interspecific behavior, especially when one species is at a disadvantage. The older laws, while based on difference, established protocooperation or mutualism in economic and custodial matters.

The dominance, distance, and control that white, middle- and upper-class Western men exert over other species in their environment extends to women of their own species. Models from interspecific interactions may provide useful parameters for analyzing behaviors including women's health and reproductive technologies when men view women as (an) other (species).

PRINCIPLES OR THEORIES OF ECOLOGY USEFUL FOR THE CRITIQUE OF FEMINISM

1. *Diversity and variety provide a healthy and stable environment*. A fundamental principle of ecology is that diversity and variety exist within environ-

ments and species and that diversity both in terms of numbers of species and types of niches filled by any one species provides a more healthy, stable environment in which survival is enhanced.

Feminists have been slow to recognize the strength and importance provided by diversity and variety. First, we were slow to recognize that diversity among women exists. Because many of the leaders of feminism, particularly of its academic arm, Women's Studies, were white, educated, middle-class, Western women, we erroneously assumed that our experience represents that of all women. This led to alienation from feminism of women of color, working-class women, and women from emerging nations because we assumed the universality of the white, middle-class, Western female experience and failed to describe the diversity of women's experience when race, class, sexual preference, and ethnic origin are considered (Dill, 1983).

Earlier recognition of the ecological principles of the existence of diversity and its importance for survival might have saved feminism from being perceived as a movement to benefit only a small group of women. Feminists have spent the past several years becoming educated to the extent of diversity in women's lives and are struggling to broaden the movement to include all women. Inclusion of all women is necessary for the survival of feminism. Numerous ecological studies of hybrid corn and other species have documented that reduction of variety within a species to one or two subspecies makes that species vulnerable to extinction. With reduced variety, a disease or environmental change that is detrimental or fatal to the remaining subspecies may wipe out the entire species. If the diversity of women's experience had been represented earlier in feminism, it would currently be a more powerful, stable, healthy movement.

2. *Individuals have different needs and will pass through different stages of development during their life span.* During different chronological stages of the life cycle, many plant and animal species have entirely different forms that bear little resemblance to other stages in the life cycle of the same individual. During a particular stage the requirements from and contributions to the environment by that individual may differ from those of other individuals or from those of itself at other stages of development. For example, the larval form, the tadpole, requires and contributes to a different environment from that of the adult form, the frog.

The information from ecology about developmental stages may be instructive to feminism. Feminism needs to be inclusive of women at all stages and ages of the life cycle. Just as the leaders of the current phase of feminism were overwhelmingly white, middle class, and Western, they were also of a relatively uniform age (from about 20–45) when the movement began. Only as the leaders have begun to age, has feminism begun to give serious attention to menopause, osteoporosis, health care, and housing for the aging. Currently, many young women are failing to identify with feminism, which they do not see as addressing the issues of their generation. A manifestation of their position is their self-definition as post-feminist (Wallis, 1989). Along with most feminists, I bristle at the term "post-feminist" because I also do not feel that feminism has yet arrived in any meaningful way in our society. However, another way to view the term is to recognize its use by young women as a way of representing themselves at a different stage or age of development in which they do not see themselves included in the current definition and concerns of feminism.

3. *Succession involves one composition and organization of communities being replaced by another until a relatively stable, self-maintaining community is established.* Ecologists have observed a succession of species that occurs in a raw environment devoid of life such as a newly formed volcanic isle or a disturbed patch of previously inhabited environment, such as a forest after a fire. The kinds of species differ, the numbers of species increase, and the trophic structure becomes more complex as succession progresses over time.

    Succession might provide a model for the life cycle of feminism. Two decades after the beginning of the late-twentieth-century wave of feminism, changes have occurred in the surrounding environment of the early 1990s to make it very different economically, politically, and socially from the environment of the early 1970s. At least some part of this difference may be due to the effect of feminism itself on that environment. It is not surprising that although some issues of concern to feminism now in the United States are the same as they were 20 years ago (equal pay for equal work, day care), or have reemerged as again significant (fight for abortion), many are new and different (feminization of poverty, ecofeminism). Changes in issues, structure and complexities in the environment at different stages are part of the life cycle of feminism itself.

4. *Depending on the environmental circumstances, survival will sometimes be enhanced by maximizing differences between the sexes, in other environmental situations survival will be enhanced by minimizing differences between the sexes.* Many species of birds such as the North American grouse and mallard ducks and mammals such as northern sea lions and African lions demonstrate sexual dimorphism through emphasis on differences in external appearance and behavior between males and females. Most amphibians, reptiles, and other species of birds and mammals have little difference in external appearance between the male and female of the species. Each strategy has an advantage: sexual dimorphism supposedly confers reproductive advantage; similarity between the sexes protects against predators.

    Because some differences do exist between males and females in our current society, the question for feminism is whether to maximize or minimize these differences. Perhaps the best strategy for survival, suggested by the ecological examples discussed earlier in this chapter, will vary depending on the surrounding environment.

5. *Survival comes first.* When environmental resources are scarce and species live in marginal environments, survival comes first. For example, radiation into other environmental niches, life span, and even reproduction may be severely restricted or even terminated under conditions of scarce resources.

Feminists in developed countries have often had problems understanding the different needs and priorities of women in developing countries. Our priorities of comparable worth, day care, abortion, and lesbian rights hold little relevance or meaning for their lives; our ideas of "development" often destroy their lives and environments (Shiva, 1989). Statements of women from Africa that water is a women's issue, of women from Ethiopia that food is woman's priority, and from women in El Salvador that "disappeared" persons are the major problem become more comprehensible to women in developed countries when we understand that survival comes first.

6. *The power of the information gained from the microenvironmental studies may be limited or lost unless it is integrated into the more holistic framework of the macroenvironment.* Reductionism or the study of one or two variables or species may yield considerable information that might not be obtained without isolating those species or variables from the complexities and interactions of their surrounding environments. Serious errors in interpretation may occur, however, if the hypotheses resulting from reductionistic approaches are not reconsidered and retested in the more complex system. For example, on initial study the Canadian lynx and the snowshoe hare did seem to follow the predator–prey oscillation curve predicted by Lotka and Volterra in their mathematical model. However, this assumption is too simplistic, as predators are not usually numerous enough to bring about the rapid decline of prey at the time that decline begins. Further study revealed that other factors in the environment such as hares eating toxic shoots of plants that emerge first in a disturbed environment, (Starr & Taggart, 1984) appear to trigger the decline.

    Similarly in feminism, gender provides a very powerful lens through which to view the world of human institutions and interactions. The lens of gender reveals distortions in androcentric perspectives. However, gender itself may be reductionistic and lead to distortions of perception when its intersection with other interlocking complex political phenomena such as race or class is not considered. For example, the work of Carol Gilligan (1982) reveals significant androcentric bias in the work of "human" developmental theorists whose models were based solely on the study of males. Until her theories are tested in adolescent girls of differing races, classes, and ethnic backgrounds it will not be clear to what extent they only represent the experience of adolescent girls who are largely white and middle to upper class. Gender, race, and class form a complex system that shapes women's experience. Consideration of one factor such as gender without regard to its interaction with other significant factors may bias the perception.

7. *All organisms in the system, no matter how small or minor are important to keep the environment healthy and functioning.* In recent years a new movement known as deep ecology has arisen within ecology. Its basic principle rests on the equality, including the equal right to life, of all organisms, no matter how small. This theory poses dilemmas for women,

particularly for feminists. A logical extension of deep ecology would suggest, for example, that the fetus has an equal right to survival as the woman. Perhaps even the AIDS virus or other fatal disease-causing micro organisms have equal survival rights compared to human beings and other "higher" organisms.

I accept that our hierarchical view of nature, which posits human beings as "higher" than most organisms, is anthropocentric and likely to be flawed. However, I am unwilling to accept the practical consequences such as no abortion, birth control, or antibiotics of some possible applications of deep ecology. The suffering from the consequences of these applications would be borne more heavily by women and children.

Although rejecting some possible applications based on theories of deep ecology, feminists might reconsider the importance of resisting hierarchy and valuing the work done by all women. Working-class women, housewives, and clerical staff have critiqued the extent to which professional women both inside and outside the academy have exploited feminism for their own career advancement to the exclusion of other women. The feminization of poverty, gender stratification of the labor market, and failure to achieve comparable worth demonstrate the continued need to fight the hierarchy that allows only a few women to have financial security.

8. *In coevolution, changes in one species necessitate changes in the other species that interact with that species in close ecological fashion.* For example, predators and prey exert continual selection pressure on each other. Warning coloration, mimicry, and camouflage represent coevolutionary changes in one species in response to another.

Although men may treat women as a(n) other (species), human males and females clearly belong to the same species from a biological viewpoint. In that sense it is not appropriate to apply the term coevolution to their behavioral changes. Use of the term as a metaphor may be instructive.

Although feminism has lobbied for societal change in the roles of both men and women, the major behavioral changes have occurred in the lives of women without correspondingly significant changes in the lives of men. In 1989 in the United States, 57.8% of women worked outside the home including 68% of women with children under 18; in 1960 34.8% of women were in the work force, which included only 28% of women with children under 18 (Wallis, 1989). Numerous studies (Berk, 1985; Cowan, 1983; Machung, 1989; Oakley, 1974; Strasser, 1984) have documented that men have failed to take significantly more responsibility for child care and housework as women have entered the workforce. Although some recent studies have shown that men do a bit more housework when their wives work (Wallis, 1989), other studies continue to reveal that men whose wives work outside the home do less housework than husbands of full-time housewives.

This double burden of work has left many women (Hewlett, 1986; Wallis, 1989) angry with feminism for not pointing out the exhaustion and pitfalls from trying to have it all. Blaming feminism for the resistance of employers to change, the feminization of poverty, the failure of noncustodial fathers to pay child support, and the lack of governmental response to needs for daycare and parental leave ignores the political and economic male power structure that controls U.S. society (Woliver, 1988). However, significantly changing the behavior of one sex without a corresponding change in the behavior of the other sex will cause severe stress and dysfunction in the system. A current issue facing feminism is how to deal with this crisis. Will the behavior of men change? Will women return to their previous status quo behavior? Or will other corresponding changes in the behaviors of both men and women occur?

9   *Competition is less severe when some environmental niches are unoccupied.* Studies of adaptive radiation of a species in new environments that result from volcanoes, earthquakes, or other natural phenomena that produce uninhabited land, reveals that new species can evolve, establish a niche, flourish and survive in the types of environments in which they might not compete if all niches were filled. The adaptive radiation of the finches on the Galapagos Islands initially documented by Darwin (1967) provides the classic example of this type of adaptation. Similarly women and women's studies have tended to fare better in newer fields and in fields and institutions in which resources are less constrained.

10.   *Cooperation and positive symbiotic relationships enhance survival in hostile environments.* The study of ecology reveals numerous examples of species that survive and/or flourish in different environments because they have evolved a positive relationship with another species.

These interactions may vary from neutral to positively necessary. In protocooperation, the interaction is beneficial but not obligatory. In mutualism, one species benefits from the interaction but the other neither garners direct benefits nor is harmed. (See the beginning section of this chapter for a fuller discussion and definition of these terms.)

Women's Studies in the academy and feminism in the wider world are more likely to survive in this time of political conservatism and backlash by forming coalitions that are protocooperative, mutualistic, or commensual with other groups. Mansbridge (1986) discusses the extent to which movements that are loosely knit and embrace constituencies that do not necessarily agree on all points or doctrines are more successful than sects that form tightly knit, cohesive groups that concur on all points of political philosophy. Feminism may survive and meet more of its agenda by joining with other groups to support specific issues. Using this strategy Jesse Jackson developed his "rainbow coalition" to support issues important to women, people of color, lesbians, gays, and poor people; Women's Studies should join with African-American studies to cooperate on strategies for programs not traditionally included in the curriculum. Both Women's Studies and Ethnic Studies might join what appear as unlikely groups, such as an honor's college or institutes for public policy, for interdisciplinary support.

In adopting these strategies, feminism would be paralleling the techniques of a political party and movement in West Germany, The Greens. The Greens formed coalitions with other groups and built their movement on four principles: democracy, ecology, nonviolence, and social responsibility. Electing 27 members to the West German national parliament in 1983, the Greens are now perceived as important in other parts of the world as an ecology party that embraces feminist principles. "Greens in the United States have generally expanded this list (of four principles) to include an explicit emphasis on decentralization—the need to reorient both politics and economics toward the local community level. There is often a strong link to the feminist vision of a society that guarantees equal rights to all and embodies the need for personal as well as political transformation" (Tokar, 1987).

Ecological and biological theory can be strengthened by feminist critiques and principles that question traditional and androcentric approaches to science and the environment. Similarly, feminist theory can benefit from critiques based on the principles of biological and ecological theory for insights to dilemmas and issues in feminism today. In their fusion as ecofeminism both theories can intertwine and complement to form a strong framework for praxis. Ecofeminists represent an activist group in which political practice and theory inform and transform each other to create a better environment for women and all living beings. It serves as a model for the future beneficial dynamic relationship of biology and feminism.

REFERENCES

Abbott, P., & Sapsford, R. (1988). *Women and social class*. New York: Routledge.

Almquist, E. (1975, June). Untangling the effects of race and sex: The disadvantaged status of Black women. *Social Science Quarterly, 56*, 129–42.

Barash, D. (1977). *Sociobiology and behavior*. New York: Elsevier.

Barrett, M. (1988). *Women's oppression today: Problems in Marxist feminist analysis*. London: Verso.

Bergmann, B. R. (1986). *The economic emergence of women*. New York: Basic Books.

Berk, S. F. (1985). *The gender factory: The apportionment of work in American households*. New York: Plenum Press.

Chodorow, N. (1978). *The reproduction of mothering: Psychoanalysis and the sociology of gender*. Berkeley and Los Angeles: University of California Press.

Cowan, R. S. (1983). *More work for mother: The ironies of household technology from the open hearth to the microwave*. New York: Basic Books.

Darwin, C. (1967). *On the origin of species: A facsimile of the first edition*. New York: Atheneum.

Davies, K. (1988, Spring). What is ecofeminism? *Women and Environments, 10*, 4–6.

Dill, B. T. (1983). Race, class, and gender: Prospects for an all-inclusive sisterhood. *Feminist Studies, 9*(1), 131–150.

Dinnerstein, D. (1976). *The mermaid and the minotaur*. New York: Harper & Row.

Farnham, C. (1987). Introduction: The same or different? *The impact of feminist research in the academy*. Bloomington: Indiana University Press.

Fausto-Sterling, A. (1985). *Myths of gender*. New York: Basic Books.

Gilligan, C. (1982). *In a different voice: Psychological theory and women's development*. Cambridge, MA: Harvard University Press.

Gould, S. J. (1981). *The mismeasure of man*. New York: W. W. Norton.

Griffin, S. (1978). *Women and nature: The roaring inside her*. New York: Harper & Row.

Griffin, S. (1989). Split culture. In J. Plant (Ed.), *Healing the wounds: The promise of ecofeminism* (pp. 7–17). Philadelphia, PA and Santa Cruz, CA: New Society Publishers.

Haraway, D. (1978). Animal sociology and a natural economy of the body politic, Part I: A political physiology of dominance; Animal sociology and a natural economy of the body politic, Part II: The past is the contested zone: Human nature and theories of production and reproduction in primate behavior studies. *Signs: Journal of Women in Culture and Society, 4*(1), 21–60.

Harding, S. (1986). *The science question in feminism*. Ithaca, NY: Cornell University Press.

Hein, H. (1981). Women and science: Fitting men to think about nature. *International Journal of Women's Studies, 4*, 369–377.

Hewlett, S. A. (1986). *A lesser life: The myth of women's liberation in America*. New York: William Morrow & Co.

Hooks, B. (1989). *Talking back: Thinking feminist, thinking Black*. Boston: South End.

Hubbard, R. (1983). Social effects of some contemporary myths about women. In M. Lowe & R. Hubbard (Eds.), *Woman's nature: Rationalizations of inequality*. Elmsford, NY: Pergamon Press.

Hynes, H. P. (1984). November-December). Women working: A field report. *Technology Review*, 37ff.

Hynes, H. P. (1989). *The recurring silent spring*. Elmsford, NY: Pergamon Press.

Keller, E. F. (1982). Feminism and science. *Signs: Journal of Women in Culture and Society, 8*(3), 589–602.

Keller, E. F. (1983). *A feeling for the organism: The life and work of Barbara McClintock*. New York: W. H. Freeman.

Keller, E. F. (1985). *Reflections on gender and science*. New Haven, CT: Yale University Press.

Keller, E. F. (1987). Women scientists and feminist critics of science. *Daedalus, 116*(4): 77–91.

King, Y. (1983). Toward an ecological feminism and a feminist ecology. In J. Rothschild (Ed.), *Machina Ex Dea: Feminist perspectives on technology*. New York: Pergamon Press.

King, Y. (1989). The ecology of feminism and the feminism of ecology. In J. Plant (Ed.), *Healing the wounds: The promise of ecofeminism* (pp. 18–28). Philadelphia, PA and Santa Cruz, CA: New Society Publishers.

Lamke, Leanne K. (1982, December). The impact of sex role orientations of self-esteem in early adolescence. *Child Development, 53*, 1530–1535.

Lancaster, J. (1975). *Primate behavior and the emergence of human culture*. New York: Holt, Reinhart and Winston.

Lerner, G. (1986) *The creation of patriarchy*. New York: Oxford University Press.

Machung, A. (1989). Talking career, thinking job: Gender differences in career and family expectations of Berkeley seniors. *Feminist Studies, 15*(1), 35–38.

Mansbridge, J. (1986). *Why we lost the ERA*. Chicago: University of Chicago Press.

Merchant, C. (1979). *The death of nature: Women, ecology and the scientific revolution.* New York: Harper & Row.

Oakley, A. (1974). *The sociology of housework.* Bath: The Pittman Bath Press.

Rix, S. (1989). *The American woman, 1988–89: A status report.* New York: Norton.

Rosser, S. V. (1986). *Teaching science and health from a feminist perspective: A practical guide.* Elmsford, NY: Pergamon Press.

Rosser, S. V. (1988). Women in science and health care: A gender at risk. In S. V. Rosser (Ed.), *Feminism withing the science and health care professions: Overcoming resistance.* Elmsford, NY: Pergamon Press.

Rosser, S. V. (1989). Teaching techniques to attract women to science. *Women's Studies International Forum, 12*(3), 363–378.

Rosser, S. V. (1990). *Female friendly science.* Elmsford, NY: Pergamon Press.

Rubin, L. (1976). *Worlds of Pain: Life in the working class family.* New York: Basic Books.

Ruether, R. (Ed.). (1974). *Religion and sexism: Images of women in the Jewish and Christian traditions.* New York: Simon & Schuster.

Sapiro, V. (1990). *Women in American society* (2nd ed.). Mountain View, CA: Mayfield Publishing Company.

Shiva, V. (1989). *Staying alive: Women, ecology, and development.* London: Zed Books.

Starr, C., & Taggart, R. (1984). *Biology: The unity and diversity of life* (3rd ed.). Belmont, CA: Wadsworth Publishing Company.

Stichter, S. B., & Porpart, J. L. (1988). *Patriarchy and class: African women in the home and the workforce.* Boulder, CO: Westview Press.

Stimpson, C. (1973, September). The new feminism and women's studies. *Change,* 43–48.

Strasser, S. (1984). *Never done: A history of American housework.* New York: Pantheon Books.

Symons, D. (1979). *The evolution of human sexuality.* New York: Oxford University Press.

Tokar, B. (1987). *The green alternative.* San Pedro, CA: R & E Miles.

Wallis, C. (1989, December). Onward, women! *Time,* 80–89.

Webster, D., & Webster, M. (1977). Neonatal sound deprivation affects brain stem auditory nuclei. *Annals of Otolaryngology, 103,* 392–396.

Weiss, R. (1984, February). The impact of marital dissolution on income and consumption in single-parent households. *JMF, 46,* 115–128.

Weitzman, L. (1979). *Sex role socialization.* Palo Alto, CA: Mayfield Publishing Company.

Weitzman, L. (1985). *The divorce revolution: The unexpected social and economic consequences for women and children in America.* New York: Free Press.

Wilson, E. O. (1975). *Sociobiology: The new synthesis.* Cambridge, MA: Harvard University Press.

Wilson, E. O. (1978). *On human nature.* Cambridge, MA: Harvard University Press.

Woliver, L. (1988, Fall). The Equal Rights Amendment and the limits of liberal legal reform. *Polity, 21*(1): 183–200.

BIBLIOGRAPHIC ESSAY
BY
FAYE CHADWELL

BIBLIOGRAPHIES
AND GUIDES TO
THE LITERATURE

An excellent starting point for the researcher new to this area of study is Londa Schiebinger's essay, "The History and Philosophy of Women in Science: A Review Essay" (*Signs 12* [Winter 1987]: 305–332). Schiebinger categorizes the literature into four areas: recovery of women's accomplishments, history of women's access and status in science, study of women's nature—mostly through the biological sciences, and the masculine nature of science and thereby its biased essence. While discussing these four areas, Schiebinger contrasts the three points of view she sees in the literature: women cannot participate in science; women's absence in science is an employment/education issue; and not only must more women be recruited into science to better it, but also science must change its masculine, or biased and distorted, basis. Another fine review of this literature is Sue Rosser's "Feminist Scholarship in the Sciences: Where Are We Now and When Can We Expect a Theoretical Breakthrough?" (*Hypatia* 2 (3) [Fall 1987] 5–17). Rosser identifies six categories: (1) teaching and curricular transformation in science, (2) history of women in science, (3) current status of women in science, (4) feminist critiques of science, (5) feminine science, and (6) feminist theory of science. Other important bibliographies include two by University of Wisconsin Women's Studies librarian Sue Searing: a 54-page bibliography, *The History of Women and Science, Health and Technology: A Bibliographic Guide to the Professions and the Disciplines* (1980 Madison, WI: University of Wisconsin System Women's Studies Librarian) and her "Further Readings on Feminism and Science" (1986, in Ruth Bleier, Ed., *Feminist Approaches to Science* pp. 191–195. NY: Pergamon Press). See also Faye Chadwell's four-part bibliography covering not only feminist critiques of science, but also feminist pedagogy, women scientists, recruitment of women scientists, and feminist theory (1989, Rosser, Sue. *Female Friendly Science* pp. 123–147. NY: Pergamon); the bibliography "Philosophical Feminism: A Bibliographic Guide to Critiques of Science," compiled by Alison Wylie, Kathleen Okruhlik, Sandra Morton, and Leslie Thielen-Wilson, includes a section on the biological sciences, but also has sections on the core literature, related criticism from the social sciences, feminist epistemology and theory, and nonfeminist critiques of science (*RFR/DRF 19* (12), 2–36); and Mary Sue Henifen's "Bibliography: Women, Science, and Health," (1979, in Ruth Hubbard, Mary Sue Henifen, & Barbara Fried, Eds., *Women Look at Biology Looking at Women*, pp. 213–268. Cambridge, MA: Schenkman; updated in 1982, Ruth Hubbard, Mary Sue Henifen, & Barbara Fried, *Biological Woman, The Convenient Myth*. Cambridge, MA: Schenkman). Preceding all these sources, Michele L. Aldrich wrote an early review of the literature focusing on statistics on women in science, women, and the history of science, women as students of science, and conferences and major studies on women in science (1978. "Women in Science." *Signs 4*, [Autumn] 126–135). These guides to the literature and bibliographies will provide more comprehensive coverage of the numerous journal articles in this field than can be suitably accommodated in the framework of a bibliographic essay.

HISTORY OF WOMEN IN THE BIOLOGICAL SCIENCES

Women have always participated in scientific research. Who are they and how does a scholar find information on these scientists? Several commendable reference sources will identify biographical sources on women in science. Patricia Joan Siegel and Kay Thomas Finley compiled a substantial bibliography organized by the sciences with listings of citations for individual women (1985, *Women in the Scientific Search: An American Bio-Bibliography, 1724–1979.* Metuchen, NJ: Scarecrow). Carolyn Herzenberg's *Women Scientists from Antiquity to the Present: An Index* actually contains two indexes. One is a list of women scientists with their field, dates, and nationality along with a key to the sources in Herzenberg's 130-source bibliography with information on these. Another index lists by field and then provides the names of women scientists in that field (1986, West Cornwall, CT: Locust Hill Press). Marilyn Bailey Oglivie produced a resourceful biographical dictionary with entries for women scientists through the nineteenth century (1986, *Women in Science: Antiquity through the Nineteenth Century*. Cambridge: MIT Press). Ogilvie has included a useful bibliography with brief annotations. Another useful, albeit dated, bibliography is Audrey Davis's *Bibliography on Women: With Special Emphasis on Their Roles in Science and Society* (1974, NY: Science History Publications).

Several collections of biographies are available that emphasize female scientists who have excelled in their respective fields. Marcia Bonta has authored a work covering 25 women naturalists, botanists, entomologists, ornithologists, and ecologists (1991, *Women in the Field: America's Pioneering Women Naturalists*. College Station, TX: Texas A & M University Press). The collection, *Women of Science: Righting the Record*, covers women in archeology, geology, astronomy, mathematics, engineering, physics, biology, medical science, chemistry, and crystallography. The essays included seek to uncover women heroes in the sciences as well as those women who developed questionable or inadequate theories, whose ideas were superseded or credited to men, whose work was minimalized, or who did minor, but useful work (1990, G. Kass-Simon & Patricia Farnes, Eds. Bloomington, IN: Indiana University Press). Continuing earlier work, Marianne G. Ainley has edited a collection focusing on Canadian women scientists (1990, *Despite the Odds: Essays on Canadian Women and Science*. Montreal: Vehicule Press). A special issue of *SAGE*, "Science and Technology," offers several articles on black women scientists (1989, *6*, [Fall]). Not as recent, Margaret Alic's work begins studying mostly European women in science beginning with prehistory and discussing goddesses and gatherers and concluding with Marie Curie (1986, *Hypatia's, Heritage: A History of Women in Science from Antiquity through the Nineteenth Century*. Boston: Beacon Press). Olga Opfell's work on "lady laureates" is in its second edition and covers any women who has won a Nobel Prize so women scientists are included (1986, *The Lady Laureates: Women Who Won the Nobel Prize*. Metuchen, NJ: Scarecrow Press). Lois B. Arnold's work *Four Lives in Science: Women's Education in the 19th Century* concentrates mainly on Maria Martin Bachman, Almira Hart Lincoln Phelps, Louisa C. Allen Gregory, and Florence Bascom (1984, NY: Schocken Books). Consult also Elizabeth O'Hern for re-coverage of 20 women, who contributed significantly to medical science (1985, *Profiles of Pioneer Women Scientists*. Washington, D.C.: Acropolis Books). Edna Yost's *American Women of Science* is an older source with information on Lillian Gilbreth, Ellen Swallow Richards, and Florence Sabin among others (1943, Philadelphia: Lippincott). Yost also authored *Women of Modern Science* (1966, NY: Dodd, Mead). Londa Schiebinger mentions several older, though important, sources:

Christine de Pizan's *The Book of the City of Ladies* (1405, reprint 1982, Earl Jeffrey Richards, trans. NY: Persea Books); Christian Friedrich Harless' *Die Verdienste der Frauen um Naturwissenschaft Gesundsheits–und Heilkunde so wie auch um Lander-Volkerund Menschenkunde von der altesten Zeit bis auf die neuste (The contribution of women to the natural sciences, health, and healing).* (1830, Gottingen: Van der Hoeck-Ruprecht); and a work by an American, John Augustine Zahm, who used the pseudonym H. J. Mozans (1974, *Women in Science: With an Introductory Chapter on Women's Long Struggle for Things of the Mind*. Cambridge, MA: MIT Press, reprint).

Several well-written book-length biographies have uncovered and celebrated individual women's accomplishments that had been ignored or minimalized. Among these are Anne Sayre's biography of Rosalind Franklin, *Rosalind Franklin and DNA: A Vivid View of What It Is Like to Be a Gifted Woman in an Especially Male Profession*, which exposes how Franklin's contributions to Crick and Watson's work were seriously undervalued (1975, NY: Norton). Evelyn Fox Keller's biography of Barbara McClintock, *A Feeling for the Organism: The Life and Work of Barbara McClintock* details the Nobel Prize winner's work with genetic transposition, particularly as McClintock's approach set her apart from her male counterparts (1983, San Francisco: W. H. Freeman). Robert Clarke's biography of Ellen Swallow (Richards) attempts to reestablish Swallow as a key figure in the beginnings of ecology, if not the founder of ecology (1973, *Ellen Swallow: The Woman Who Founded Ecology*. Chicago: Follett). Succeeding Swallow, Rachel Carson is the subject of H. Patricia Hynes's work, examining Carson's classic *Silent Spring* and providing a feminist reading of it (1989, *The Recurring Silent Spring*. NY: Pergamon).

Although historical analyses have shifted away from the great-person approach, by far most biographical studies still maintain this type of focus. Researchers trying to locate those sources with more emphasis on social history should locate Patricia Phillips' *The Scientific Lady: A Social History of Woman's Scientific Interests, 1520–1918* providing information on the intellectual pursuits of women in Great Britain (1990, NY: St. Martin's Press). A significant work is Margaret Rossiter's *Women Scientists in America: Struggles and Strategies to 1940*, which concentrates on ordinary women's work in science (1982, Baltimore, MD: Johns Hopkins). Specifically Rossiter posits that in the 1880s and 1890s when doors to higher education were opening for women, the possible feminization of science proved threatening enough to cause barriers to rise and create sex-segregated areas in the sciences. Pnina G. Abir-Am and Dorinda Outram have edited *Uneasy Careers and Intimate Lives: Women in Science, 1989–1979*, a collection of essays documenting how ordinary rather than exceptional botanists, ornithologists, physicians and others try to balance their personal and professional lives (1987, New Brunswick, NJ: Rutgers University Press). Another source with a similar focus in Vivian Gornick's *Women in Science: Portraits from a World in Transition* (1983, NY: Simon and Schuster). Finally, though not feminist in approach, S. Phyllis Stearner's *Able Scientists-Disabled Persons* is a unique source providing information on 27 contemporary scientists, who contend with some type of disability. One-third are women including Stearner herself (1984, Oakbrook, IL: John Racila Association).

STATUS AND RECRUITMENT OF WOMEN IN THE BIOLOGICAL SCIENCES

It should not be surprising that women scientists earn less money, obtain fewer doctoral degrees, and garner less recognition than do their male counterparts. Several sources provide quantitative analyses of this phenomenon and describe the many barriers or obstacles women face in the scientific disciplines. An excellent source to consult is the National Science Foundation's report *Women and Minorities in Science* (1986, Report 86–300, Washington, DC: National Science Foundation). A more recent source is *The Outer Circle: Women in the Scientific Community*, edited by Harriet Zuckerman, Jonathan R. Cole, and John T. Bruer (1991, NY: Norton). This collection of mostly comparative studies documents the position of women in science in terms of performance, productivity, rank, salary, and recognition, includes interviews with geneticist Salome Waelsch, astronomer Andre Dupree, and biochemist/virologist Sandra Panem, and theorizes about why differences between men and women exist. Another significant work in this area is *Women in Science: A Report from the Field* (1985, Jane Butler Kahle, Ed., Philadelphia: Falmer). This collection focuses on education and employment of women primarily in biology. Ann E. Haley-Oliphant contributed "International Perspectives on the Status and Role of Women in Science," providing a global viewpoint (pp. 169–192), while Mildred Collins and Marsha Lake Matyas added "Minority Women: Conquering Both Sexism and Racism" (pp. 102–123). Willie Pearson analyzes the status of blacks in American science and considers how race is an influential factor in black scientists' careers (1985, *Black Scientists, White Society, and Colorless Science.* Millwood, NY: Associated Faculty Press). His book includes the noteworthy chapter, "On Being Black, Female, and Scientists" (pp. 137–161). Violet B. Haas and Carolyn C. Perrucci edited a collection of papers from a 1981 National Conference on Women in the Professions: Science, Social Sciences, and Engineering held at Purdue University (1984, *Women in Scientific and Engineering Professions.* Ann Arbor, MI: University of Michigan). An early work is *Covert*

Discrimination and Women in the Sciences, a collection of papers from an AAAS symposium addressing five questions: what is discrimination, what can hinder women, what keeps women out of science, what goes on between individuals and institutions regarding tenure and promotion, and are men's and women's performance judged differently (1977, Judith Ramaley, Ed., Boulder, CO: Westview Press for the AAAS).

As statistics were gathered, feminists next began developing strategies and programs to counteract both covert and overt discrimination against women. Based on a 1986 NWSA conference session, Sue V. Rosser's *Resistance of the Science and Health Care Professions to Feminism* explores forms of resistance to women in science and the reasons for resistance with the hope of overcoming obstacles (1988, NY: Pergamon Press). Judith Whyte details the Girls into Science and Technology or GIST project based at Manchester Polytechnic from 1979–84, a project established to discover why girls underachieved in the sciences and how to correct the situation (1986, *Girls into Science and Technology: The Story of a Project*. Boston: Routledge and Kegan Paul). Sheila Humphreys collaborated with Barbara Gross Davis on yet another work *Evaluating Intervention Programs: Applications from Women's Programs in Math and Science* (1985, NY: Teachers College, Columbia University). Finally, Humphreys edited a compilation of papers from an AAAS symposium in 1980. This work provides strategies for effective intervention to increase the participation in science of high school, college, and reentry women (1982, *Women and Minorities in Science: Strategies for Increasing Participation*. Boulder, CO: Westview).

FEMINIST PEDAGOGY

If science is not representative because there are not enough women scientists, then will it necessarily be enhanced if women continue to do science as usual? Several sources propose means of changing the curriculum to invite more women into science programs and, more importantly, to change women's as well as men's ways of doing and thinking about science. Two noteworthy sources to consult regarding changes in the curriculum are Sue V. Rosser's valuable works *Teaching Science and Health from a Feminist Perspective: A Practical* and *Female Friendly Science: Applying Women's Studies Methods and Theories to Attract Students* (both by NY: Pergamon, 1986 and 1989, respectively). The former is an excellent resource for the science teacher wanting to bring feminist critiques of science into the classroom, especially in biology, health, women's studies, and science education classes; it includes a useful bibliography and sample syllabi. The latter discusses various critiques of science, including feminist approaches, methods for attracting more women, and sexism in textbooks. Another useful, probably indispensable source for women's studies and biology classes is Ethel Sloane's textbook *Biology of Women* (1985, 2nd ed. NY: Wiley). See also Jan Harding's *Switched Off: The Science Education of Girls* (1983, York, England: Longman Resources Unit). Jane Butler Kahle and Faith M. Hickman have also published the helpful *New Directions in Biology Teaching* (1981, Reston, VA: National Association of Biology Teachers). Those journal articles of particular interest to science educators and women's studies faculty, should be: J. Koch's "A Feminist Agenda for Teaching the Natural Sciences" (1987, *Women's Studies International Forum* 10 (5), xxxvii; Anne Fausto-Sterling and Lydia L. English's "Women and Minorities in Science: An Interdisciplinary Course" (*Radical Teacher*, *30* [Jan. 1986], 16–20); in collaboration with Nancy Lowry and Mary Sue Henifen, Amy Woodhull's "Teaching for Change: Feminism and the Sciences" (1985, *Journal of Thought* 20(3), 162–173); Carol C. Halpern and Marlene Samuelson's "Our Progress and Struggles as Feminists Teaching Biology" (1985, *Feminist Teacher*, 1(4), 10–14); Nancy Goddard and Mary Sue Henifen's "A Feminist Approach to the Biology of Women" (1984, *Womens Studies Quarterly*, 12, (11–18); Mary Jo Strauss's "Feminist Education in Science, Mathematics, and Technology" (1983, *Women's Studies Quarterly* 11 [Fall] 23–25). See also Anne Fausto-Sterling's "Course Closeup: The Biology of Gender" (1982, *Women's Studies Quarterly* *10*, (17–19) and Ynestra King's "Feminist Pedagogy and Technology—Reflections on the Goddard Feminism and Ecology Summer Program (1981, *Women's Studies International Quarterly*, 4(3), 370–372). Two other pertinent essays are: Mariamne Whatley's "Taking Feminist Science to the Classroom: Where Do We Go from Here?" (1986, In Ruth Bleier, Ed., *Feminist Approaches to Science*, pp. 181–190. NY: Pergamon Press) and Hilary Rose's "Integrating the Feminist Perspective into Courses in Introductory Biology" (1985, In Marilyn R. Schuster & Susan R. Van Dyne, Eds., *Women's Place in the Academy: Transforming the Liberal Arts Curriculum*, pp. 258–273. Totowa, NJ: Rowman and Allenheld). Numerous authors have discussed feminist pedagogy in general and some are noted in Faye Chadwell's bibliography in Sue Rosser's *Female Friendly Science* (1990, pp. 123–147. NY: Pergamon Press).

FEMINIST CRITIQUES OF THE BIOLOGICAL SCIENCES

Arguments for excluding women from science often originate from biological theories or studies purporting that women are not biologically suited or equipped to participate in science. These same biological theories have been used to argue and conclude, not only that women cannot be scientists but also that women are biologically inferior, are incapable of performing "male" tasks, are better suited to be mothers . . . and so the list goes on. Most feminist critics of such biological theories and of biology itself generally agree on this abuse or misuse of biology and its theories. Going a step further many discuss how in turn racial, class, social, economic, and other political factors wield a tremendous impact on the construction of such theories and on biology or science. Recent works have examined the literature or discourses produced by biologists or scientists. Marina Benjamin edited a recent collection of essays, *Science and Sensibility: Gender and Scientific Enquiry, 1780–1945* (1991, Cambridge: Basil Blackwell). This source's various essays discuss women, not exceptional women, scientists practicing in their disciplines and emphasize how science personified nature as female and then extrapolated from this idea to define gender roles in society. Ludmilla Jordanova takes a look at scientific and medical writings, particularly images from the eighteenth through the twentieth century, as these images depicted the differences between men and women (*Sexual Visions: Images of Gender in Science and Medicine between the Eighteenth and Twentieth Centuries*. Madison, WI: University of Wisconsin Press). Donna Haraway's book *Primate Visions: Gender, Race, and Nature in the World of Modern Science* pulls together some of her previously published and always thought-provoking essays to provide an analysis of the scientific discourse within primatology, particularly the primate sciences in the twentieth century (1989, NY: Routledge). Cynthia Eagle Russet examines the scientific literature of nineteenth- and twentieth-century America and Great Britain on sex differences (1989, *Sexual Science: The Victorian Construction of Womanhood*. Cambridge: Harvard University Press). In the context of the Victorians' time, Russet examines how Victorian scientists used their science of gender differences to establish and control social and political policy and even how feminists of the time or their allies dealt with science. *Body/Politics: Women and the Discourses of Science* contains essays illuminating how science and scientific discourse in traditional and popular forms continue acting against the feminine body since the beginning of the nineteenth century in social, political and economic arenas (1990, Mary Jacobus, Evelyn Fox Keller, & Sally Shuttleworth Eds., NY: Routledge). Susan Leigh Star has continued her work on brain research with *Regions of the Mind: Brain Research and the Quest for Certainty* (1989, Stanford, CA: Stanford University Press). Ruth Hubbard has recently published *The Politics of Women's Biology*, which collects some of her previously published essays (1990, New Brunswick, NJ: Rutgers University Press). Its chapters are chiefly concerned with the sociology of science, feminist criticisms of subject matter, and the application of biological knowledge in reproductive technologies.

Beginning in 1976, Ruth Bleier's work in the area of gender-differences research proved immeasurable. She edited *Feminist Approaches to Science*, a collection of nine essays examining primatology, endocrinology, and neurology and proposing ways feminism might transform science (1986, NY: Pergamon Press). *Science and Gender: A Critique of Biology and Its Theories of Women* is representative of her research as it focuses on how science has aided in the creation of an elaborate mythology regarding the biological inferiority of women (1984, NY: Pergamon Press). Lynda Birke's *Women, Feminism, and Biology: The Feminist Challenge* discusses science's emphasis on competition rather than cooperation and draws on ecofeminism to establish a model for feminist science (1986, NY: Methuen). Anne Fausto-Sterling's *Myths of Gender: Biological Theories about Women and Men* examines those areas in biology that have focused on gender differences: sociobiology, and research on brain differences, genes, and hormones and shows how much of this questionable research results from poor scientific methods but nonetheless is used to maintain the status quo (1985, NY: Basic Books). Virginia Sapiro edited *Women, Biology, and Public Policy*, which focuses on the biological significance for formulating or implementing public policies (1985, Beverly Hills, CA: Sage Publications). Anne Innis Dagg's *Harem and Other Horrors: Sexual Bias in Behavioral Biology* is a critique of animal behaviorists who study mammals other than humans and then theorize from these studies about human behavior and society (1983, Waterloo, Ontario: Otter Press). Marian Lowe and Ruth Hubbard coedited *Woman's Nature: Rationalizations of Inequality*, a collection of essays important for the variety of ethnic and cultural points of view it provides (1983, NY: Pergamon Press). Janet Sayers's *Biological Politics: Feminist and Antifeminist Perspectives* (1982, London: Tavistock) examines the basis of antifeminist thought in biology and the use of biology to sustain, even advance, social inequality. Ruth Hubbard also worked with Mary Sue Henifen and Barbara Fried as editors of *Biological Woman, the Convenient Myth: A Collection of Feminist Essays and a Comprehensive Bibliography* (1982, Cambridge, MA: Schenkman). This work contains essays published previously in another collection edited by Ruth Hubbard, Mary Sue Henifen, and Barbara Fried (1979, *Women Look at Biology Looking at Women*. Cambridge, MA: Schenkman). A similar collection, published a year later by the Brighton Women and Science Group examines the use of scientific theories to control, dispower, and manipulate women (1980, *Alice through the Microscope: The Power of Science over Women's Lives*. London: Virago Press). Marian Lowe also edited *Genes and Gender II: Pitfalls in Research on Sex and*

Gender with Ruth Hubbard. This work's essays concentrate on sex and gender research, mostly in hormone studies (1979, NY: Gordian Press). See also *Genes and Gender I* (1978, Ethel Tobach and Betty Rosoff, Eds., NY: Gordian Press). Evelyn Reed contributed her critiques of sociobiology, primatology, evolutionary theories, and anthropology in *Sexism and Science* (1978, NY: Pathfinder Press).

Several sources do not focus exclusively on biology and its theories, but still are worthwhile for their critical discussions of science and its foundations in Western philosophy. Relevant sources include Lorraine Code's *What Can She Know?: Feminist Theory and the Construction of Knowledge* with its reworked material criticizing "mainstream epistemology" produced within the disciplines of biology and some social sciences (1991, Ithaca, NY: Cornell University Press). Susan J. Hekman tackles the divisiveness of feminist and postmodernist thought in relation to modernist ideology and proposes constructing an argument for a postmodern approach to feminism to overcome the division (1990, *Gender and Knowledge: Elements of a Postmodern Feminism*. Boston: Northeastern University Press). Using the work and thought of contemporary empiricist W. V. Quine, Lynn Hankinson Nelson attempts to reopen the dialogue between feminist critics of science and empiricism with the possibility of reconciling differences (1990, *Who Knows: From Quine to a Feminist Empiricism*. Philadelphia: Temple Univ. Press). Helen Longino's latest book is *Science as Social Knowledge: Values and Objectivity in Scientific Inquiry*, a continuation of her work analyzing the scientific claim to objectivity (1989, Princeton, NJ: Princeton University Press). Alison Jaggar and Susan Bordo coedited the source *Gender/Body/Knowledge: Feminist Reconstructions of Being and Knowing* (1989, New Brunswick, NJ: Rutgers University Press). Jaggar also wrote *Feminist Politics and Human Nature* (1983, Sussex, England: Harvester Press). Nancy Tuana edited the collection *Feminism and Science*, which includes essays previously published in two special issues of *Hypatia* (1987, *2*(3); 1988, *3*(1)), devoted to feminism and science (1989, Bloomington, IN: Indiana University Press). Consult also the special issue of *Communication and Cognition* (1988, *21*(2)). Marsha Hanen and Kai Nelson edited *Science, Morality, and Feminist Theory*, actually a supplementary volume of the *Canadian Journal of Philosophy* (1987, Calgary, Alberta: University of Calgary Press). Another scholar producing challenging criticism is Sandra Harding. She has edited *Discovering Reality: Feminist Perspectives on Epistemology, Metaphysics, Methodology, and Philosophy of Science* with Merrill B. Hintikka, an excellent collection illustrating the enormous range of feminist viewpoints critiquing science (1983, Dordrecht, Holland: D. Reidel). Harding also edited *Sex and Scientific Inquiry* with Jean F. O'Barr, a series of essays previously published in *Signs* and emphasizing criticism of the natural sciences (1987, Chicago: University of Chicago Press). Individually Harding authored

The Science Question in Feminism, an exploration and analysis of the major trends in feminist critiques of science and their resulting tensions, conflicts, inadequacies, and values (1986, Ithaca, NY: Cornell University Press). In addition to her biography on Barbara McClintock, Evelyn Fox Keller wrote *Reflections on Gender and Science*, which examines the association between the construction of gender and the construction of science (1985, New Haven, CT: Yale University Press).

Feminist critiques of science have even reached ecology in the form of ecofeminism. Carolyn Merchant's latest book *Ecological Revolutions: Nature, Gender, and Science in New England* discusses two major transformations of the local ecology, human society, and human consciousness in New England between 1600 and 1860 (1989, Chapel Hill, NC: University of North Carolina Press). Merchant's earlier provocative work *The Death of Nature: Women, Ecology, and the Scientific Revolution* examines the major thinkers Bacon, Hobbes, and Newton and the changes wrought in science and society between 1500–1700 (1980, San Francisco: Harper and Row). Another important source in this area to consult is H. Patricia Hynes's previously mentioned work *The Recurring Silent Spring* (1989, NY: Pergamon). See also Ynestra King's essay ''Toward an Ecological Feminism and a Feminism Ecology.'' (1983, Joan Rothschild, Ed., in *Machina Ex Dea: Feminist Perspectives on Technology*, pp. 118–129. NY: Pergamon Press).

INDEX

THE AUTHOR

Sue Rosser, a Ph.D. in zoology, is Director of Women's Studies at the University of South Carolina at Columbia and Professor of Family and Preventive Medicine in the Medical School there. She has edited collections and written numerous journal articles on the theoretical and applied problems of women and science. Author of the books *Teaching About Science and Health from a Feminist Perspective: A Practical Guide* (1986), *Feminism Within the Science and Health Care Professions: Overcoming Resistance* (1988), and *Female-Friendly Science* (1990) from Pergamon Press. Dr. Rosser is also the Latin and North American coeditor of *Women's Studies International Forum*.